Poul Jorgensen's
BOOK OF FLY TYING

Poul Jorgensen's BOOK OF FLY TYING

A GUIDE TO FLIES FOR ALL GAME FISH

POUL JORGENSEN

JOHNSON BOOKS: BOULDER

ISBN 1-55566-004-5 (cloth)
ISBN 1-55566-002-9 (paper)
LCCCN 88-83072

Cover Design by Molly Davis
Photographs by Poul Jorgensen

Printed in the United States of America by
Johnson Publishing Company
1880 South 57th Court
Boulder, Colorado 80301

Foreword

Some years ago I read a book by the celebrated German psychiatrist Erich Fromm in which he set forth five elements of character required to master any art. These traits are: supreme concern for that art, concentration, discipline, patience, and practice.

Armed with that perception of what predisposes one to mastery, I was able to answer a question I had pondered about myself as to why I have never mastered such arts as knitting, drawing, or photography. Simple! I have not yet acquired or nurtured these traits in myself and am, therefore, a Jack-of-all-trades, master of none.

Having had my consciousness raised on the subject of character traits, I was able to do two things: learn to appreciate other traits of my own nature that I do possess and take a fresh look at those elements of character in others.

About eight years ago, I met Poul Jorgensen. As our friendship developed and I spent increasing amounts of time talking and listening to him, traveling with him, and observing Poul at his work, I had a first-hand look at mastery in action. Poul approaches each aspect of his projects with total concern and with such concentration that attempts to engage him in conversation at such times fall on deaf ears. I was fascinated to discover how he has disciplined his hands and mind to great precision through many years of practice at the fly tying vise. If one fly fails to meet his mark of excellence, he has the consummate patience to begin again with ever-evolving patience and more attention to detail and technique, until the end result satisfies. In matting and framing of angling art, in bookbinding, in photography . . . in all of Poul's pursuits, he manifests these traits of mastery.

Poul's efforts to perfect his art benefit those collectors in this country and abroad who own his flies or his frames or read his books on fly tying. His own rewards lie in the satisfaction of work well done and in awards such as the "1978 Book Of The Year" award given to him by the international angling fraternity United Fly Tiers for his book *Salmon Flies* (Harrisburg, Penn.: Stackpole Books, 1978).

Poul Jorgensen's Book of Fly Tying started with one concept and ended two and a half years later with quite another. Originally Poul commenced what was to be an updating of *Dressing Flies for Fresh and Salt Water* (Rockville Center, N.Y.: Freshet Press, 1973). But as the revision progressed, he became interested and excited about new materials, new flies, and ever more effective fly tying techniques. The book grew longer and longer, the publisher grew less and less patient. The book progressed in what seemed slow motion until, at last, it was complete. The whole process reminded me of giving birth; there was that kind of love, the level of struggle and effort in producing a book of this size and technicality.

One might say, "Well, then, it is hopeless for me to attempt this complicated fly tying stuff. I don't have 'IT'." Not at all! If I have learned one thing in my role as observer, both of Poul and of my talented author/fly tier brother, Dick Talleur, it is that these traits and skills can be taught and they can be learned and nurtured toward mastery.

Through my friendship with Poul, I have been privileged to meet and be in close association with many of the outstanding talents in the world of flyfishing. I continue to be intrigued with the outpouring of love for this many-faceted sport and all of its accompanying arts and crafts. At first glance, flyfishing appears to be one great mystique. Upon further investigation, we learn that this flyfishing game has something for everybody. For the harried business man or woman, escape from the tensions of office life. For the nature lover, excursions into the wilds of Montana or Alaska . . . sweet days astream in the welcoming rivers of the Catskills. For those who love photography, endless opportunities to capture the fish, fishermen, river scenes, and country charm on film. For travel buffs, fishing can take the angler from the austere landscape of Iceland to coral-strewn Christmas Island, from lush New Zealand to the scenic rivers of Norway. For those who love not so much to fish as to *talk* about fishing, I know of no sport in which the sharing of knowledge and the exchange of "fish tales" is so integral a part of the whole. If collecting is your pleasure, there are reels, rods, flies, and fine works of angling art or items of historical significance to be sought out and treasured. If you enjoy participation in conservation, there are organizations and projects to involve yourself in for the reclamation of streams and fishing areas.

Of all these varied aspects of flyfishing, none holds more fascination for me than the art of fly tying. In the book you now hold in your hand, Poul Jorgensen shares his experience, skill, knowledge, love, and quintessential artistry in the hope that you, the fly tier, will grow with him in mastering techniques that lead to beautiful flies, and the joy, pride, and satisfaction that can be yours at the fly tier's vise.

Carol Talleur

Danbury, Connecticut
September, 1987

Other books by the author:
Dressing Flies for Fresh and Salt Water
Modern Fly Dressings for the Practical Angler
Poul Jorgensen's Modern Trout Flies
Salmon Flies

Chapters by the author appear in these books:
Masters of the Nymph
Masters of the Dry Fly

Preface

Most authors who write books probably do so with the intention of making a profit. That's the American way of being rewarded for long hours of hard work. In the field of flyfishing and fly tying, however, it is more a work of love for the sport or art than a money-making proposition.

So now that you know that this fly tying author does not ride around in a limousine or live a lavish lifestyle, let me tell you the real reason I write books. Quite simply, I do so to share my knowledge and more than thirty years of experience with my fellow fly tiers . . . young and old, beginners and advanced. Thus, I help assure for future generations the continuity of that art which a lot of us love the most . . . fly tying.

To get the full benefit from a "how-to" book, one must start at the beginning and learn all the basics from the outset. Start by leafing through the pages to familiarize yourself with the format, which in this case can best be described as "progressive." If you start from the beginning and "practice" your way through, you will learn all the techniques needed to tie flies for all the gamefish you may encounter.

As you progress, you will discover that any book you choose is merely a guide to work from. If you practice enough, you will start to develop a style of tying that will be all your own. Even though the basic steps are the same as others use, your tying will have a unique flavor and flair which you will create as you learn. This you can be proud to pass on to the next generation. In that way it will always be possible for fly tying to survive. As my mentor, Bill Blades, so often said when he cut my flies from the hook with a razor blade, just as I thought I deserved a medal, "Fly tying is a school from which we never graduate." Thank God!

Acknowledgements

I wish to express my sincere appreciation to all the anglers, suppliers, and friends who have sent me flies, tools, and supplies and lent encouragement during the writing of this book. I am deeply grateful.

I would also like to extend a most heartfelt thanks to my friend, Lefty Kreh, for teaching me to use the camera way back when I first needed those skills and for always standing ready to offer advice and help when I needed it.

A warm "thank you" to Bob Marriott for giving me the opportunity to fish in places that were otherwise out of reach. I am truly blessed with good friends.

And last but not least, I wish to thank my publisher and editor, Scott Roederer, for the patience and kindness shown while I worked on this difficult endeavor.

Contents

This book is dedicated with gratitude to Bill W., to Dr. Bob, and to my sweetheart, Carol. They saved my life.

Chapter 1

Fly Tying Tools

I have long been of the opinion that one should use as few fly tying tools as is practical, stressing the importance of training your fingers to do the job of the many, often useless gadgets offered by suppliers. However, in fly tying, as in most other crafts, there are essential tools that you must have, and for those it pays to buy only the best. There is no point in handicapping yourself by using inferior tools, which in the end create nothing but frustration. (Note: A list of reliable suppliers of fly tying tools is found at the end of Chapter 3.)

Vise

The vise is an instrument designed to hold the hook firmly while the fly is being dressed. The vise together with a good pair of scissors are by far the most important tools in fly tying. Today there are many more vises to choose from than when I first started to tie flies. I have tried them all at one time or another and have come to the conclusion that there are two which, in my opinion, are superior to others in many ways. They are the HMH (**Fig. 1.1**) by Angling Products,

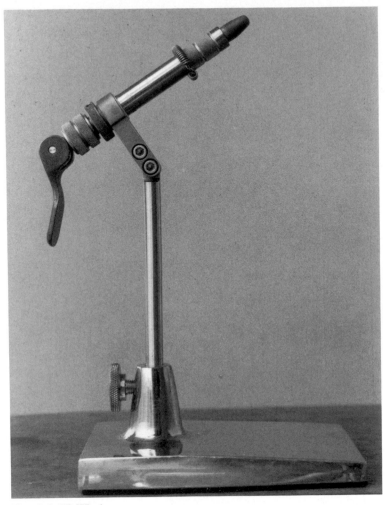

Fig. 1.1 HMH vise.

Fig. 1.2 Thompson Three-Sixty vise

Inc. and the D.H. Thompson vise (**Fig. 1.2**) by Thompson of Elgin, Illinois.

Both of these vises come with either a C-clamp for fastening them to a table (**Fig. 1.3**) or a pedestal mount so you can place them anywhere you please, even on the hood of your car. Best of all, they have different sizes of jaws (**Fig. 1.4**,

Fig. 1.5) that are easily changed, thus enabling you to tie flies from the smallest (size 28) to the largest size flies you will ever need for both freshwater and saltwater fishing. The HMH and several of the Thompson models also have rotating heads that enable you to inspect the fly from all sides while you are dressing it.

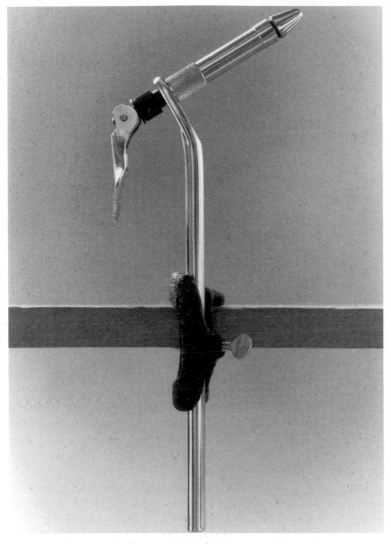

Fig. 1.3 Thompson "A" vise with C-clamp.

Later, you may consider a small hand vise so you can tie a fly right at streamside. This, however, requires a considerable amount of practice.

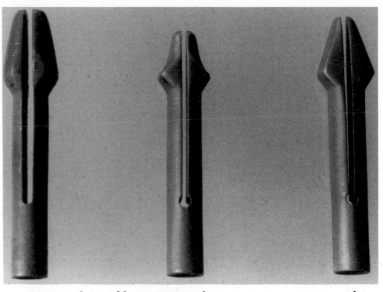

Fig. 1.4 Interchangeable HMH jaws, l. to r.—magnum, trout, midge.

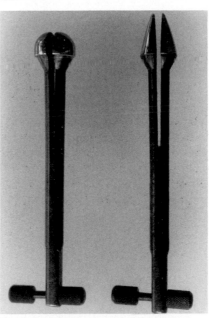

Fig. 1.5 Interchangeable Thompson jaws, super and midge.

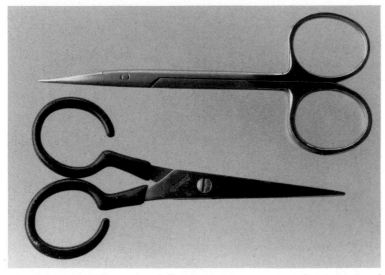

Fig. 1.6 Typical fine-pointed fly tying scissors—surgeon's iris (top) and Thompson Supreme.

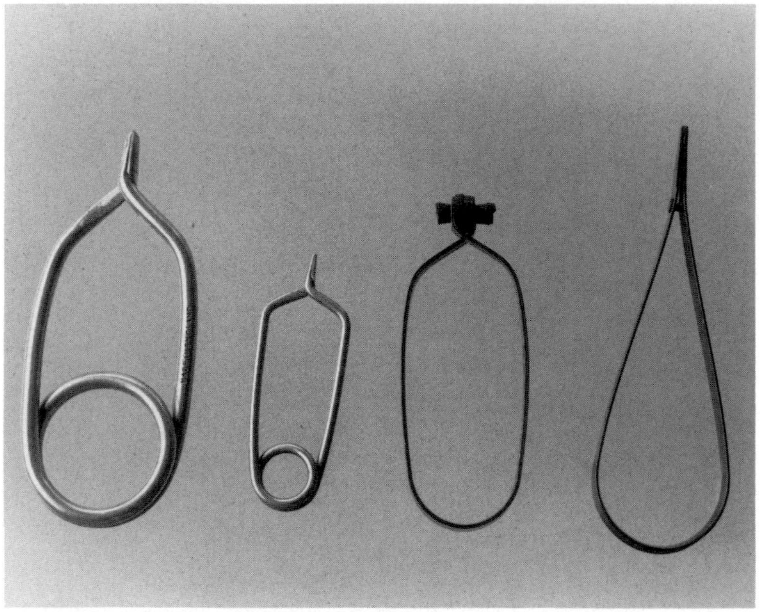

Fig. 1.7 Hackle pliers, l. to r.—English-style, midge, Thompson Non-Skid, teardrop.

Scissors

Like the vise, a pair of scissors is one of the most important tools in fly tying (**Fig. 1.6**). A pair of fine-pointed scissors is an absolute necessity for cutting hackle and other light material. They should be from 3″ to 4½″ long, with short blades that are straight or slightly curved. Surgeon's iris scissors are particularly well suited for the finer work. For heavier work, such as cutting wing feathers, deer body hair, and bucktail, it is not advisable to use your fine scissors, as they might get sprung or damaged in some other way. For coarse work, I recommend a pair of heavy-duty scissors with larger, sturdier blades.

Other Important Tools

Hackle Pliers: Hackle pliers are primarily used for winding hackle and body material (**Fig. 1.7**). The large, heavy, English-style pliers can also serve as a weight when spinning several types of dubbing. This technique is explained in later chapters.

Just a few words about the English-style hackle pliers. There are several inferior imitations on the market today, so make sure that you check the surfaces and ends of the jaws to make sure they are finely polished and without sharp edges that will cut the hackle while it is being wound.

Thompson's Non-Skid Pliers (one of my favorites) have round jaws that are fitted with rubber. They are excellent for most work but are not heavy enough for spinning dubbing. I recommend that you also get a pair of English-style midge pliers for winding hackle on very small flies. A very lightweight pair of hackle pliers, such as the teardrop type, can also be useful.

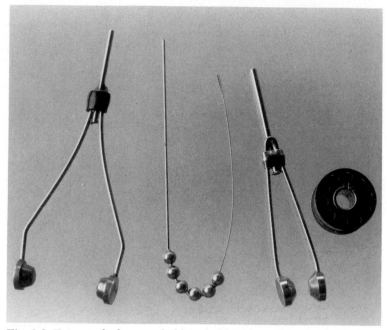

Fig. 1.8 Tying tools, l. to r.—bobbin, bobbin threader, mini-bobbin and spool.

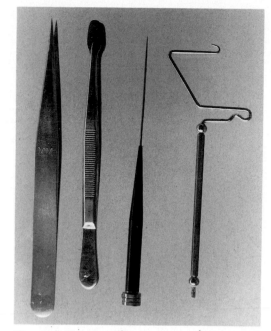

Fig. 1.9 Tying tools, l. to r.—fine-pointed tweezers, wide-jaw tweezers, dubbing needle, Matarelli whip finisher.

Bobbin: The main function of the bobbin is to hold the thread spool while the thread is being used (**Fig. 1.8**). When hanging from the hook shank by the thread, it also acts as a weight to prevent the material from unraveling, thus eliminating the need for the manual half-hitch knot. Matarelli and D.H. Thompson make fine bobbins that are similar in construction. A bobbin consists of a tube for the thread with finely polished ends to prevent it from fraying. It has two spring steel arms with cone-shaped balls on the end to hold the spool. Even the narrowest spools can be used in this type bobbin since the pressure can be adjusted by bending the arms. Both companies make several sizes of bobbins, but the two most popular are the regular and the mini size.

Bobbin Threader: This is a handy tool for threading the bobbin (**Fig. 1.8**). I prefer the Matarelli, as it has a threader on one end and a stainless steel wire on the other to clean out wax that builds up in bobbin tubes.

Tweezers: Tweezers are handy for many things (**Fig. 1.9**). The wide-jaw models are very similar to those used by stamp collectors. I use those to hold feathers when they are being tied in and to bend the legs on very realistic flies, etc. Fine-pointed tweezers are good for picking up small hooks and feathers.

Dubbing Needle (Bodkin): The dubbing needle is used to spread and pick out fur dubbing evenly on the tying thread, to separate hackle fibers and wing quill sections, and to apply head cement and lacquer (**Fig. 1.9**).

Whip Finisher: In the old days, a whip finish was always made with the fingers, but Matarelli has designed a unique tool that enables you to finish off the head on even the smallest dry flies without winding down any of the fibers (**Fig. 1.9**). Its use is demonstrated in the Beginner's Tying Practice, Chapter 4.

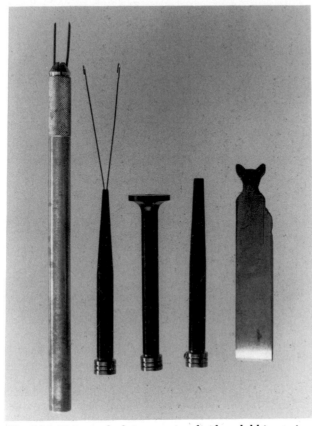

Fig. 1.10 Tying tools, l. to r.—wing divider, dubbing twister, hair packing tool, half-hitch tool, wing burner.

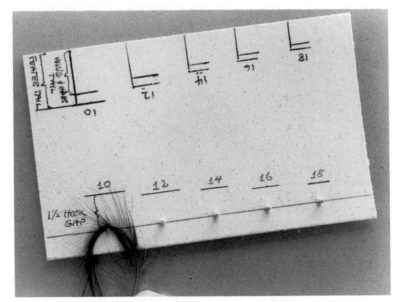

Fig. 1.11 Homemade hackle guage.

Wing Divider: This is an adjustable tool that can be set to separate wing feather strips at different widths (**Fig. 1.10**). It enables you to make left and right wing strips that are exactly the same size.

Dubbing Twister: The dubbing twister is a very practical tool for spinning fur on a hook (**Fig. 1.10**). The fur is first dubbed on the thread; then a loop is formed with the twister in the end of it. Twist the tool and the thread loop is twisted into the dubbing, forming a very neat tapered dubbing for either dry flies or nymphs.

Hair Packing Tool: This tool is used when spinning deer and elk hair bodies when each application of hair must be packed tightly together on the shank (**Fig. 1.10**). It can be used on hair-bodied flies such as those described in Chapter 15.

Half-Hitch Tool: Like the Matarelli whip finisher, this tool is designed to finish off heads on dry flies (**Fig. 1.10**). It consists of a rod 3″ to 5″ long and about the diameter of a pencil. The ends are tapered and have holes in them to accommodate the hook eye and the fly head. Frequently, when the hackle is wound and tied off, several fibers crowd the eye, making it difficult to finish the head. That's where this tool comes in handy as demonstrated in the Beginner's Tying Practice, Chapter 4.

Wing Burner: This tool comes in different sizes and can be used to burn both feathers and latex (**Fig. 1.10**). The only wing burners I use are for stonefly wings. They are the only ones I have found that are accurate enough.

Fig. 1.12 Hair stacker.

Hackle Gauge: Being able to select the right size hackle for dry flies is very important. There are several inexpensive devices on the market, or you can easily make your own (**Fig. 1.11**).

Hair Stacker: To align the hair after it's cut from the skin, this tool is a must (**Fig. 1.12**). Although I rarely use it, there are times when I would not want to be without it. Place the hair in the funnel-like top, tips first. Bang the stacker on the table several times, and the hair tips are aligned. Hold the tool sideways and carefully remove the funnel from the bottom. You can then grasp the hair tips and take the whole bunch out with your fingers.

Hackle Guard: This tool holds the hackle out of the way while the head is finished. It is a very useful tool when tying small flies.

Fig. 1.13 Minichop for blending furs.

Fur Blender: In my book *Modern Fly Dressing For The Practical Angler* (New York: Winchester Press, 1976) I introduced an Italian fly tier from Pittsburgh named Tony Marasco who, as far as I know, was the first to discover the unique method of blending fur in a small coffee grinder. I now use a more modern blender called Mini Chop (**Fig. 1.13**). It's small and has very sharp blades that will chop and blend anything you put in it. If you use yarn, cut it in ½" lengths for best results.

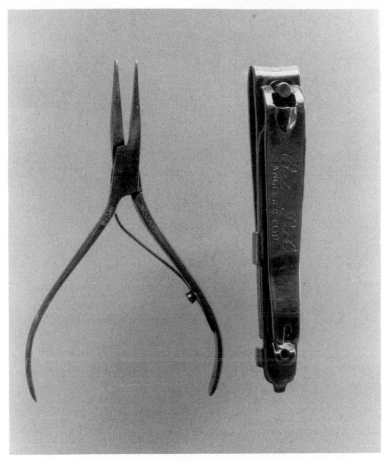

Fig. 1.14 Additional tools—needlenosed pliers and nail clippers.

Miscellaneous Tools: In addition to the specialized fly tying tools mentioned above, you will also need an X-Acto saw, several small jeweler's files, fine sandpaper, nail clippers, and a small pair of needle-nosed pliers (**Fig. 1.14**). I am sure there are a few more things you will need as you progress in your tying, but they can always be added later.

Chapter 2
Fly Tying Hooks

Although some rather primitive methods of catching fish with hook and line have been known to man for thousands of years, the hook-making industry did not begin to develop until the middle of the seventeenth century when needlemakers in Redditch, England incorporated hook making into their industry. Fish-hook manufacturing then quickly spread to other countries, particularly Norway.

While Redditch, at one period of time, had a half-dozen significant hook manufacturers, most of them are now out of business, leaving Partridge as the only large-scale hook maker left to carry on the tradition of this famous town. Together with Mustad of Norway, the two companies each make a complete line of hooks, using only the finest tempered steel—a line that includes hooks specifically designed for fly tying.

While there are other hooks on the market today, they have not been proven in the field, and I am satisfied that a selection of fly tying hooks by Mustad and Partridge will cover all your needs and enable you to tie all the flies presented in this book, as well as other favorite patterns of your own. I have, however, described two hooks manufactured

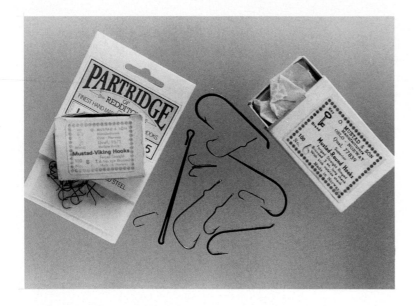

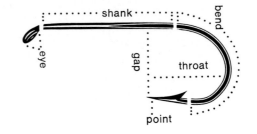
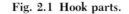

Fig. 2.1 Hook parts.

Fig. 2.2 Limerick bend.

Fig. 2.3 Sproat bend.

Fig. 2.4 Round bend.

in Japan by Tiemco. They are included because of their unique design.

To succeed in fly tying, it is important that you become thoroughly familiar with the many sizes and shapes of hooks you will be using, because as you will soon discover, each hook is designed individually for very specific uses. The dry fly, for example, is an insect imitation that is designed to float on the surface. Its floating ability depends entirely on the material used and the light-wire hook selected for the dressing.

Flies fished below the surface, such as nymphs, wet flies, and streamers, imitate immature underwater insects or bait fish and should be tied on heavier hooks in order to sink them to the depth where the fish are feeding. Here, incidentally, is where I have difficulty with some of the newer books on the market. I find that their fly patterns designed for sub-surface fishing call for hooks with too light a wire, which requires you to wrap lead on the shank to be able to get them to sink far and fast enough. I personally do not like weighted flies, although it is sometimes necessary to use weight, even with Partridge and Mustad hooks, when fishing very fast and deep water.

Hook Identification

To aid in correctly identifying hooks, manufacturers use a code letter "X" in addition to size and style numbers. All manufacturers produce hooks in a standard diameter wire for each hook size. Many hooks are also made with wire that is either lighter or heavier than the standard diameter.

Wire for dry fly hooks, for example, may be smaller in diameter and therefore lighter than the standard, while wire for a wet fly hook of the same size may be larger in diameter and therefore heavier. If a wet fly hook is designated as being 1X, 2X, 3X, or 4X stout, it means that the diameter of the wire used is equal to the standard diameter wire of hooks one, two, three, or four sizes larger. Dry fly hooks are marked 1X, 2X, 3X, and 4X fine, meaning that the wire is the same as the standard wire for hooks one, two, three, or four sizes smaller. This may all seem very complicated, but after a while it becomes just routine to identify the various styles of hooks.

Generally speaking, you will rarely need hooks heavier than 2X stout, except for some saltwater flies. If additional weight is needed to sink the fly, I prefer to choose a fly line with a sink tip or, in some cases, even a full sinking line rather than adding lead wire to the hook shank before the fly is dressed.

Hook lengths varying from standard length are indicated as being 1X to 12X long or 1X to 5X short. The same progressive method is used as is used for wire diameter identification.

The position of the hook-eye is also important to the tier. Up-eyed hooks are often used for small dry flies to insure maximum hooking efficiency. Small hooks are now also available by popular demand with "ringed" eyes, eyes that are parallel to the hook shank. I prefer up-eyed hooks for most of my dry flies, particularly those that float without hackle or ones tied parachute style. I have studied photographs of flies from underwater and when the eye is in the surface film, as it is when the eye is turned down, there is a great deal of distortion that makes the fly look somewhat blurred. However, this is a personal preference and not standard by any means.

For nymphs, wet flies, and most freshwater streamers, I use hooks with the eye turned down, but I use hooks with the eye turned up for salmon flies and some flies that are designated for steelhead fishing. Saltwater flies are nearly always tied on ringed-eye hooks.

Salmon hooks are considerably stronger than average hooks, since extra-heavy wire is used in their construction.

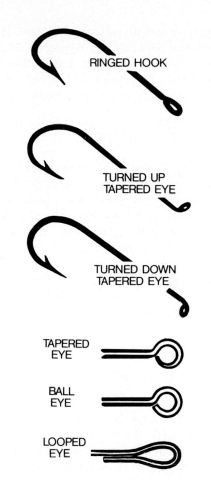

Fig. 2.5 Styles of hook eyes.

They are also usually 1X long. "Low-water salmon flies," however, are an exception; they are tied on finer wire and are 2X long.

Flies for saltwater fishing must be tied on stainless steel hooks, not tinned or nickel-plated hooks, to prevent rust and corrosion. Stainless steel hooks don't rust when sharpened, plated hooks do. Hooks for these large saltwater flies are made of heavy wire and usually range in sizes 6 to 6/0, either regular length or 5X short, depending on the fly being dressed.

Depending to some degree on the time of year the flies are used, steelhead flies can be dressed on a variety of hooks, all usually made with heavy wire. Lately there is a tendency to tie steelhead flies on salmon hooks, which makes a lot of sense, since the fish is almost as large and strong as a salmon.

Selected Fly Tying Hooks

The following descriptions of hook styles and their applications should be considered a general guide, for there are many more hooks on the market to choose from. The ones I have listed are those I have found most practical and best suited for my style of fly tying. They all have one thing in common, though; no matter what the manufacturers tell us about their high standard of quality control, most hooks are dull. Perhaps they mean to leave sharpening to the user. I take time to sharpen all my hooks before I dress them and suggest that you do the same.

Dry Fly Hooks

Mustad #94840: Round bend, turned-down tapered eye, bronzed, 1X fine wire. This hook is considered the standard hook for traditional dry flies and for those who prefer a slightly heavier hook for western-dressed flies such as the Wulff patterns. Sizes 6-28.

Mustad #94833: Round bend, turned-down tapered eye, bronzed, 3X fine wire. Good for sparsely-dressed flies and for those who prefer a light-wire hook. Sizes 6-22.

Mustad #7957B: Similar to the #94840 except that it is made with regular wire rather than 1X fine wire and has a 1X long shank. It is used mostly in the West. Sizes 6-20.

Mustad #94859: This is the same hook as #94840 except that it has a ringed eye, specifically designed for midges. The ringed eye does not interfere with hooking the fish on these small flies. Sizes 18-28 only.

Mustad #94838: Round bend, turned-down tapered eye, bronzed, 1X fine wire, 2X short shank. Excellent for dry caddisflies, beetles, variants, and other flies requiring a shorter hook shank. Sizes 10-20.

Mustad #94842: Round bend, turned-up tapered eye, bronzed, 1X fine wire, regular length. A very fine hook for no-hackle, parachute, and extension-body flies. I also use this hook for hoppers and crickets. Sizes 8-28.

Partridge Code L3B: Very similar to the #94842. I often prefer this hook, particularly since it has a wider gap and is made with 4X fine wire. Very good for extension-body flies like the Jorgen-Betts spinner/duns described in Chapter 5.

Mustad #94831: Round bend, turned-down tapered eye, bronzed, 2X fine wire, 2X long shank. A very good hook for wooly worms, hoppers, large mayflies, etc. Sizes 4-16.

Mustad #9523: Round bend, turned-up tapered eye, bronzed, 1X fine wire, 5X short shank. This hook has a wide range of uses, such as caddis worms, spiders, variants, extension-body flies, etc. Sizes 2-16.

Partridge Code K3A: Swedish dry fly hook. Modified sproat shape, turned-up eye, bronzed, 4X fine wire, 2X long shank. This hook has a multitude of uses for large mayflies, caddisflies, and emergers. The hook floats with the bend up out of the water. Sizes 10-18.

Nymph, Wet Fly, and Streamer Hooks

Mustad #3906: Sproat bend, turned-down tapered eye, bronzed, heavy wire, regular length. This is a standard wet fly/nymph hook that can also be used for caddis pupae, etc. Sizes 2-20.

Mustad #3906B: This hook is the same as #3906 but with 1X long shank. It is a very good hook for longer nymphs and wet flies. Sizes 4-18.

Mustad #9672: Round bend, turned-down tapered eye, bronzed, regular wire, 3X long shank. Used for large wet flies, stonefly nymphs, small streamers, and small nymphs. Sizes 2-18.

Mustad #9671: This is the same as #9672 but only 2X long shank. Sizes 2-18.

Mustad #38941: Sproat bend, turned-down tapered eye, bronzed, regular heavy wire, 3X long shank. Excellent hook for stonefly nymphs, muddlers, matukas, and other streamers. Sizes 2-16.

Partridge Code CS2: Very similar to the Mustad #38941. Sproat bend, turned-down eye, black, 2X long shank, and heavy wire. Very good for streamers and steelhead flies. Sizes 2-8.

Mustad #3665A: Limerick bend, turned-down tapered eye, bronzed, regular heavy wire, 6X long shank. Used for streamers, stoneflies, etc. Also good for longer nymphs in smaller sizes. Sizes 2-14.

Mustad #9575: This hook is the same as #3665A but with a looped eye. I prefer this one for some stoneflies and sculpins. Sizes 2-12.

Partridge Code CS17: Very similar to Mustad #9575, but it's black and a little wider in the gap. Excellent for large black stoneflies, sculpins, and large streamers. Sizes 1-6.

Mustad #94720: Round bend, turned-down eye, bronzed, regular wire, 8X long shank. Good for Gray Ghost streamers, large bucktails, etc. Sizes 2-8.

Partridge Code CS5: Round bend, ringed eye, black, heavy wire, 4X long shank. This hook was designed for Keith Fulsher's Thunder Creek series. Sizes 4-8.

Mustad #79580: Round bend, turned-down tapered eye, bronzed, regular wire, 4X long shank. This is a good hook for those who prefer streamers and large nymphs tied on a little shorter hook than #3665A and who want a round bend. Sizes 6-14.

Partridge Code K2B: Yorkshire caddis hook, slightly up-turned eye, bronzed. The best caddis pupae hook made. Sizes 8-16.

Partridge Code K12ST: Sedge/caddis hook, black, regular wire, 3X long shank. About the same shape as the Code K2B, but with a ringed eye. It is very popular for long-shanked nymphs, caddis pupae, and many of the popular emerger patterns. Sizes 8-14.

Partridge Code K4A: This hook is designed for grub and shrimp patterns. Special curved shank, turned-down eye, wide gap, 2X fine wire, slightly offset. Can also be used for caddis pupae. Sizes 8-18.

Tiemco TMC 200: Special shape, bronzed with ringed eye. The shank is straight, and the hook is a little longer than typical and made of thinner wire. Excellent for nymph emergers. Sizes 4-20.

Tiemco TMC 400T: A very special shape, similar to the TMC 200 but has humps designed specifically for swimming and rising nymphs. A very nice hook for imitator nymphs. Sizes 8-14.

Bass, Pike, and Landlocked Salmon Hooks

Mustad #33903: Cork popper hook. Sproat bend, ringed eye, bronzed, special kink in 1X long shank. Sizes 2-14.

Mustad #37187: Stinger hook. Special wide gap, straight shank, ringed eye, bronzed. A special wide-gap hook for deer hair poppers. Sizes 1/0-10.

Mustad #1404: Similar to the #37187, except it has a vertical kink in the middle of the shank for use with cork bodies. Sizes 1/0-10.

Mustad #3366: Sproat bend, 1X fine wire, tapered, ringed eye, bronzed. An inexpensive but very good hook for deer hair poppers. Sizes 2/0-6.

Mustad #79666: Keel hook. Special hook designed for up-side-down flies such as small hammerheads, muddlers, etc. Sizes 2-10.

Mustad #3191: Carlisle hook. Ringed eye, bronzed, offset sproat bend. This is the hook I convert into a keel hook for large deer hair flies for bass and northern pike. Sizes 5/0-4.

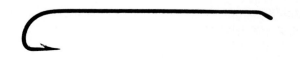

Partridge Code CS12: Carrie Stevens, super heavyweight streamer hook. Limerick bend, turned-down looped eye, bronzed, 12X long shank. Excellent for large bass, pike, and landlocked salmon flies. Sizes 2/0-4.

Saltwater Hooks

Mustad #34007: O'Shaughnessy bend, ringed eye, stainless steel, heavy wire, 1X long shank. Used for tarpon and other saltwater game fish. Sizes 6/0-8.

Mustad #9175: O'Shaughnessy bend, righted eye, cadmium-plated and tinned, 3X short shank, extra strong. For use on saltwater flies where a short shank is required. Sizes 2/0-6.

Salmon and Steelhead Hooks

Mustad #9174: Sproat O'Shaughnessy bend, ringed eye, bronzed, 1X strong wire, 3X short shank. This hook is often used for tying the popular Glo-Bug egg and sperm flies used in salmon and steelhead fishing in Alaska and elsewhere. Sizes 2-8.

Partridge Code M: Standard single salmon hook. Turned-up looped eye, sproat bend, black japanned 2X stout wire, standard length. For all types of the heavier salmon flies, steelhead flies, matukas, and other flies used in deep or fast water. Sizes 5/0-12.

Partridge Code N: Low-water salmon hook. Basically the same as Code M, except it has 1X stout wire and 2X long shank. My favorite hook for most hair-wing salmon flies. Sizes 5/0-12.

Partridge Presentation Code N: For presentation flies. Very large low-water hooks which can be converted to gut-eyed flies for the old classic salmon flies. Sizes 9/0-6/0.

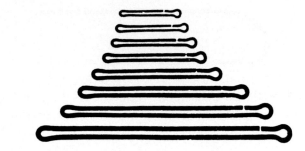

Partridge Code P: This hook is the double version of the single salmon hook, Partridge Code M. Preferred by many salmon anglers for balance and hooking. Sizes 3/0-12.

Partridge Code V1B: Double Waddington shank. Black, leading eye turned-up.

Partridge Code Q: Double version of low-water Partridge Code N.

Partridge Code 01: Single Wilson dry fly hook. Black, turned-up looped eye, 1X fine wire, 4X long shank. Excellent hook for large salmon dry flies such as the Wulff patterns, McDougals, Palmer flies, etc. The same hook is also available in doubles (Partridge Code 02). Sizes 4-12.

Partridge Code X2ST: Black treble for Waddington shanks, straight oval eye, 4X long shank.

Length of Waddington shanks and suggested hook sizes:

1/2″—	size 12
5/8″—	size 10-12
3/4″—	size 8-10-12
1″—	size 6-8-10-12
1 1/4″—	size 4-6-8-10
1 1/2″—	size 2-4-6-8-10
2″—	size 2-4-6-8-10
2 1/2″—	size 2-4-6-8

Partridge Code CS6: Blind-eye salmon hook, black, Dublin style. A gut-eye is attached before dressing the fly. Very popular for display flies. Sizes 7/0-2/0.

Partridge Code CS10: Bartleet salmon fly hook. Black, medium wire, 2X long shank, fine tapered looped eye, slightly curved shank. Good for both salmon and steelhead flies. Very popular in larger sizes for display flies. Sizes 3/0-6.

Chapter 3
Fly Tying Materials

Many people are somehow led to believe that before venturing into fly tying, they must first obtain feathers and fur from almost every bird and animal in existence. This is, of course, not true. In fact, some of my angling friends carry all their tying materials and tools in a small sewing box and are able to tie all the flies they need. It's undoubtedly true that some tiers make a point of owning everything in the suppliers' catalogues, regardless of whether they need it or not, but I suggest that quality be given priority over quantity.

Many feathers that were used in fly dressings originated many years ago are no longer available, owing to import restrictions or laws protecting the various birds from which they were obtained. In such cases, one must find substitutes, a task which is not always that easy.

This state of affairs, however, should not discourage you from venturing into fly tying. There are so many new and exciting materials available today, in fact, that if I were to include them all, they would take up at least half the pages of this book. In this chapter, then, I will include only the materials necessary to tie the flies in the various chapters throughout the book. I strongly recommend that you get some suppliers' catalogues, or better yet, visit their stores. It's always better, when possible, to hand pick materials than to order by mail.

Sundries

Wax: I prefer non-sticky wax for extra waxing of tying thread when making fur dubbing. Overton's Wonder Wax or Thompson's Tacky Dubbing Wax are two examples. Both come in handy screw-top containers.

Head Cement: A good, clear head cement is applied to the head of the fly to prevent the tying thread from unraveling. I use several types. Price's Head Cement is the best I have used for heads on salmon flies and streamers. For dry flies, nymphs, and after each application of spun deer hair, I prefer a thin, penetrating cement such as The Pharmacist Formula or Fritz Von Schlegell's Special Formula that comes in a unique bottle with flow control and brush. Price's Head Cement tends to thicken rather quickly in the bottle, so I suggest you get some thinner with it. Hard-as-Nails fingernail polish is also good for saltwater flies.

Lacquer: For painting fly heads, cork poppers, and so on, a good lacquer can be obtained from your supplier in the following colors: black, white, yellow, orange, brown, red, green, and blue.

Epoxy: Epoxy is used for gluing wiggle eyes on cork or deer-hair poppers and for attaching the hook in a slotted cork head. Any good five-minute epoxy available at drug and hardware stores will do nicely.

Feather Spray: A clear spray is used on wing quill segments so that the fibers will stick together. It is commonly used on segments for wing cases on nymphs, hoppers, and caddis pupae. I use either Krylon or Tuffilm by Grumbacher. Both come in aerosol spray cans and can be purchased at art supply stores or from your material supplier.

Tying Thread

The brand of tying thread one chooses to use is a matter of personal preference, but it is advisable to obtain it from a reputable supplier who deals in silk and nylon thread specifically made for fly tying.

I have tried most of the different tying threads over the years and have come to the conclusion that prewaxed 6/0 thread will cover your needs for most nymphs, dry flies, salmon flies, and streamers. It is available in the following colors: black, white, beige, dark brown, claret, light and dark olive, cream, primrose, gray, orange, red, tan, and fluorescent red.

For spinning deer hair and tying large streamers and saltwater flies, you will need a heavier thread, such as prewaxed Monocord, available in black, gray, white, yellow, green, brown, orange, blue, and tan.

Kevlar Super Thread is the strongest thread I have found. It is fairly thin and is prewaxed. I use it for spinning deer hair and tying large streamers and saltwater flies. It is available in yellow, olive, black, red, and bronze.

A relatively new product is the D.H. Thompson's Monobond kit. The kit consists of one dozen small metal spools, each filled with assorted colors of either 3/0, 6/0, or super-strength waxed thread. A fourth kit contains rayon floss. Both the floss and thread fit the Thompson mini-bobbin. It's the most convenient assortment I have ever used.

Body Materials

Floss: This is a flat, narrow, ribbon-like material made of silk or rayon. Heavy, single-strand floss is used for large trout flies, streamers, steelhead flies, and salmon flies. Lighter two- and four-strand floss can be separated into single strands for use on smaller flies. Floss is available in the following regular or fluorescent colors: white, yellow, orange, burnt orange, red, brown, gray, olive, light olive, green, light yellow, purple, claret, pink, Silver Doctor blue, lavender, cream, and beige. When using floss, it must always be untwisted so it is flat before it is wound, or it will not be smooth and nice looking.

Yarn: Almost any yarn can be used for fly tying, but there are several types that have proven particularly effective. Among the most popular are Glo-Bug yarn, polypropylene, Sparkle Poly, Mohlon, crewl wool, Angora yarn, and Antron, all of which are used for bodies on flies. Most of these yarns come in a multitude of colors, some of which are fluorescent.

Chenille: Chenille is a fuzzy, water-absorbent material that looks very much like a pipe cleaner. There are many types of chenille available from suppliers. It comes in fine, medium, or large diameters. Chenille is used in many western flies, such as Wooly Worms, Wooly Buggers, and Montana Nymphs. Like the yarns, it comes in many popular colors. Fluorescent chenille is used for some of the flies designed for fishing in Alaska. I also use tinsel chenille for some streamer bodies. It comes in both gold and silver.

Tinsel: The French make excellent silver and gold tinsel that can be obtained from your supplier in narrow, medium, and wide stock. Unfortunately, the really good stuff is somewhat scarce today. Most of what you can get today is Mylar, which is gold on one side and silver on the other. Since it is thin and flat, it is used mostly for solid tinsel bodies, but it can also be used for ribbing on salmon flies and other patterns.

Flat, embossed tinsel is used on streamers and has a scale-like appearance that makes it very effective. Oval tinsel is a very narrow, flat tinsel wound over a cotton core and flattened. It is used almost exclusively for ribbing and tags, particularly for salmon and steelhead flies. It comes in fine, medium, and large diameters.

Round tinsel is made in the same manner and for the same purpose but is not flattened. In England, the round tinsel is often referred to as "twist". Lace, which is two or three strands of round tinsel twisted together, is often used in classic salmon flies. Wire, in silver, gold, and copper, is not really tinsel but is often used in nymphs and salmon flies, as well as some other flies.

Mylar Tubing: Braided Mylar tubing is used for bodies on both freshwater and saltwater streamers. It is available in three diameters: 1/16", 1/8", and 3/16". Most of the brands have a center core consisting of several strands of cotton thread. This thread is removed so the tubing can be slipped on the hook shank and tied down at the front and rear. Mylar tubing is excellent for flashy extension bodies on saltwater flies. In addition, I have used this type of body on large flies for bass and northern pike. They are extremely effective. In addition to the traditional colors of gold and silver, Mylar tubing is now available in a wide variety of colors.

Flashabou: Flashabou is the brand name of a thin, flexible Mylar tinsel that can be mixed in with bucktail and other wing materials for streamers, salmon flies, and saltwater flies. It comes in the following colors: copper, red, black, light blue, dark blue, silver, gold, purple, yellow, bronze, pink, and peacock herl.

Pearlescent Tinsel: This pearl-colored tinsel is used as an underbody with a thin over-wrap of narrow, clear Swannundaze. It is especially good for bonefish flies.

Crystal Hair: This special, crinkled, hair-like Mylar material is very similar to Flashabou but is much finer in texture. It comes in the same colors as Flashabou, and then some. It can be used as a substitute for polar bear when tying salmon flies and can also be twisted together and wound as whole bodies. I'm sure if you use your imagination, you can find many other uses for it as well.

Swannundaze: A hard, but flexible, nylon strand that comes in three sizes (1/32", 1/16", and 3/32"), Swannundaze is used for ribbing on nymphs and some saltwater flies. The only size I use is 1/32". It is available in the following colors: clear, light transparent amber, dark amber, light olive, dark olive, brown, black, amber, pale yellow, and orange.

Swiss Straw: A rayon material in ribbon form, Swiss Straw is a substitute for raffia. I use this for wing cases on several of my stonefly nymphs. It comes in white, black, cream, gray, tan, copper, light olive, olive, amber, golden amber, yellow, orange, insect green, and fiery brown.

Latex: This high-grade rubber material comes in small 5″ by 5″ sheets and is available from most suppliers in medium, light-heavy, and extra-heavy stock. I use only the natural cream color for stonefly bodies and some wing cases. Place the latex between two pieces of thin cardboard for best results when cutting to size. I use waterproof marking pens to color the latex.

Microfibetts: These are very fine synthetic fibers with tapered tips. I use these for tails on the Jorgen-Betts spinners and duns. They are available from some suppliers in yellow, clear, olive, light dun, dark dun, cream, tan, and brown.

Fur

Animals supply the fly tier with natural shades of fur, many of which closely resemble the colors of the insects that are important to the angler. Pieces of skin from the animals listed here will give you most of the shades you need. Other colors are created by bleaching and then dying natural fur or are available in synthetic fibers.

Red Fox: This fur is available in gray, tan, fawn, and creamy white. The pinkish-colored belly fur from the female red fox is in much demand for the well-known Hendrickson dry fly. Fox fur is very long, and in some instances, it is gray at the base, cream in the middle, and tan at the tip. Such fur can be cut in sections and is excellent for the spinning method used when dressing fur nymphs, spinners, and emergers.

Mink: Light brown, dark brown, reddish brown, rusty brown, and tan furs are found on this animal. Most of the colors have a gray cast and make fine fly bodies.

Otter: This is a very fine-textured fur in cream and creamish gray. The guard hairs are often used for tails and wings on fur flies.

Opossum (Australian): This fur comes in black, gray, light tan, and creamy yellow. It is rather short fur and is very good for the special legs/thorax dubbing method I use for very small caddis pupae. The fur from the neck is particularly good for this use.

Beaver: Beaver fur has brownish-gray to blue-gray shades. It is used in some nymph patterns.

Muskrat: The underfur from this animal is most widely used for flies such as the Blue Dun, Dark Cahill, and Dark Hendrickson. It's a very nice blue or blue-gray shade.

Mole: This little animal has the truest blue underfur obtainable. It's very fine for smaller flies.

Hare's Ears and Mask: These have rusty-brown to dark-gray underfur with speckled guard hairs. Its texture and short length make it a little difficult to dub unless the spinning loop method is used. For flies such as the Gold-Ribbed Hare's Ear and for the body on some March Brown nymph patterns, the guard hairs are generally left in the fur and are picked out as legs after the body is dubbed on.

Squirrel: Some parts of this skin are used as a substitute for hare's ear, but it is more often used for fine tails.

Rabbit: Your supplier has small pieces or whole rabbit skins in many colors. I usually buy whole skins and cut them into pieces the size of a cigarette pack. I can then very economically dye pieces any color I need. When tying some of my fur nymphs and pupae, the most important color you need for legs and thorax dubbing is the natural brown. Use the fur and guard hairs from the back portion of those skins and cut it in thin layers.

Seal: If you are lucky enough to have some on hand, seal is the finest and most translucent fur you can use for salmon flies and nymphs. But, because of import restrictions, this important material is difficult, if not impossible, to obtain. Fortunately, there are good substitutes available. (See the section on synthetics below.)

Zonker Strips: These are long, thin strips of rabbit skin with hair attached. They are used for tying the Zonker-type of streamer flies. They come in the following colors: natural grizzly, natural brown, natural gray, natural white, purple, yellow, gold, olive, black, chartreuse, rust, and brown. They are also available in fluorescent colors.

Blended Furs and Synthetics

In looking over the list of blended fur that is available today, it seems that everybody is in the blended fur business. The following blends are the ones I have found best for my style of tying, but it's entirely possible that you may prefer something else. I suggest that you order a package or two of each kind and make up your own mind.

Seal-Ex: Some years ago, when faced with the absence of natural seal's fur, I developed a very fine synthetic substitute called Seal-Ex. It has a very high translucency and dubs more easily than real fur. For various reasons, I stopped making it for a while, but I have now redesigned it so it is more suitable for today's dubbing methods. It comes in black, red, yellow, buff, creamish white, golden amber, yellowish cream, light orange, hot orange, brownish black, Isonychia, light golden brown, medium brown, dark brown, olive brown, fiery brown, pale olive, medium olive, dark olive, pale olive gray, pale amber, claret, pale green, grass green, Green Highlander green, and Silver Doctor blue.

Buggy Nymph Dubbing: A fine, synthetic short-fibered dubbing that can be mixed with natural fur in the fur blender if particular effects are needed. It is available in the following

colors: rust, mint, blue dun, drake brown, lava brown, silver black, gray, spruce, sage green, tan, gold, black, copper, dark brown, light brown, light hare's ear, Isonychia, dark hare's ear, olive, light olive, aqua green, brownish olive, golden stone, cinnamon, tan damsel, pale olive, maize, light ginger, and blue olive. It may come as a surprise to Tim Paxton, who developed this fine product, that I find it excellent for dry flies as well as for nymphs.

Blended Rabbit Dubbing: One brand of this natural fur blend comes from Rocky Mountain Dubbing Company. It has the guard hair in it and is excellent for nymphs. Like the Buggy Nymph Blend, it is short-fibered and can be blended in the fur blender to create special shades when needed. It comes in red, blue, purple, yellow, pale yellow, green, dark green, gold, orange, olive, pale olive, dark olive, golden olive, rust, brown, dark brown, tan, pink, chartreuse, gray, dark gray, black, natural white, and natural brown.

Fly-Rite: This is a most popular synthetic dry fly dubbing. It's 100% polypropylene and very easy to work with. It is available in the following 40 colors: white, black, dark olive, bright yellow, rust, chocolate brown, dark gray, golden olive, golden yellow, Blue-Winged Olive, orange, cream, Grannom green, golden amber, light olive, chartreuse, golden brown, rusty orange, light tan, dark tan, light gray, Cahill tan, Olive Sulfur, Tiny Blue-Winged Olive, Cream Variant, Adams gray, Speckled Dun, dark reddish brown, Western Olive, March Brown, Pale Morning Dun, rusty olive, orange sulfur, Quill Gordon, inch-worm green, ginger cream, Gray Drake, pale watery yellow, medium brown, and caddis pupae green.

Camel Blend: This is actually the natural underfur from a camel's coat. It is a soft, easy-to-dub material, used for all types of dry flies. It's available in yellow, brown, rusty brown, dark brown, olive, dark olive, Cahill cream, black golden stone, Adams gray, camel, and squirrel belly.

Home-Made Dubbing: Much like a painter mixes his paint, the fly tier must know how to mix his fur to produce particular

Fig. 3.1 Matched duck primary wing feathers.

amounts of cream and tan are mixed. If olive with a brownish cast is needed, olive is chosen as the base color, and brown is added in small quantities until the desired effect has been obtained.

To make your own dubbing blend, start at your local yarn shop or department store. There you will find most of the wool and synthetic yarns that the pre-packaged dubbings are made from. Next, go to your local furrier and ask if you can buy some of the scraps lying around in his shop. With these items on hand, plus a small fur blender (such as the Mini Chop mentioned in Chapter 1), you are ready to create your own dubbing. The only thing to remember is that the yarn should be cut in short pieces, about ½″ or so, or the blender will not separate it. Also, when blending yarn and fur together, chop the yarn in the blender first; then add the fur.

Wing and Tail Feathers

The primary and secondary flight feathers of birds, as well as their tail feathers, are used for wings and other parts of artificial fishing flies of all kinds. To get the correct curvature for wings on your flies, you must cut the segments from a left and right wing feather (**Fig. 3.1**). Matched feathers are available from your supplier, or you can buy whole wings for a better selection of feathers.

The following descriptions will help you identify the feathers given in the materials lists for the flies described in this book.

Duck: These flight feathers come in white, gray, and blue-gray (slate), depending on the species of duck from which they are taken. The blue secondary feathers with white tips are used on some flies, like the McGinty. Duck quills are very good for some medium-sized and small flies. The white feathers can be dyed any color.

Turkey: Turkey wing quills are very large. Some have gray and white bars, others are solid brown or mottled brown. The mottled brown quills are used for flies like the Muddler

colors and shades. It is virtually impossible for anyone to set a rule for the quantity of different color furs or yarn needed to produce a certain shade, since the outcome depends entirely on the colors of the basic furs or yarns used. If a dressing calls for a creamish-tan fur body, it's safe to assume that even

Minnow and several hopper patterns. The large turkey tail feathers are cinnamon or very dark mottled brown with white tips. While some of these feathers are 9″ to 12″ in length, the smaller ones, 6″ to 7″ long, are much softer. Use them for wet flies and some salmon flies. Some turkey tail feathers nowadays are white. They come from birds raised in hatcheries and are dyed many colors. These dyed feathers are primarily used in fully-dressed salmon flies.

Goose: Goose wing quills are dark gray or white and are excellent for large flies. They are available in many dyed colors. Goose shoulder feathers (called nashurias) are very soft, white feathers and range in length from 4″ to 7″. Since they usually have the quill in the middle of the feather, you can get both the left and the right wing for a fly from the same feather. They are used when tying presentation salmon flies. They are available from your supplier in black, yellow, red, orange, green, blue, and purple.

The leading edges (short side) of a goose's gray or white primary wing feathers have some short, pointed quills tightly packed along the quill stem. They are called "goose biots" or "dyed, stripped goose", depending on whom you buy them from(**Fig. 3.2**). I use these for legs on realistic stoneflies and for tails and feelers on some of the more fishable stoneflies. They come dyed in black, fiery brown, amber, dun, pale yellow, olive, and orange. They also come in white so you can dye them any color you need.

Hen: The wing quills on hens vary in color, depending on the breed, but the most widely used colors are cinnamon, brown, and speckled brown. They are excellent for wing cases on nymphs.

Crow: All of the feathers from this bird are black. They are far superior to dyed feathers for smaller flies requiring black feathers.

Ostrich Herl: Although this type of herl is rarely used for whole bodies, except in some midge flies, it is an important item for butts on salmon flies. Like peacock herls, ostrich

Fig. 3.2 Goose biots.

herls are found on each side of a rather long, heavy stem. It's best to buy a whole feather so you can choose the herl sizes you need. Ostrich herl comes in natural black or white and in dyed black, red, green, and yellow.

Mini-Ostrich Herl: These are feathers 6″ to 8″ long with 2″ or 3″ short-fibered herls on each side of the stem. Their dun-gray color makes them very effective for tails on some of the larger burrowing nymphs, such as the Hexagenia. They can also be used for tying very small midges, in which case they are wound as hackle or whole bodies. If your supplier doesn't have them, check the household goods department in stores, as these feathers are often used in feather dusters.

Ring-Necked Pheasant: The entire skin and tail of this bird can be used by tiers for one thing or another. The metallic-black feathers on the neck are used for some black beetles, and the white feathers from the same area can be dyed red

Fig. 3.3 Peacock eye, stripped peacock eye, peacock sword, and herl.

and used for substitute Indian crow. The body feathers have all kinds of markings, some of which make them ideal for stonefly wing cases and other uses. The fibers from the tail are used for tails on nymphs, legs on hoppers—you name it.

Golden Pheasant: This bird provides the most important supply of feathers for salmon and steelhead flies, streamers, and legs on deer hair hoppers. Like the ring-necked pheasant, every feather can be used. However, I do not recommend that you buy a whole bird skin. Instead, I suggest you buy a skin without the tail, crest, and tippets. Those should be purchased separately. I use the yellow back feathers for

wing cases on some stoneflies, while the rest of the feathers are rarely used except in classic salmon flies. By far the most important thing to get is the golden-yellow crest, which is used most often for tails on salmon flies. The golden-yellow tippets with black bars are used for tails and in wings on trout flies and some salmon flies.

Amherst Pheasant: The only feathers from this bird that you need for tying the flies in this book are the center tails, which have black and white (silver) markings, and the tippets (neck feathers) that are white with two black bars. These feathers are used mostly for salmon flies.

Peacock: This bird provides the tier with some very important feathers for all kinds of flies (**Fig. 3.3**). The gray-mottled secondary wing feathers are used mostly for salmon flies. The long tail feathers provide bronze-green herls on each side of the stem that are used in wings on flies such as the Gray Ghost and several other streamer flies.

The peacock eye itself provides the two-toned quill used for the Quill Gordon dry fly and other important patterns. Since only the quill (stem) is used, the flues (colored fibers) must first be removed. However, you need not worry about that, since you can now purchase the quills already stripped. The bronze herls closest to the eye are the heaviest and are used as butts on Royal Wulffs, salmon flies, and other important artificials. The shorter sword feathers with no eyes are used for tails on some hair-wing salmon flies, such as the Blue Rat and Rusty Rat patterns, and for whole wings on some wet flies.

Blue Kingfisher: These are sold in whole skins only. The small, blue back feathers are used in tails and for cheeks on some salmon flies.

Heron: The soft, long-fibered, gray and black body feathers from this bird are highly sought after for some steelhead and salmon flies. However, they are not available in the United States because all heron species are protected. As a substitute, I can suggest that you use the long-fibered rump feathers from a common ring-necked pheasant, which can either be used in their natural color or dyed black. Chicken hens also have some soft tail and rump feathers that make an excellent gray heron substitute.

Indian Crow: This feather, commonly used in salmon fly patterns, is no longer available. A small neck feather from a young chicken dyed red can be substituted. These feathers are the ones with rounded tips that are found almost on top of the bird's head. The white feathers from the neck of a ring-necked pheasant can also be dyed and used as a substitute.

Jungle Cock: These feathers are rarely available from suppliers at this time. If you are lucky enough to find some, I suggest you keep them in a safe and use them only for presentation flies. In most cases, they are left out or substituted for with whatever the tier finds most suitable. See the section on guinea fowl, below, for one substitute. Some tiers also use feathers from a ring-necked pheasant. Others use teal flank feather.

Flank and Body Feathers

Marabou: These feathers are naturally white and come in two sizes. The longer feathers are 4″ to 6″ long, while the short ones, often called "blood marabou" are 3″ to 4″ long. The shorter feathers are much preferred, since the soft, fluffy fibers are nicely bundled together, ready to be tied in as wings on many of the better-known streamers. They are available in natural white, black, yellow, hot orange, olive, dun gray, red, blue, brown, and fluorescent colors, as well.

Wood Duck: The lemon-colored feathers with very fine, dark bars are among the most sought after feathers for wings on dry flies such as Quill Gordons, March Browns, Hendricksons, and many others. They are not always available, and dyed versions using other feathers are often substituted. The black-and-white barred flank feathers from the same birds are mostly used for wings on salmon flies and for tails and cheeks on some streamers.

Bronze Mallard: These feathers are the large, brown-speckled shoulder feathers. They are used for wings and tails on some wet flies, salmon flies, and steelhead flies.

Teal: Teal feathers have the same texture as wood duck feathers but are white with heavy black bars. They are used in many trout, salmon, and streamer patterns.

Mallard: The breast feathers are white with fine gray bars. The larger side feathers have more pronounced dark gray bars on a light gray base. These large feathers are used for the abdomen portion on some mayflies, in which case, they are dyed a lemon wood duck color.

Silver Pheasant: The body feathers are silvery-white with irregular black bars. They are most often used for the sides and cheeks of streamers like the Gray Ghost. They can also be dyed blue and used as a substitute for blue jay on some salmon fly patterns.

Guinea Fowl: The breast and flank feathers are used as throat hackle on many flies. They come in two different marking patterns, black with white spots (which can be trimmed and used as substitute jungle cock) or gray speckled. Both feathers are found on the same bird. Like the silver pheasant, they can be dyed Silver Doctor blue and used instead of blue jay.

Grouse and Partridge: The body feathers come in different shades with brown and gray markings. They are excellent for legs on wet flies and nymphs.

Hen and Rooster Body Feathers: These feathers are very fine for making cut wings for dry flies and legs for wet flies and nymphs. It's best to get the whole skin if possible. This enables you to choose the right curvature and texture when cutting wings. The most useful colors are light and dark blue dun.

Dry Fly Hackle

In the pioneering days of fly tying in America, the fly tier had to raise his own roosters or wait until a neighbor's bird was old enough to be killed in order to obtain hackle. Today, one can order rooster and gamecock necks from a long list of suppliers. Among the best of these are Metz necks. In addition, some smaller capes from India are also good.

The quality of the hackle used for floating the dry fly is very important, and the tier should take his time in studying the necks, as well as the individual hackles. A good dry fly hackle is rather long and slim, with a minimum of web at the spine. The fibers should be shiny and even in length. They should stand straight out from the stem when the hackle is held by the tip and one's fingers are run down the center stem a few times.

In time, you will be able to spot good dry fly hackle just by looking at the neck (**Fig. 3.4**). The location of the different sizes of hackle vary a great deal from neck to neck. When you get a new neck, I suggest you examine it and find the different locations of the hackle sizes.

The following necks in their natural colors and shades are most important. In addition to the natural necks mentioned, I suggest that you check your supplier's catalog for dyed dry-fly necks.

White: These necks are usually not pure white. They often have a creamy shine on top. I prefer these cream-tinged hackles, as they are usually of a better grade than the pure white ones.

Cream: Cream necks are often difficult to separate from white ones. They can best be described as being between white and very pale ginger. The late Art Flick, author of *The Streamside Guide to Naturals and Their Imitations*, recommends this shade for the Light Cahill.

Black: Natural black necks used to be very hard to get, but with modern genetic methods of raising birds, this has changed. They are now as available as any other shade. Some blue dun roosters have almost black necks, but they are generally of very poor dry fly quality.

Light Ginger: A pale tan shade.

Dark Ginger: A very light brown color.

Natural Red: A brown to reddish-brown shade.

Coachman Brown: This flat brown to mahogany-colored neck is specified for most of the coachman patterns.

Coch-y-Bondhu: Dark brown with black center and tips.

Furnace: Brown to dark brown with a very pronounced black center. They are very effective for streamer wings.

Badger: White to cream with a black center. Some of the hackles have a pale golden edge and black center. These are sometimes referred to as golden badger or badger variant.

Blue Dun: The natural necks are hard to describe correctly, as they come in many different shades, from almost black to a very pale gray. The shades I use most frequently are light blue-gray, medium-gray, and a dark shade with a rusty shine, which is particularly good for Quill Gordons and other darker patterns.

Grizzly: The necks come from Plymouth Rock stock and are usually marked with white and black bars, although several other shades are available. These variant shades range from ginger to brown or combinations thereof, all with the Plymouth Rock barred effect. They are strictly freaks and are referred to as red or ginger grizzly variants.

Cree: This is a tri-colored neck. The hackles have three distinct shades of barring—cream or light ginger, natural red, and dark gray to almost black. These necks are very scarce. With a cree neck, you can tie an Adams or Flick Multi-Variant without using grizzly hackle.

Chinchilla: These necks are marked like the Plymouth Rock (grizzly), but the bars are dun-gray on white.

Honey Dun: A pale honey color with brownish-gray center markings.

Fig. 3.4 Grizzly dry fly neck.

Fig. 3.5 Types of hackle, l. to r.—dry, wet, hen, saddle, and spade.

Other Hackle

In addition to dry-fly hackles, several other types of hackle are important. These include webby hackle and hen necks

Fig. 3.6 Grizzly saddle patch.

used for wet flies, saddle hackle used for streamers, and spade hackle used for heavily-dressed flies (**Fig. 3.5**).

Saddle Patches: Saddle patches come from the same birds that provide necks and are very important (**Fig. 3.6**). Saddle patches supply the spade hackles for tails on dry flies, hackle for heavily-dressed flies, and the long hackles needed for wings on streamers and bugs for both freshwater and saltwater.

Hen Necks: These make excellent wet fly hackle, cut-wings, and so forth (**Fig. 3.7**). They are available in natural colors as well as any dyed color you can think of. Some of the necks imported from India have very fine markings that make them very highly sought after for legs on nymphs and stoneflies. Ask your supplier to send some sample feathers.

Strung Saddle Hackles: These hackles are an absolute must for tying streamers, bass bugs, salmon flies, and steelhead flies. They are 3 1/2″ to 6″ long with lots of web at the butt section of the hackle. They are available in white, black, and all the colors you need for dressing the flies in this book, in both regular dyed colors and fluorescent colors.

Pure Quality Dyed Necks: These are usually very poor quality dry fly necks that are dyed in all the colors that you will need, including fluorescent colors. They are used for body hackle and beards on salmon flies and steelhead flies but can also be used for matukas, bass bugs, and other patterns.

Saddle and Neck Trimmings: Metz is selling these trimmings in small packages. The saddle trimmings have very fine fibers for dry fly tails, and the neck trimmings are very useful for wet fly hackle or cut-wings. I can highly recommend this material.

Hair

Bucktail: The length of the hair varies a great deal, and one should specify large, medium, or small tails when ordering. The natural tails are white with brown hair down the middle. Bucktail is also available in the following dyed colors: red, blue, purple, brown, black, orange, green, olive, and yellow.

Fig. 3.7 Hen neck.

Polar Bear: When available, this highly translucent white hair makes fine wings for streamers, salmon flies, and steelhead flies. It is available in the same colors as the bucktail described above. Since it's often hard to get, suppliers have several substitutes you can use, such as Fishair, listed below. For mixing into a salmon fly wing, for example, I substitute Crystal Hair mentioned earlier under the tinsels.

Black Bear: The hair on this animal can be used whenever a fly dressing calls for black hair. As a whole, however, it can only be classified as a coarse hair with a maximum length of about 3″ or 4″. Therefore, it's not suitable for small flies except for use as tails.

Calf Tail: These tails are white with rather short, crinkled hair that can be straightened somewhat by rolling the hair bunch between your fingers. Like the bucktail, calf tail can be dyed any color and is also available in fluorescent colors, as well. The white hair is prized for some steelhead flies and many of the Wulff patterns and western dry flies.

Fitch Tail: The guard hair on the tip section of these small tails from members of the ferret family is very soft and shiny and ranges from dark brown to black. It is used in some hair-wing salmon flies, but due to its short length, it is not suitable for flies larger than size 4.

Gray Fox: The guard hairs on the back of the gray fox are very important for the Rat patterns and other hair-wing salmon flies. The hair is grayish-black with a distinct white bar. The hairs on the tail of the same animal are much longer and are used for wings on many other flies. Save the fine gray underfur, as it makes excellent medium-gray dubbing.

Squirrel Tail: The hair on the gray squirrel's tail is speckled with a white bar and white tip. The fox squirrel's tail has reddish-brown hair with black bars, and the tail of the black squirrel is solid black. The hair on the tails of these three species is about 1″ to 2 1/2″ long. The eastern pine squirrel is much smaller. Its tail has about the same shades as that of the fox squirrel but is only about 6″ long and sometimes even shorter. The hair is therefore short, but like all the other tails, it is very important in some of the hair-wing salmon flies.

Skunk: The entire skin of a skunk supplies some of the nicest black hair you will ever see. The hair is about 1 1/2″ to 3″ in length. It's super for many streamer and salmon flies.

Woodchuck: The guard hairs are used for wings and tails on some dry flies. They are somewhat short but can be used as wings on wet flies and some salmon fly patterns. The underfur is a dark grayish-black shade that can be used for both nymphs and dry fly bodies. Some skins also have brown guard hairs on the sides that can be used for wings and tails on dry flies.

Fishair: This is a synthetic fiber designed to be used as a substitute for polar bear, which is hard to obtain. It is available in lengths from 2 1/2″ to 6″ in the following colors: gray, black, brown, red, royal blue, sky blue, peacock blue, purple, white, emerald green, moss green, fluorescent yellow, orange, chartreuse, lime green, light pink, and dark pink. It is excellent for large saltwater flies and streamers.

Deer and Elk Body Hair

It was not long ago, when I met Steve Kennerk, president of Rocky Mountain Dubbing Company, that I learned a valuable lesson about deer and elk hair (**Fig. 3.8**). To most fly tiers, deer hair is deer hair, and elk hair is elk hair. But not to Steve. He carefully studies the hair from different parts of the animals and considers how old the animals were, their sex, and when they were killed. The following is what he recommends for tying.

Hair Texture:
Fine—will not flare; excellent for wings and tails.
Medium—will flare to a limited degree, maximum 45 degrees; good for tying caddisfly wings and other dry flies.
Coarse—will flare to almost 90 degrees; used for clipped-hair flies.

Deer:
Texas Whitetail—texture fine; hair length 3/4″ to 1 3/4″.

Deer Neck Hair—texture medium soft; hair length 3/4″ to 1 3/4″.

Fig. 3.8 Coarse elk hair, left, and deer hair.

Deer, Early—texture medium stiff; hair length 1/2″ to 3/4″.

Deer, Yearling—texture fine, soft; hair length 1 1/2″ to 2 1/2″.

Deer, Rump—texture coarse; hair length 1 1/2″ to 2 1/2″.

Elk:

Elk Bull—texture medium; hair length 1″ to 2″.

Elk Cow—texture extra coarse; hair length 1 1/2″ to 2 1/2″.

Elk Hocks—texture medium fine; hair length 1/4″ to 1/2″; good for tails and wings on flies sizes 18 to 24.

Elk Mane—very long hair often used for tails on western flies and bass bugs; natural, dyed red, black, and bleached creamish-white.

Bass Hair—very coarse hair; hair length 1 1/2″ to 2″; a must for tying bass bugs; available in orange, red, chartreuse, green, blue, yellow, and pale yellow.

Elk and deer hair are generally available in the following colors: brown, golden brown, dark brown, gold, dun, green, olive, orange, purple, red, rust, yellow, black, and bleached.

Fig. 3.9 Accessories, l. to r.—lead wire, wiggle eyes, lead eyes, cork bodies, and bead chain eyes.

Miscellaneous Materials

Some of the most common fly tying accessories are listed here (**Fig. 3.9**). A look at any fly tying catalog will show you that there are many, many other accessories available, but these are the ones the beginning fly tier will find most helpful.

Cork Bodies: These come in many sizes and are used for bass poppers. Most of the ones available come pre-slotted and shaped, ready to use.

Rubber Legs: Some bass poppers have rubber legs to give them more life-like action. Rubber legs come in small, medium, and large diameters. The colors are black, brown, orange, white, yellow, gray, and chartreuse.

Lead: Lead is available in either tape or several diameters of round wire. It is used to sink the flies to the level where the fish are feeding. Lead is wrapped on the hook shank for extra weight.

Bead Chain Eyes: Bead chain eyes are used on several saltwater and steelhead flies. They are available in gold or silver and come in small, medium, large, and extra large sizes.

Wiggle Eyes: Wiggle eyes are very effective when added to cork or hair bass bugs. White or yellow, they are 5mm, 6mm, 7mm, or 10mm. They are usually glued on with five-minute epoxy.

Lead Eyes: There are two types of lead eyes, plain lead or nickel-plated. They are available in the following diameters: 5/32″, 6/32″, 7/32″, and 8/32″. When added to the front of a fly, these not only add extra weight but also force the fly to ride point up, making it virtually snagless.

Beamoc Foam: This is a closed cell "mini-foam" that can be trimmed to any shape with scissors or cutting tools. It floats forever and is available in black or white. The white can be tinted any color with a waterproof marking pen. As of now, it is available only from my company, Artistic Fishing Flies, listed under suppliers.

Felt-Tip Marking Pens: The use of waterproof marking pens in fly tying is nothing new. It is an easy method of achieving two-toned effects and markings when copying insects with distinctly different colors on top and bottom. I use Pantone markers for most of my work, and they are available from suppliers or from art stores. The color number of a Pantone pen used in specific patterns is often mentioned in fly tying books.

Storage of Materials

To preserve your necks, fur, hair, and other supplies, keep them in closed containers with plenty of moth balls or moth crystals added. I use zip-lock bags whenever the material will fit. If not, any larger plastic bag will do, just as long as you are able to close it in some way. Material can be very expensive and should be taken care of. There is nothing more disheartening, to say the least, than to find that your best natural blue dun neck has been the main course at a moth dinner.

Material Suppliers

Marriott's Fly Fishing Store
2634 W. Orangethorpe #7
Fullerton, California 92633

Fig. 3.10 Material supply store (courtesy of Mariott's Fly Fishing Store).

D.H. Thompson
11 N. Union St.
Elgin, Illinois 60120

Thomas & Thomas
22 Third St., P.O. Box 32
Turners Falls, Massachusetts 01376

Hunter's Angling Supplies
1 Central Square
New Boston, New Hampshire 03070-0300

Kaufmann's Streamborn
P.O. Box 23032
Portland, Oregon 97223

Donegal
677 Route 208, P.O. Box 569
Monroe, New York 10950

Beaverkill Angler
Broad Street
Roscoe, New York 12776

Poul Jorgensen's Artistic Fishing Flies
Cottage Street, P.O. Box 382
Roscoe, New York 12776
(For Seal-Ex dubbing and Beamoc Foam.)

Bob Johns International
6086 Nicolle St., Unit D
Ventura, CA 93003
(For Partridge hooks and select materials.)

Chapter 4

Beginner's Tying Practice

Before we get down to the buisness of fly tying, it might be wise for you to review carefully the chapters on materials and tools. I also want to clear up any confusion as to what an artificial fly represents.

Ever since man discovered that fish could be attracted by a few feathers properly arranged on a hook, he has involved himself in a study of the feeding habits and diet of fish. By careful selection of feathers and fur, it becomes possible to produce fishing flies that suggest, in one way or another, insects, bait fish, or other underwater life on which fish feed.

Early flies were designed to be fished below the surface and are known today as wet flies. Nymphs and streamers are also fished wet, but they are of much more recent development.

Although wet flies may occasionally be mistaken for small bait fish, they are meant to represent various forms of insect life, in many cases the nymphal stages of mayflies or stoneflies. In other cases, wet flies were originated to imitate adult terrestrial or adult aquatic insects that, for one reason or another, become submerged.

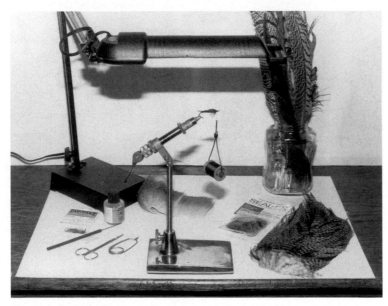

Fig. 4.1 A typical tying set-up.

The fly tier should have some basic knowledge of entomology and would benefit from collecting some specimens of insects whenever he goes fishing. They are invaluable references when tying specific patterns.

At the outset though, I would suggest you spend most of your time developing your tying skill through constant practice. Each chapter in this book will explain a series of steps which, in the end, will enable the beginner and advanced tier to assemble all the fly patterns described here, plus of course, other patterns found elsewhere.

Most of the tying methods I use are the ones that I learned from the late Bill Blades. In addition, I have learned from other fly tiers, so naturally there are many techniques that reflect on the old masters' techniques. I have also developed some methods myself over the years. Modernization of American fly dressing has added new tools, materials, and procedures that were not used in Bill's tying days. Some of these I use and others I do not. In any event, as Bill so often said, "Fly tying is a school from which we never graduate." Personally, I would like to add that that is very fortunate, indeed!

Getting Started

The first and most important consideration when setting up shop is the vise. I sincerely hope you have selected the very best vise that you could afford and have studied its use. As a small humorous footnote to this, I might add that I hope you have selected the biggest room in the house for your fly tying. If you get bitten by the fly tying bug, you might need it.

Clamp your vise on a table or board in front of you and adjust it to a comfortable height with the jaws pointing to the right. (Please note that instructions and photos are geared to right-handed tiers. Adjustments will have to be made by left-handed tiers. In this case, the jaws of the vise should point to the left if you are a left-handed tier.) If your vise does not have a C-clamp but is mounted on a pedestal, it is usually pre-adjusted to the correct height.

To ease the strain on your eyes and make working conditions more efficient, you should have good overall room lighting and a high intensity lamp to illuminate your immediate

Nymphs, such as those presented in later chapters, are extremely important to trout fishermen and to anglers who fish lakes for bass and sunfish, since they represent the immature stage of mayflies and other insects you may see flying around the waters you are fishing.

Streamers do not represent insects at all but are imitations of the various bait fish found in both freshwater and saltwater. Their dressings are not nearly as critical as those of dry flies, nymphs, and wet flies.

The more recently developed dry fly is designed to imitate adult insects. When ready to hatch, the mayfly, for example, sheds its nymphal skin and becomes a dun. This form of mayfly is ordinarily represented by a dry fly fished on the surface rather than underwater. This transformation, with a few exceptions, usually takes place in the surface film, and mayflies, at that moment, are very vulnerable to hungry fish. Most of them, however, do escape and fly to safety. After a certain period of time, they undergo a second and final transformation and return to the stream or lake to mate and lay eggs, after which they die. This final stage of mayfly is known as a spinner and, like the dun, is imitated by a dry fly.

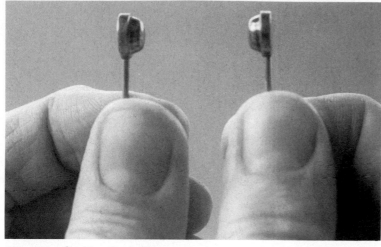

Fig. 4.2 Adjusting the bobbin.

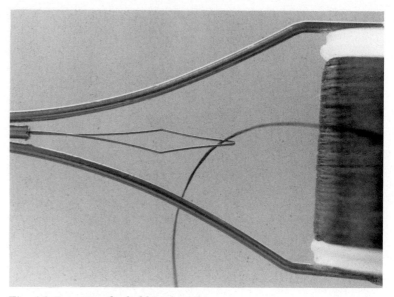

Fig. 4.3 Inserting the bobbin threader.

work area. I use one of the new lamps with two small fluorescent tubes that do not get hot at all. A typical tying set-up is illustrated in **Fig. 4.1**.

Threading the Bobbin

I can highly recommend that you buy a Matarelli bobbin. It's among the best that I have ever used and can be purchased in most fly fishing shops that sell materials, tools, and supplies. The standard size is a good all-around size for thread sizes 6/0 and larger. When making your purchases, do not overlook the D.H. Thompson mini-bobbin that fits the small metal spools that come in sets as described in Chapter 3. I am never without a couple on the table, ready to go with different size threads.

At the same time you should purchase a Matarelli bobbin threader/cleaner that matches the size bobbin you have purchased. A bobbin threader serves two purposes. It has a fine wire loop on one end of a length of bead chain to aid in pulling thread through the tube and a stainless steel wire cleaner on the other end to clean out wax build-up in the tube. You will find that the Matarelli bobbin threader also fits the Thompson mini-bobbin very nicely.

When you get the bobbin, you will notice that it is not open wide enough to accommodate the spool (except the Thompson mini-bobbin, which is fitted exactly for the small metal spools). The best way to open the bobbin wide enough is to grasp a stem with each hand and pull outward as shown in **Fig. 4.2**. You may have to do this several times until the brass holders in each end of the stems are far enough apart to hold the spool with light pressure. The pressure should be heavy enough to wind the thread tightly on the hook, yet light enough for the spool to rotate.

Now, remove the label from the thread spool and place it between the two brass holders. Insert the bobbin threader's wire loop in the front of the tube and put the thread in it as you would a needle's eye (**Fig. 4.3**). Pull the threader with the thread out of the tube as shown in **Fig. 4.4**, and you are all set to go. If you decide to become really serious about fly tying, you may want to purchase additional bobbins so you don't need to change spools when different colors of thread are needed.

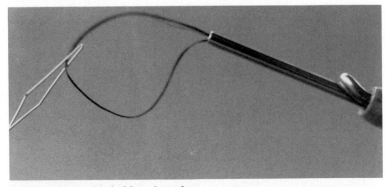

Fig. 4.4 Using the bobbin threader.

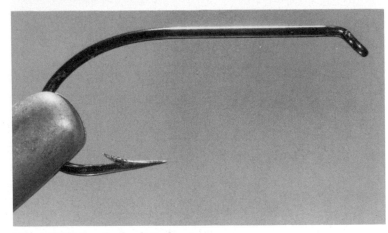

Fig. 4.5 Placing the hook in the vise.

Attaching the Tying Thread

Placing the hook in the vise and attaching the tying thread are the very first steps you will take, regardless of the type of fly you are tying. For the purpose of clarity, and since this is just practice, I will show you the procedure on a rather large hook and will use a piece of fly line instead of tying thread. I suggest, however, that you use tying thread when practicing.

Place a hook, let's say a size #10 Mustad #94840, in the vise with the shank parallel to the work surface. Clamp it in

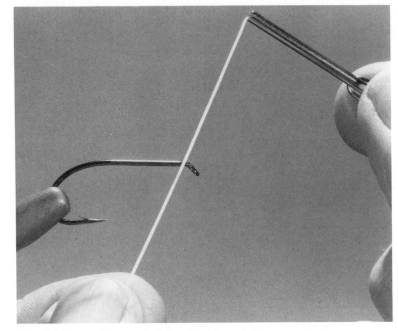

Fig. 4.6 Preparing to wind the thread.

tightly, burying just a small portion of the bend in the jaws, as shown in **Fig. 4.5**.

This is the way I always place the hook in the vise. I want the hook point and barb exposed at all times because they are often used as reference points during the tying instructions throughout this book. When you get used to it, it becomes just routine to manipulate the tying thread around the hook point. When the hook is fastened, hold the eye of the hook between your fingers and try to move it up and down. The hook should not move in the vise; you should feel only the spring in the steel.

Now, draw out about 6″ of tying thread from the spool, holding the bobbin in the right hand and the loose thread between the thumb and first finger of the left hand. Tighten the thread and lay it against the hook shank close to the eye as shown in **Fig. 4.6**.

The length of thread extended between the end of your bobbin and the thumb and first finger should be about 3″. Hold the thread tight and take five or six turns with your

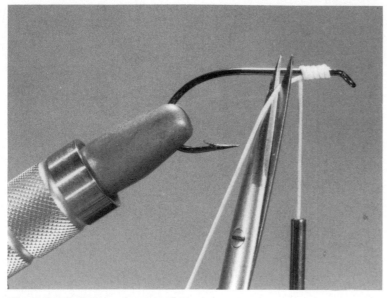

Fig. 4.7 Winding on the thread.

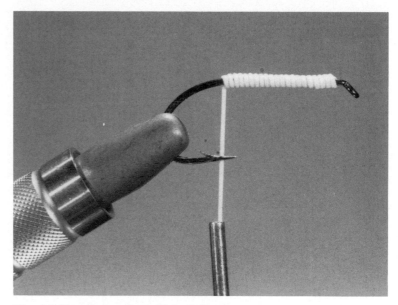

Fig. 4.8 Completing the initial winding.

bobbin hand in a clockwise direction and away from you. Wind it on the hook over the end of the thread held with the left hand. The windings should be next to each other and should be wound toward the rear, as shown in **Fig. 4.7**.

After five or six turns, the excess portion of thread held with your left hand should be cut off close to the windings with your scissors. Continue winding the thread neatly down the shank to a position approximately above the hook point as shown in **Fig. 4.8**.

The Whip Finish

Finishing the head and tying off are normally the last things you do when tying a fly. However, if you come to that point and you don't know how to do it, you are stuck, so I will teach you how to do this before going any further. There are three methods you can use:

1. The manual way.

2. The Matarelli tool method.

3. The half-hitch tool method (the best method for smaller flies).

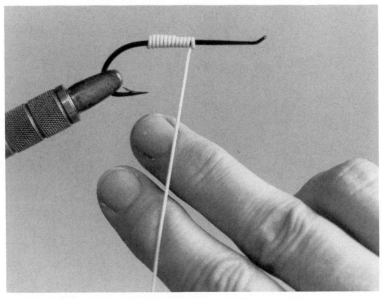

Step 1 Positioning the fingers.

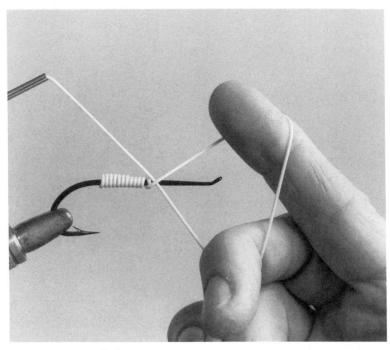

Step 3 Forming the loop.

The Manual Whip Finish

Step 1: Hold the tying thread tight toward you and place the index and middle fingers of your right hand underneath the thread close together.

Step 2: Separate the fingers while twisting the thread on the middle finger.

Step 3: Twist your hand clockwise, thus forming a loop. Continue twisting until the loop appears as shown in the photo. Hold the loop open with your index and middle finger. Note that the thread from the bobbin is against the hook, and the thread held by your index finger is on the outside.

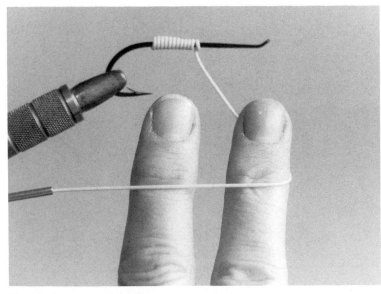

Step 2 Beginning the twist.

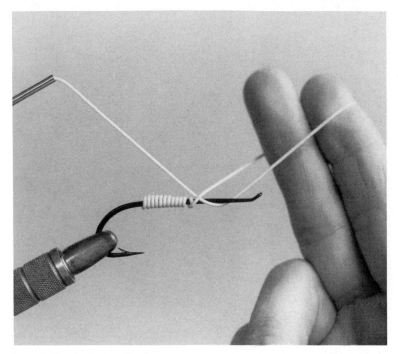

Step 4 Manipulating the loop.

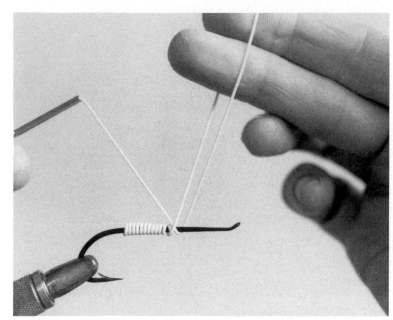

Step 5 Preparing for the first turn.

Step 4: Move the loop back, with upper part over the hook and lower part under. Move the middle finger close to the index finger and hold the thread as shown.

Step 5: Twist your hand and hold the loop to the rear, as shown.

Step 6: Move the loop directly down.

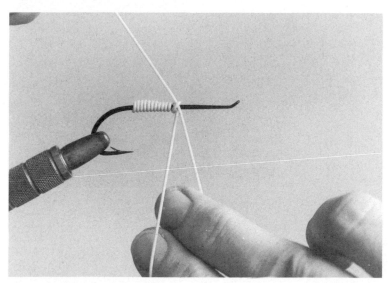

Step 6 Making the first turn.

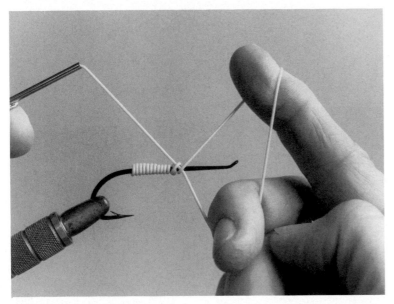

Step 7 Opening the loop.

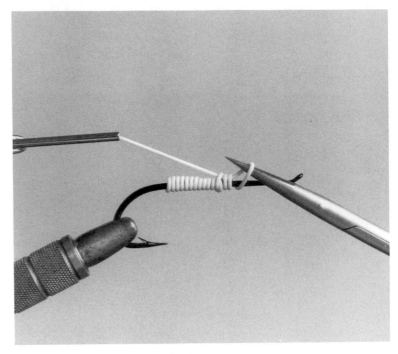

Step 9 Completing the whip finish.

Step 7: Open the loop with your fingers on the near side, and the first turn is completed.

Step 8: Apply four or five more turns in the same manner; then insert your dubbing needle or scissors in the loop and remove your fingers.

Step 9: Pull the thread tight with your bobbin hand as you remove the dubbing needle or scissors, and the whip finish is complete. Cut the surplus thread, and you are ready to apply head cement.

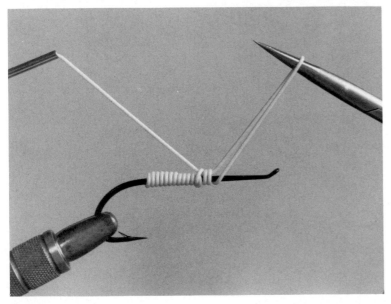

Step 8 Inserting the scissors.

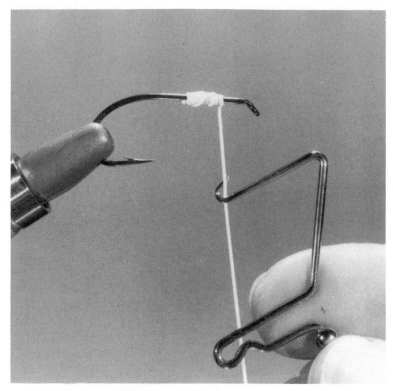

Step 1 Positioning the tool.

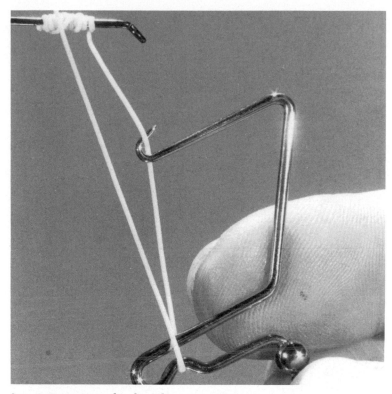

Step 2 Positioning the thread.

The Matarelli Tool Method

Judging from the amount of photos and written instructions given here, it may appear to you that the Matarelli whip finish tool is very difficult to use. Actually, if you were sitting next to me, I could teach you to use it in just a few minutes. But on paper, there are no shortcuts. It takes what it takes.

Step 1: Before you start the whip finish, you should have about 6″ of tying thread between your bobbin and the head

of the fly. To prevent the tool from turning when you first start out, hold the tool in the palm of your hand and place your thumb and index finger as shown. Hold the tying thread tight with your bobbin hand and engage the hook of the tool about 2″ from the head of the fly and lay the other end of the thread behind the lower notch near your index finger.

Step 2: While still holding the tool as described, bring your bobbin and the remainder of thread up past the hook close to the fly head.

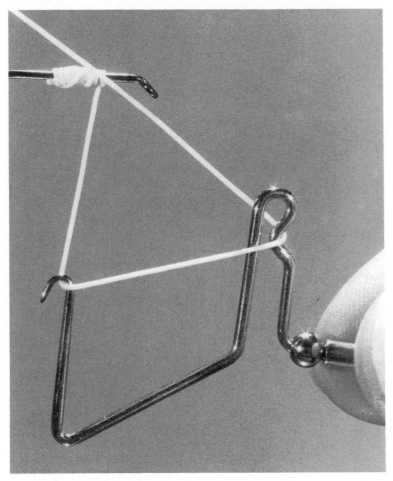

Step 3 Rotating the tool.

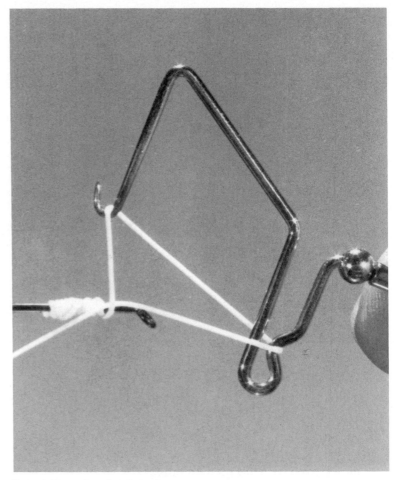

Step 4 Trapping the thread.

Step 3: Maintain the tension on the thread with your bobbin hand while allowing the tool to rotate naturally in its handle until both tool and thread appear as shown. Make sure the thread is still close to the fly head.

Step 4: While still maintaining pressure on the thread, move the tool to a position above the hook as you apply pressure in a downward direction with your bobbin hand, thus trapping the thread coming from the bobbin against the fly head.

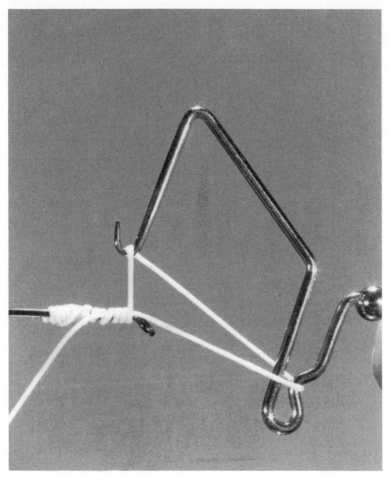

Step 5 Rotating the tool.

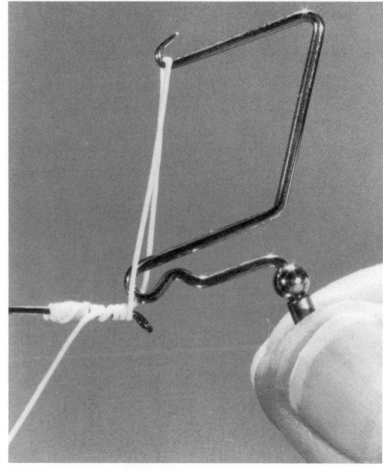

Step 6 Releasing the thread.

Step 5: Rotate the tool around in a clockwise direction until the desired number of turns are made (four or five should do it). If more thread is needed to do this, release it from the spool and gently pull the tool away from the wraps already applied.

Step 6: To release the thread from the lower notch, move the tool to a position above the fly head. Then move the tool handle to a vertical position, as shown, and the thread will slide off the notch while remaining engaged in the hook.

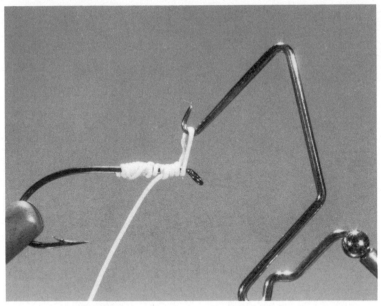

Step 7 Disengaging the tool.

Step 7: Pull the loop tight with your bobbin hand and disengage the tool hook. Now pull the windings completely tight, and you are ready to apply head cement.

The Half-Hitch Tool Method

Using the half-hitch tool is by far the simplest method you can use to tie off a fly when it is finished. Unfortunately, it only works well for small flies, particularly small dry flies. When purchasing a half-hitch tool, you should check the

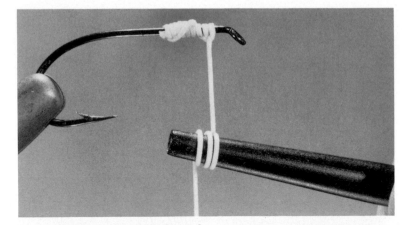

Step 1 Winding thread on the tool.

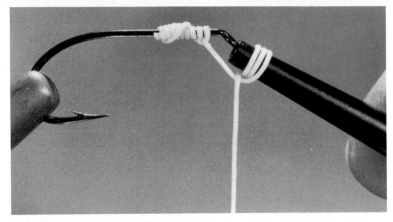

Step 2 Positioning the tool.

holes in the end. They should be big enough for a hook eye to enter. Actually, the best half-hitch tool you can use is a ballpoint pen with the ink cartridge removed.

Step 1: Release about 3″ of thread between the bobbin and the head of the fly. Hold the thread tight toward you and place the end of the tool in the middle on top of the thread. Hold the tool still and take two or three turns of thread around it in a clockwise direction (over and away from you).

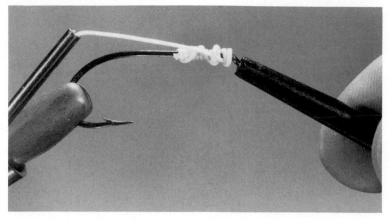

Step 3 Completing the knot.

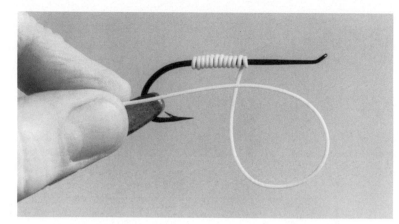

Step 1 Forming the loop.

Step 2: Hold the bobbin still and roll the tool upward to a point directly in front of the hook eye.

Step 3: Place the hole in the end of the tool over the hook eye and slide the windings onto the shank by pulling the bobbin toward the rear. Repeat the whole procedure a couple of times. Then tighten the windings, and you are ready to apply head cement.

The Manual Half-Hitch Knot

When I started tying flies many years ago, Bill Blades, my teacher, did not use a bobbin, so naturally I was taught to tie flies without one. Instead, we used an 18″ length of tying thread and a half-hitch knot to prevent the windings from unraveling every time we had to attach a new piece of material. Today, most tiers use a bobbin, but there are times when a half hitch comes in handy, so I will include it here in the beginning of the tying practice.

Step 1: Release 4″ to 6″ of tying thread between the hook shank and bobbin and form a loop as shown.

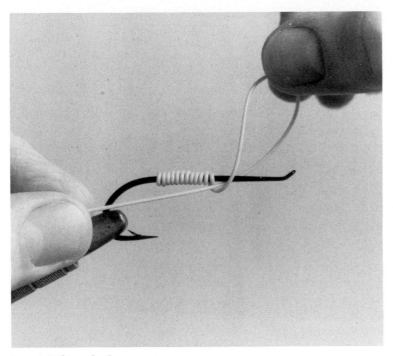

Step 2 Lifting the loop.

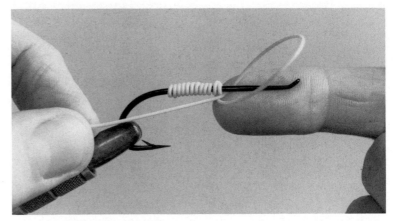

Step 3 Trapping the thread.

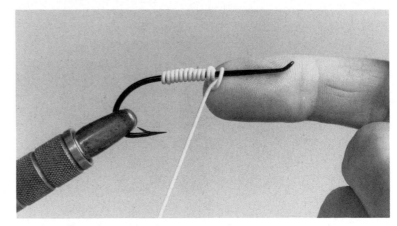

Step 4 Pulling the knot tight.

Step 2: Place your thumb and index finger of your bobbin hand where the thread coming from the fingers crosses the thread coming from the hook and lift the loop over the hook shank.

Step 3: Place your finger on the thread, trapping it tightly between the finger and the hook shank.

Step 4: Pull the loop tight with your bobbin hand, and the half hitch is completed.

Your First Fly

When I got interested in flyfishing, there were three flies the old timers always talked about—the Adams, the Royal Coachman, and the Wooly Worm—but not necessarily in that order. Being a follower then, I was never without them, and they always took fish, whether I was fishing for trout or or bluegill.

When I started to tie my own flies and became a little more independent, I found that there were literally thousands of flies to choose from, many of which I suppose, would have taken fish as well. Now, like most other experienced anglers, I tie a small but very carefully chosen selection of patterns as the season progresses for both freshwater and saltwater fishing, including the old timers' three favorites.

There are a couple of reasons why I have chosen the particular fly you are about to tie as your first lesson in fly tying. First, it's a very easy fly to tie. Second, it has taken more trout than any other fly I have used.

I am lucky enough to live in the Catskill mountains in the town of Roscoe, New York (now called Trout Town U.S.A. by the Federation of Fly Fishermen). The Willowemoc River runs past my backyard and joins the Beaverkill a mile or so downstream at Junction Pool. This is heaven for fly fishermen who come from all over the world to visit this area and try their luck in the famed rivers. Many stop by my house for a chat about flies and the fish taken . . . or not taken.

A gentleman came by one day to tell me that he had been fishing the Beaverkill for two days and had not seen a fish or had a single strike. The poor man was convinced that the river was fished out. Well, you just don't fish out 30 miles of river, so I grabbed a couple of peacock herl nymphs and took him to a spot on the river with lots of rocks and pocket water.

Within an hour we had hooked and released 18 fish between us, picking the pockets with a simple-looking herl nymph that didn't even have a name. It was not until later when a friend of mine invited me to fish some private water on the upper Beaverkill that the fly got its name. I outfished my dry-fly fishing companion six to one that day.

Fig. 4.9 The Insult.

"What in the world are you using?" he asked. When I showed him the beat-up herl nymph, he looked at me in disgust and said, "What an insult!" I thanked him for finally finding a fitting name for this fish-getting herl nymph, which today is known as "The Insult" (**Fig. 4.9**).

Tying the Insult

HOOK:	Mustad #9672, 3X long, size 10
THREAD:	Black, prewaxed 6/0
TAIL:	Small bunch of brown hackle fibers, 1/2 as long as the body with two short sections of peacock herl stump 1/2 the length of the tail fibers
BODY:	Three strands of heavy peacock herl
HEAD:	Black tying thread

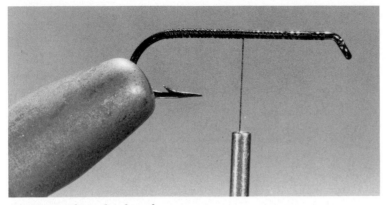

Step 1 Attaching the thread.

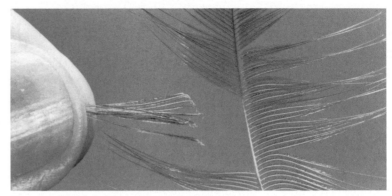

Step 3 Aligning and removing the tail fibers.

Step 2 Selecting and preparing the hackle.

Step 1: Place the hook in the vise and attach the tying thread as explained earlier in this chapter. Wind it to a point above the barb of the hook and then back to the middle of the hook and let the bobbin hang with about 2″ of thread between it and the hook shank.

Although the material used for tails on artificial flies may vary from pattern to pattern, the tying method remains the same and is applicable to both wet and dry flies. Whenever there is a variation from that, it will be explained in the directions for the fly where such a difference exists.

Before continuing, you should thoroughly familiarize yourself with Chapter 3, in which the difference between wet and dry fly hackle for tails and other uses is described. Since you will be tying a nymph, the hackle you select can be of rather poor quality with plenty of web.

Step 2: Select a large brown rooster neck hackle. The fibers in the middle of the hackle should be at least as long as the hook shank. Hold the hackle by the tip and stroke it down the center stem several times until the fibers stand out at a right angle from the stem, as shown.

Step 3: Gather 10 to 15 fibers between your thumb and index finger. In the process of doing so, try to hold the fibers at a 90-degree angle from the stem to get the tips of the hackle fibers lined up as evenly as possible. Now, while holding the hackle close to the fibers to be pulled off, grasp the fibers you have gathered very firmly with your two fingers and pull them off the stem with a downward motion. Once the fibers are off the stem, hold them tight between your fingers and don't let go of them.

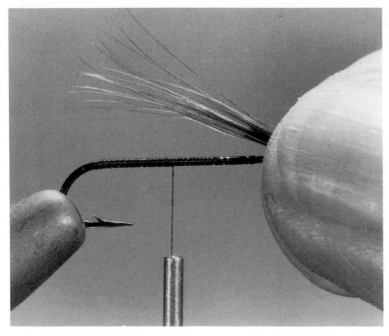

Step 4 Aligning the tips.

Step 5 Judging the tail length.

Step 4: Work the fibers into a tight bunch between your fingers. Then grasp them firmly by the butt ends with the fingers of your other hand and let go with the hand that pulled them off. While holding them tightly together, check to see if the tips are even. If not, carefully even them up, pulling out a few fibers if necessary. The tail fibers are now ready to be tied on the hook.

Step 5: The bunch should now be manipulated in such a manner that the tips are projecting to the rear beyond the bend; they should project, in this case, a distance equal to about 1/2 the length of the body. Keep your fingertips right above the barb of the hook.

Step 6: Now grasp the fiber tips with the fingers of the other hand and tilt the fibers at an angle as shown without moving them sideways in either direction. The fibers should be on the near side of the hook.

Step 6 Preparing to attach the tail.

Step 7 Attaching the tail.

Step 9 Attaching the herl with a slack loop.

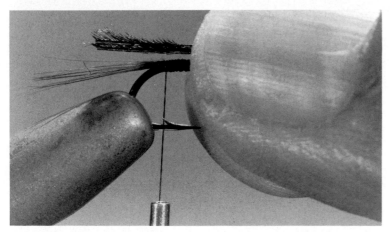

Step 8 Preparing the peacock herl tail section.

Step 7: Carefully take three or four turns of tying thread around the fibers and the hook shank moving the thread over and away in a clockwise direction. The turns should be fairly tight but loose enough to allow you to manipulate the fibers so they are positioned directly on top of the shank. After the thread is wound forward, hold the tips of the fibers and wind the thread back toward the rear with close turns. Stop when you reach the point above the barb and let the bobbin hang there. This completes the first part of the tail.

Step 8: Cut two 1″ sections from the center of a peacock herl and hold them together with the ends even. Now hold them directly on top of the tail you just tied on, with the ends reaching to the middle of the hackle tail.

Step 9: Hold the peacock herl in that position with the thumb and index finger of the other hand while straddling the hook with your fingers, as shown. Be sure you continue to hold the fibers tight between your fingers. Now bring your tying thread straight up between your thumb and the hook. Hold it there with a little pressure.

While holding it there, bring it over the top to the other side, forming a slack loop. Pull the thread straight down between the hook and your index finger on the far side. A loop is thus formed over the material and the shank of the hook. Tighten the loop. Repeat the procedure a few more times, binding down the fibers on the shank. Move your fingers to the rear, take a couple of extra turns around the material, and let the bobbin hang at the tie-in spot right above the barb.

Step 10 Attaching the body herl.

Step 10: The surplus ends of the tail material are left as long as possible to serve as padding for the body. If they are excessively long, they may be cut with scissors, but do not cut them farther back than 1/3 of the hook length measured from the eye. Select three heavy peacock herls about 5″ long and hold them together with the tips even. Hold them at an angle as shown and tie them in together on the near side of the hook, with three or four turns of thread. Tie them in at the same spot where the tail was tied in.

Since peacock herl is very fragile, it must be reinforced with tying thread. To do this, release twice as much thread from the bobbin as the length of the herl and double it over your finger. Use the bobbin to bring the thread back to the tie-in spot. Take a couple of turns of thread around the shank to secure the loop. Leave the loop behind and wind the tying thread forward to a point 1/8″ from the eye, binding down the butt ends of both the herl and tail material in the process. Let the bobbin hang. (The 1/8″ measurement will vary, depending on the size fly you are tying.)

Step 11 Using the reinforcement loop.

Step 11: Twist the thread loop together a little. Now bunch the thread and strands of herl tightly together side by side and clamp your hackle pliers on the end, as shown. Be sure the thread is clamped in with the herl. Twist the herl and thread together by turning the hackle pliers five or six times in a counterclockwise direction. Don't wind it too tight, or you will break the herl.

Step 12 Winding the body.

Step 13 Finishing the head.

Step 12: Using the hackle pliers, start to wind the herl on the shank, over and away in a clockwise direction. Make the turns close together and brush the flues back after each turn. Every two or three turns, give the hackle pliers an additional twist counterclockwise. Keep winding the herl on the hook until you reach the point where the tying thread is hanging. Tie off the herl at this point with three or four turns of thread; then cut the surplus herl with your scissors.

Step 13: Wind a small head with a half dozen turns of thread and tie it off with one of the whip finish methods explained earlier in this chapter. Cut the tying thread with your scissors,

apply some head cement with a dubbing needle or small brush, and your Insult is finished.

Now that you have tied your first fly, I would like to repeat the statement from Bill Blades I made at the start of the Beginner's Tying Practice: "Fly tying is a school from which you never graduate." I would, therefore, suggest that you practice a couple more times on this easy fly which incorporates some of the most important steps in fly tying, steps you will need to learn to near perfection before you go any further.

Chapter 5
Dry Flies

I have often heard it said that if you can tie a good dry fly you should have no trouble tying anything else. I completely disagree with this theory. Tying a dry fly is not nearly as difficult as it is made out to be. In fact, it's fairly simple if you are willing to follow the tying instructions given here and learn each step thoroughly before going on to the next.

Since dry flies are designed to float on the water's surface, there are two very important factors to be considered. First, they must be proportionately well balanced, and second, the hook and material must be carefully selected. A poorly dressed dry fly may catch a fish now and then, but it will quickly fail to float, defeating the purpose for which the fly was designed in the first place.

There are literally thousands of flies on record for having caught a fish or two, but in my view most of them are totally unnecessary. In this chapter, then, I will only teach the techniques that are used in dressing flies you are most likely to use, followed by a list of tested patterns for fishing both eastern and western waters.

The "key fly", if I may call it that, is the American March Brown, for which each tying step is carefully explained. When describing additional fly styles, I will not repeat certain tying

A. Feather tail length = 2½x hook gap.

B. Hair tail length = 2x hook gap.

C. Hook gap.

D. Wing length = 2x hook gap.

E. Wing tie-in position = ⅓ shank length from eye.

F. Hackle length = 1½x hook gap.

G. Shank length = from eye to above barb.

H. Hook length.

I. Wing spread = 1½x hook gap.

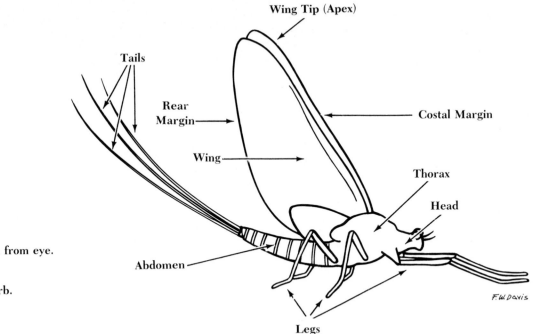

Fig. 5.1a Anatomy of a mayfly adult.

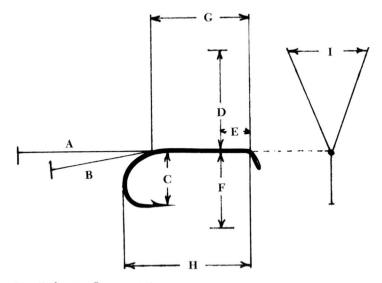

Fig. 5.1b Dry fly proportions.

steps but, instead, will refer back to the instructions for the American March Brown, giving new instructions only for changes in the body, hackle, and wing style.

Before you start to tie the American March Brown, or any other fly for that matter, I suggest that you re-read the beginner's tying practice in Chapter 4. To help you determine the correct proportions for the American March Brown and similar flies, I have included a drawing showing the anatomy of a mayfly adult (**Fig. 5.1a**) and a chart showing dry fly proportions (**Fig. 5.1b**). You should study these before beginning the tying instructions and refer back to them when necessary.

The Flank-Feather Wing Dry Fly

I never could understand how the American March Brown got its name, since according to the wonderful little book, *Art Flick's New Streamside Guide* (New York: Crown Pub-

Step 1 Attaching the tail.

lishers, Inc., 1978), the fly it imitates (*Stenonema vicarium*) hatches from mid-May to mid-June, at least in the East. The name makes just about as much sense as many other elements of flyfishing.

But the fact remains that it is a very important fly almost anywhere one plans to fish. Since it is also a large fly, it is somewhat easier for the beginner to tie while learning the art of dressing a dry fly.

For these reasons and because it incorporates nearly all of the procedures used in tying dry flies, I have chosen the American March Brown as the "key fly." When you can dress the March Brown, you can dress any other fly with a flank-feather wing and many other dry fly patterns. Just study and practice the setting of the other wing styles covered in later instructions.

Tying the American March Brown

HOOK:	Mustad #94840, sizes 10 to 12
THREAD:	Orange, prewaxed 6/0
TAIL:	Dark ginger hackle fibers
WINGS:	Well-marked wood duck flank feather
BODY:	Light fawn-colored fox fur
HACKLE:	Grizzly and dark ginger wound together
HEAD:	Orange tying thread

Step 1: Select 10 to 12 stiff hackle fibers from a spade or large neck hackle and tie them in on top of the shank. (Study

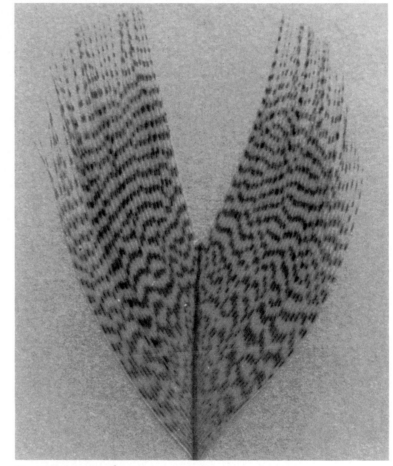

Step 2 Preparing the wings.

the drawing of dry fly proportions in this chapter for tail length and see the detailed tie-in procedure in the beginners' tying practice, Chapter 4.) Trim excess tail material in the middle of the shank and wind the thread over the butt ends to a position 1/3 of the shank length back from the eye. The wing is to be tied in at this point.

Step 2: Select a well-marked, lemon-colored wood duck flank feather and pull off the lower fibers on both sides of the stem. The remainder of the feather should be about double

Step 3 Attaching the wings.

Step 5 Dividing the wings.

Step 4 Setting the wings.

the wing length of the fly you are tying. (See drawing of dry fly proportions in this chapter.) Trim out a piece of feather at the tip end by cutting the center stem as shown. The depth of the notch should be slightly more than the fly's wing length.

Step 3: Gather the fibers in a tight bunch between the thumb and index finger of your left hand. The fiber tips exposed in front of your finger tips should be slightly longer than the fly's wing length. Hold the fibers tight on top of the shank and fasten them with four or five tight turns of tying thread close against your finger tips. The wing will be just as tightly fastened with a few turns of thread as with a dozen. Make sure that all the fibers are on top of the hook shank and positioned 1/3 of the shank length from the eye.

Step 4: Gather the wing fibers with your left hand and hold them back while taking four or five turns of thread in front and close against their base. As shown in the photo, I also press down and back at the base so the fibers stand up by themselves. Trim the excess material on a long slant behind the wing to serve as an underbody.

Step 5: Divide the wing fibers into two equal-sized bunches using the tip of your scissors or dubbing needle. Grasp one bunch with the thumb and index finger on one hand and do likewise with the other bunch using the other hand. Pull the fibers out to each side of the shank as shown. Let the tying thread hang in front of the wing by the bobbin, and you are ready to set the wing permanently.

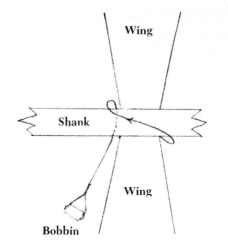

Step 6 Beginning the crisscross.

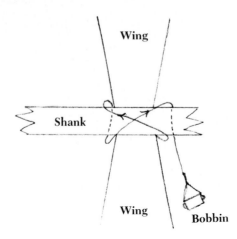

Step 7 Completing the crisscross.

Setting the Wing

To set the wing permanently, you should apply some crisscross windings to keep the fibers separated, followed by the figure-eight technique that will set the wings in their final upright and divided position.

For better illustration, I will demonstrate this procedure with drawings rather than photos, as the technique must be learned properly if you are to succeed in tying winged dry flies.

Step 6: Having completed Step 5, the tying thread must be in front of and close against the base of the wings. Now,

bring the thread up in front of the near wing and take it over the middle and down behind the far wing. This completes the first half of a crisscross, as shown in the drawing.

Step 7: Pull the completed half-crisscross tight and bring the tying thread under the shank and up behind the near wing. Continue by taking it over the middle and down in front of the far wing, as shown. This completes the crisscross that separates the wings. Pull the thread tight and apply another crisscross in the same manner. When using very coarse wing material, I often use several more crisscross windings.

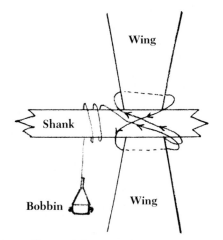

Step 8a Making a figure-eight.

Step 9 Front view of divided wings.

Step 8b Side view of divided wings.

Applying The Figure-Eight

Step 8: Hold the thread up in front of the near wing and take it over the middle and down behind the far wing. Let it hang by the weight of the bobbin and grasp the far wing firmly with the thumb and forefinger of your left hand. Lift

it up to the angle you want it to sit at. While still holding the wing firmly, grasp the bobbin and take a turn of thread around the base of the wing close to the shank in a clockwise direction, as shown in the drawing. Come all the way around, then over between the wings and down behind the near wing.

While still holding the thread tight, let go of the far wing and grasp the near one with your left hand. Raise the wing up like you did the other one and move the tying thread around the base of the near wing in a counterclockwise direction. Come all the way around with the thread tight, then over between the wings down behind the far wing. Take a couple of turns of thread around the hook shank behind the wings to secure the thread. This completes the figure-eight, and the wings should now sit as shown in the photo.

Step 9: The front view of the wings shows how they should sit after completing Steps 6, 7, and 8. The wings should angle equally from the sides of the shank in relation to the hook bend, and the wing tips should be separated by about 1 1/2 hook gaps. If the wings you have completed are like the ones in the photo, apply some penetrating cement on the windings, and the wings are set permanently. If not, correct them by twisting them into place and adding additional figure-eights before applying the cement.

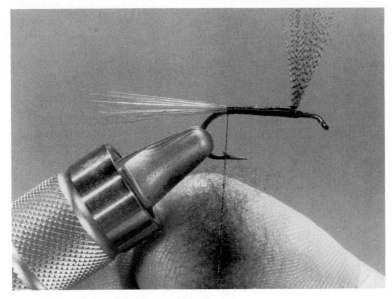

Step 10a Applying dubbing to thread.

Step 10b Tightly dubbed thread.

Step 10: Wind the thread over the trimmed butts to the bend, thus forming an underbody. Hold the thread toward you and, with your index finger about 1/2″ from the hook, place a small amount of fur on the thread, as shown in the Step 10a photo. Roll the fur on the thread between your index finger and thumb in one direction only, working clockwise, while applying pressure. At the end of each roll, release the pressure on your fingers and start a new roll. The result will be a thin, compact layer of fur wound around the thread as shown in the Step 10b photo.

Step 11: Continue to add more fur in the same manner, increasing the amount for each application and slightly overlapping the previous roll until the desired length of tapered dubbing is made. For a size 10 fly, it should be about 2 1/2″ long.

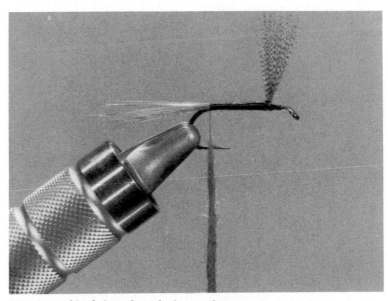

Step 11 Dubbed thread ready for winding.

Step 12 Winding on the dubbing.

Step 14 Preparing the hackle.

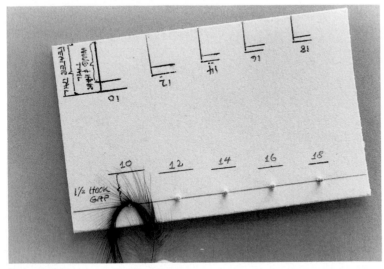

Step 13 Measuring the hackle.

Step 12: Wind the dubbing on the shank in a clockwise direction so it forms a neat taper. Leave a space for the hackle between the dubbed body and the rear of the wing.

Step 13: Select a grizzly and a dark ginger hackle from good-quality dry fly necks. The size of the hackle for a given hook size is determined by the length of the fibers in the middle of the top half of the hackle. On a dry fly, they should be 1 1/2 to 2 hook gaps long. Measure the fiber length by bending the hackle feather with the stem resting on the pin of a hackle gauge, such as the homemade one shown. This measurement can be made before pulling the hackle from the neck.

Step 14: If you use genetic necks, cut the two hackles in half, using only the top portion and discarding the rest. Pull off a few fibers from the butt ends, exposing about 3/16″ of hackle stem. If you use India necks, you may have to use the best portions of two grizzly and two dark ginger hackles, as they are much shorter than genetic hackles.

Step 15 Attaching the hackle.

Step 16 Winding the hackle.

Step 15: Place one hackle on top of the other with the "good" side (the side that faces up on the neck) up. Tie them in behind the wing with three or four tight turns of thread; then bind the stems down on the side or underside of the hook with the same number of windings in front of the wing. Trim the excess stems, if any, so they don't block the eye. Let the thread hang by the weight of the bobbin midway between the eye and the front of the wing.

Step 16: Grasp the tip of the top hackle with your hackle pliers and hold it up with the fibers at a right angle to the hook shank. Wind the hackle on the hook in a clockwise direction as follows: take two turns behind the wing, then a third one close against the back of the wing. Cross over on the far side as you complete that turn and continue winding with the next turn close against the front of the wing, pulling the hackle sharply toward the rear with the hackle pliers to close the gap between that turn and the one in back of the wing. Continue winding all the way around and follow up with two or three more turns in front. Tie the hackle off with three or four windings of thread.

Step 17: Cut the surplus hackle close to the tie-off windings and wind the second hackle in the same manner, moving the hackle through the first one with a side-to-side rocking motion to avoid winding the fibers of the first hackle down. Tie off the second hackle like the first one, cut the surplus,

Step 17 The finished American March Brown.

and wind a small head to cover the stem ends. Finish off with a whip finish or by using the half-hitch tool. Apply a few drops of penetrating cement, and your fly is finished. If the hackle doesn't look as good as you would like it to, don't worry . . . it takes a lot of practice to wind hackle on a dry fly.

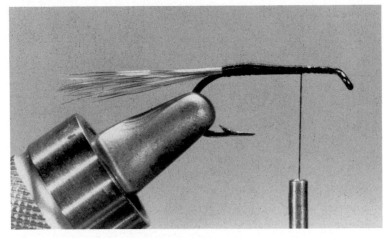

Step 1 Attaching the hackle fiber tail.

Step 2 Attaching the hackle-tip wings.

The Hackle-Tip Wing Dry Fly

Going fishing during the trout season without an Adams is like trying to drive your car without gas. Ironically enough, this fly does not represent any particular insect, but fish take it as a mayfly or a caddisfly. It can be tied in a variety of sizes from 8 to 28.

I recall a conversation I had with Ed Van Put, one of the finest dry fly anglers I've had the pleasure of meeting. As we shared a piece of water on the Beaverkill, I asked him once what he thought was the best fly to use. Without hesitation, he replied with a grin, "It doesn't really matter, just as long as it's an Adams."

The basic difference between the American March Brown and the Adams, as far as style and tying procedures are concerned, is that the Adams has hackle-tip wings while the American March Brown has flank-feather wings.

Tying the Adams

HOOK: Mustad #94840 or #7957B, sizes 10 to 20
THREAD: Black, prewaxed 6/0
TAIL: Grizzly and brown hackle fibers, mixed
WINGS: Grizzly hackle tips
BODY: Muskrat fur dubbing
HEAD: Black tying thread
NOTE: In the West the fly is often tied on a Mustad #7957B and has a tail of dark moose body hair.

Step 1: Tie in the tail on a size 10 hook and wind the tying thread to a position 1/3 of the shank length back from the eye.

Step 2: For the wings, select two well-marked grizzly saddle or neck hackles with rounded tips. Cut a 1″ length off the tip section of each hackle and place one on top of the other with the good sides together. Line up the tips and hold them with the thumb and index finger of your left hand with a little more than a wing length exposed in front of the finger tips. Place them on edge on top of the hook shank and tie them in with four or five tight turns of thread. Make sure they are tied on 1/3 of the shank length back from the eye.

Step 3 Setting the wings upright.

Step 4 Finishing the wings.

Step 3: Trim the surplus feather behind the wing on a long slant to serve as an underbody. Now pull the wing feathers up with your fingers and press a little at the base of the wings until the two solid tip portions of the hackles are standing straight up. Note the stray fibers projecting over the eye in front of the wing.

Step 4: Hold back the wings while trimming off the stray fibers in front midway between the wing and the eye. Wind some tying thread over the fiber ends close against the front of the wing. Then make several crisscross turns between the wings to hold them upright and separated. Take a couple of turns of thread directly behind and close against the wing. With close turns, wind the thread over the butt ends of the hackle until you reach the bend. Apply some cement on the windings to hold them in place permanently.

Step 5: Make the fur body. Then measure, tie in and wind the hackle as shown in the section on tying the American March Brown. Wind a small head, tie off the thread, apply some cement on the head, and your Adams is finished.

Step 5 The finished Adams.

Step 1 Attaching the tippet tail.

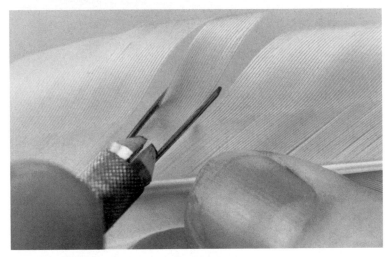

Step 2 Separating the wing quill segment.

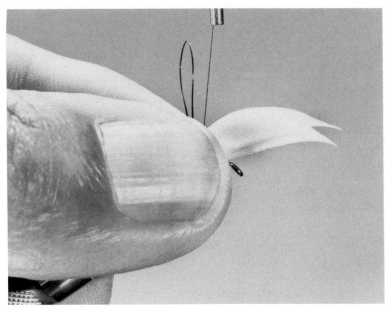

Step 3 Forming a slack loop.

The Quill-Strip Wing Dry Fly

Even some people who have never enjoyed laying out a fly line over a pool full of trout have heard the name Royal Coachman. This old, historic English fly has been tied in a variety of styles such as quill wing, hair wing, parachute hackle, and upright wing. The pattern is used in both trout and salmon fishing. It has, I suspect, accounted for more trout and salmon catches than all other dry flies put together.

The pattern I have chosen to demonstrate here is, as far as I know, the original dressing with a tippet tail and white duck quill-strip wings.

Like the Adams, this fly does not represent any natural insect, but it seems to attract fish when all else fails.

Tying the Royal Coachman

HOOK:	Mustad #94840, sizes 10 to 20
THREAD:	Black, prewaxed 6/0
TAIL:	Golden pheasant tippet
WINGS:	White wing quill strips
BODY:	Peacock herl with red floss center segment
HACKLE:	Coachman brown (dark mahogany brown)
HEAD:	Black tying thread

Step 1: Form the tail by tying in 10 to 20 fibers from a golden pheasant tippet feather in the usual fashion, and then wind the tying thread to a position 1/3 of the shank length back from the eye.

Step 4 Attaching the quill-strip wings.

Step 2: Select a left and a right primary wing feather from a white duck. (See Chapter 3 for information on this material.) One feather must come from the left wing and the other from the right wing of the bird. They must be of the same size and texture. For a size 10 hook, set your wing divider tool so there is a 3/16″ distance between the two paper clip wires. Insert the tool through the quill and draw it out toward the edge, thus separating a quill section. With your scissors, cut the section close to the feather stem. Do the same with the other feather. When taken from the same location on each feather, the pair of wing sections will be perfectly matched. While a quill section 3/16″ wide will do nicely for sizes 10 and 12 flies, the sections for larger flies or smaller flies can be made as wide or as narrow as you choose.

Step 3: Place the quill sections back to back with the convex sides together and even the tips. Hold them between your thumb and first finger with a little more than the measured wing length exposed in front of your fingers. Straddle the shank with your fingers as you place the wings on top of the hook. Now take the tying thread up between your thumb and the wing on the near side, then over and down on the other side between your first finger and the far wing, thus forming a slack loop.

Step 5 Setting and dividing the wings.

It is important to prevent the quill sections from folding when the first thread winding is pulled tight, so you must be sure to hold them firmly between your fingers. Before you pull the loop tight, come all the way around and again bring the thread up between your thumb and the wing on the near side. Now tighten the loop with an upward pull. Repeat this a couple of times.

Step 4: Move your fingers back and take a couple of extra-tight turns so the wing is securely fastened on the shank. It should now sit as shown in the photo.

Step 5: Trim the butt ends from the wings to a long taper as shown. Then lift the wings to an upright position and take four or five turns of thread in front and close against them. Divide the wings and apply crisscross and figure-eight windings as explained in the instructions for tying the American March Brown. Apply a little cement on the windings to secure them permanently.

Step 6 Winding the herl.

Step 7 Finishing the body.

Step 6: Wind the thread over the trimmed butt ends to the bend. Trim and discard 1″ from the tip ends of two medium-heavy peacock herls and tie them in together with a couple of turns of thread. Wind the thread forward to the middle of the shank, twist the herls together, and wind a herl body to the middle of the hook shank. Tie off the herl, but do not trim away the surplus—it's used later. Now tie in a 5″ length of narrow silk or rayon floss at the spot where you tied off the herl. The fly should now look like the one shown in the photo. When tying off and tying in material, just use two or three windings for each step to avoid bulk.

Step 7: Grasp the floss with your fingers and wind it toward the rear over the herl body. Use close turns and cover the herl fibers in the process. Wind the floss to a point 1/16″from the end, thus leaving a segment that forms the rear herl butt. Now wind the floss toward the front over the first layer. When you reach the tie-in spot, hold the two herl ends up and take one or two turns of floss to their right and close against them. Tie off the floss, twist the herls together and wind a second herl segment with two or three close turns. Tie off the herl and trim away all the herl and floss surplus ends. Wind the tying thread to midway between the front herl segment and the wing where the hackle is to be tied in.

Step 8: Tie in and wind two Coachman brown hackles, as explained in the instructions for tying the American March Brown. Wind a small head. Apply some cement, and the fly is finished.

The No-Hackle Dry Fly

In the book *The Treasury of Angling* by Larry Koller (The Rich Press, 1963), you will find a color plate of early American flies painted by the late Austin Hogan showing a no-hackle dun dry fly with upright quill wings. The flies date back to 1850.

Apparently, this type of fly was all but forgotten until Swisher and Richards, in their fine book *Selective Trout* (New York: Crown Publishers, 1971), re-introduced no-hackle flies to the angling world.

This style of fly has since risen in popularity among dry fly anglers who frequently fish quiet stretches of water like those in the Catskills, the Midwest, and some western spring creeks.

Almost any of the popular patterns can be converted to no-hackle flies and tied in many different sizes. My experience is that some beginners find it difficult to set the wings. If you faithfully follow the instructions presented here and practice the steps carefully, you will soon get the hang of it. By the way, don't neglect your practice. It may surprise some of you that, even after 31 years of fly tying, I practice daily. Like a concert pianist, you must constantly fine-tune your fingers and your mind if you wish to master fly tying techniques.

The mistake that some tiers make when dressing flies with this particular wing style is that they set the wings on top of the hook instead of down on each side. Therefore, of course, their flies do not look like the ones they see in photographs or in their supplier's catalog or showcase. The fish don't mind, as they don't read books.

Step 8 The finished Royal Coachman.

Tying the Dark Hendrickson

HOOK:	Mustad #94840 or Partridge L3B, sizes 10 to 16
THREAD:	Black, prewaxed 6/0
TAIL:	Dark blue dun hackle fibers, divided and splayed
WINGS:	Dark gray duck wing quill sections
BODY:	Gray muskrat fur
HACKLE:	None
HEAD:	Black tying thread

Step 1 Splaying the tail.

Step 2 Dubbing the body.

Step 1: Place a size 10 hook in the vise and attach the tying thread. Then wind back slightly down the bend. Roll a little fur dubbing on the thread and wind a small fur ball. Now

Step 3 Positioning the wings.

wind the tying thread to the middle of the shank and tie in six to eight hackle fibers as a bunch. Be sure they are measured so the tips of the fibers extend 2 1/2 hook gaps beyond the bend when fastened in the middle of the shank.

Now wind toward the rear holding the fibers bunched together on top of the shank, stopping when you reach a point 1/8″ ahead of the fur ball. Divide the fibers into two equal bunches, one on each side of the fur ball. While winding the thread tight up against the fur ball, hold the tail fibers in a splayed position separated by the fur ball. Make sure that the fibers are sitting parallel with the hook shank. Then apply a little cement.

Step 2: Dub a tapered fur body blending it nicely in the rear with the fur ball. The body should reach to 1/3 of the shank length back from the eye where the wings will be tied in. Your fly should now look like the one shown in the photo.

Step 3: Cut a quill segment from a right and a left dark gray primary duck wing feather. The width of each segment should be equal to at least 1/3 of the shank length. Setting this type of wing is a little different from those of the Royal Coachman

Step 4 Attaching the wings.

Step 5 The finished Dark Hendrickson no-hackle.

and others, even though they are fastened on in about the same way. When tying them in, they should be held in the position and at the angle that will be final once the tying thread is pulled tight.

To show this angle and to illustrate the wing position in relation to the hook shank and the tying thread, I have left out the near wing. As you can see, when the tying thread is held at a 90-degree angle to the shank and the wing is at a 45-degree angle, half the quill strip is above the shank and the other half below. Where the thread crosses the upper edge of the wing represents the finished wing length.

Step 4: Line up the wing tips and hold them on the shank between your thumb and index finger at the spot outlined in Step 2 and fasten them with thread windings, using the slack loop method (explained in Step 3 of the instructions for tying the Royal Coachman). When the wings are securely fastened, use the figure-eight method explained in setting the wings on the American March Brown but pull each turn

tight with the thread parallel to the shank. Wind forward toward the eye, being careful not to fold the wing segments over. This will splay the wing a little, which is what you want. The wings should now sit as shown. Apply some cement at the base of the wing and on the thread windings.

Step 5: Trim away the butt ends from the wings and wind some thread over the remainder. Now roll some fur dubbing on the thread and wind it on the shank in front of the wing. Then form a small head with tying thread. Apply some head cement, and your Dark Hendrickson is finished.

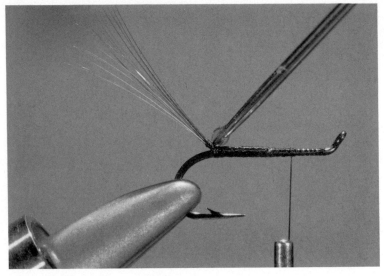

Step 1 Attaching the raised tail.

The Cut-Wing Parachute Dun

Cut-wing parachute duns are my personal favorites. I have experimented for years with different tying methods to create more realism in the wing and overall appearance of these excellent flies and to give them more durability.

I first got interested in cut-wings many years ago when working with Bill Blades. He pointed out that this type of wing was first experimented with by W.J. Dunne, an Englishman who, at that time, was considered one of Britain's greatest dry fly experts.

I have never found the contemporary methods of using wing burning tools satisfactory for shaping the wings. I personally do not use them. Instead, I have devised a method by which I can shape two wings exactly alike with a pair of toenail clippers.

My cut-wing dry flies are designed to float on their fur bodies. The parachute hackle, which is wound horizontally around the wing stems, serves not only to imitate the legs, but also to stabilize the fly so it will float upright.

I prefer to dress this fly on an up-eyed hook. I decided this after studying underwater photographs and noticing that down-eyed hooks break the surface film and distort the shape of the fly from the fish's point of view.

It is important to realize that when using this type of wing we must deal with aerodynamics. I have found that the stem of the wings must be as close to the front edge as possible with the rear margin being much wider. It acts as a rudder, thus preventing the fly from spinning the leader when being cast.

Tying the Jorgensen Isonychia Dun

HOOK:	Mustad #94842 or Partridge L3B, size 10
THREAD:	Olive, prewaxed 6/0
TAIL:	Dark ginger hackle fibers or moose hair
WINGS:	Two dark blue dun hen or rooster body feathers, trimmed to shape
BODY:	Dark reddish-brown fur dubbing
HACKLE:	Dark ginger rooster hackle, tied parachute
HEAD:	Olive tying thread

Step 1: For the tail, tie in 10 or 12 hackle fibers as a bunch. They should be as long as one full hook length when measured in raised position. When they are tied in, raise them to a 45-degree angle and take some turns of thread directly around the fibers at the base. Then fasten them in raised position with some turns of thread around the shank. Apply a little cement on the windings and advance the thread to 1/3 of the shank length back from the eye where the wings are to be tied in.

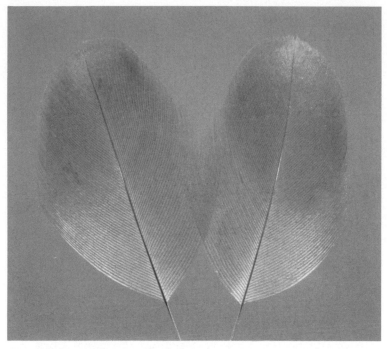

Step 2 Selecting the wing feathers.

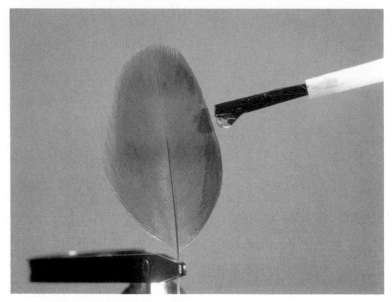

Step 3 Preparing the wing feathers.

Step 2: For the wings, select two body feathers of the same size, shade, and texture. It's important that the stems are of the same thickness. Pull off the soft and unwanted fibers from the stems, leaving two feathers of the same size that are at least twice as long as the length of the hook. Be sure the fibers are sitting directly across from each other at the base of each feather.

Step 3: Place the feathers together, one on top of the other with the dull, concave sides together. Line up the feathers so the fibers at the base are directly on top of each other. Now clamp your teardrop hackle pliers on the stems so they are close and tight against each other with the base fibers about 1/16″ from the jaws of the pliers.

Hold the feathers up to the light. The light coming through them will enable you to line up the stems directly on top of each other as if there was just one stem. When they are

lined up, apply a little nail polish on the feather tips. Re-check the stem alignment. Then apply a narrow coat of polish along the entire edge of one side of the feather only. Also apply a drop of heavy cement on the stems between the plier jaws and the lower base fibers. Set aside to dry. I usually make several wing set-ups in one sitting so they are ready when I need them.

Step 4 Sizing the wing feathers.

Step 6 Trimming the front wing margin.

Step 5 Trimming the rear wing margin.

Step 4: Draw a line across a piece of cardboard 1″ wide. The line should be one hook length from the edge. Place the cemented feathers on the cardboard with the base fibers just slightly past the line. The extra length is needed so you can trim the wing tips to shape. Now cut the feathers along the edge of the cardboard, and you have the wing length.

Step 5: Trim the unglued edge with two cuts of your toenail clippers, as shown. Then round the corners of the wing tip and base. This finishes the rear wing margin. On smaller wings, this can be done with one cut.

Step 6: Turn the feathers and trim the glued costal margin (front edge). You should note that it is trimmed closer to the stem in front, offsetting it from the center for better balance. The wings should be as wide as one hook gap. Round the corners a little. Separate the glued stems, and you have a left and a right wing which are exactly alike. The wings can also be cut with a razor blade by laying the feathers on a piece of glass or plastic. Use a very sharp blade and press down with one clean stroke, rocking the blade slightly.

Step 7 Attaching the wings.

Step 8 Positioning the wings.

Step 7: Hold the wings between your fingertips with the shiny sides together so they will flare out a little when tied in. Be sure the wing tips are perfectly aligned. Straddle the hook shank with your fingertips and place the wings on top with the stems projecting forward over the eye. Take a couple of turns of thread around the stems tight enough to hold them. Now adjust the wings so that there is a little exposed stem between the lowest fibers and the thread windings. (The exposed stem allows for winding the parachute hackle later.) Now secure the wing stems firmly on top of the shank with a few additional thread windings, making sure the wings are sitting parallel to the hook shank.

Step 8: Raise the wings to an upright position and take several turns of thread directly behind them. Now take some turns of thread directly around the wing stems to hold them together and at the same time take turns around the shank until the wings stand by themselves as shown. Trim the long ends of the hackle stems and apply some cement on the structure to set the wings permanently. Note again the exposed stem between the lower wing fibers and the shank.

Step 9 Front view of wings.

The stem is used later for the parachute hackle. Your fly should now look like the one shown in the photo.

Step 9: This photo shows the front view of the completed wings. Note the angle and curvature of the wings.

Jorgensen Isonychia Dun   75

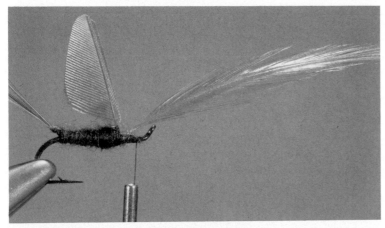

Step 10 Attaching the wing and dubbing the body.

Step 12 Tying off the parachute hackle.

Step 11 Winding the parachute hackle.

Step 10: Select a hackle with fibers that are 2 hook gaps long. Tie it in in front of the wing projecting forward over the eye in a flat position with the shiny side up. Leave a 1/8″ section of bare stem between the first fibers and the shank. Then tie over the stem behind the wing and continue to wind the thread toward the rear up against the tail. Apply a neat, tapered dubbing on the thread and wind it up to the wing. Hold the hackle out of the way and take a couple of turns of dubbing in front of the wing. Let the thread hang a short distance from the eye.

Step 11: Clamp your heavy English hackle pliers on the end of the hackle. Hold the wings with your fingers and wind the hackle on the wing stem horizontally in a clockwise direction. After the first turn, make sure that each succeeding turn is beneath the previous one. Four or five turns should be enough. When the last turn is completed, use the weight of the pliers to allow the remainder of the hackle to hang on the near side in front of the wing.

Step 12: To better illustrate the tie-off procedure, I have used a large hook and hackle. Start by lifting the front hackle fibers out of the way to expose the hackle remainder hanging on the near side of the shank. While the hackle is hanging by the pliers, hold the thread toward the rear. Now take the thread over the hackle remainder and hook, trapping the hackle stem against the shank. Take a couple of turns of thread around the hackle and hook shank. Then grasp the hackle and pull it gently to the right to tighten the hackle windings.

Step 13 The finished Jorgensen Cut-wing Parachute Isonychia Dun.

Now take some additional tight turns around the tie-off spot to secure the hackle permanently. Trim the surplus hackle and apply a one-handed whip finish. If you are unable to do this, let go of the hackle fibers and apply a whip finish with your half-hitch tool. Cut the tying thread and re-arrange the wings and hackle before applying some cement on the tie-off windings. If you wish, you can apply a little cement at the base of the wings on top of the parachute hackle for extra strength, but be careful not to get cement on the wings.

Step 13: Form a head with tying thread and apply some head cement. Your finished Jorgensen Cut-Wing Parachute Isonychia Dun should now look like the one in the photo.

The Fur Spinner

Dry flies dressed with spent (horizontal) wings are known as spinners. They imitate the last stage of a mayfly's life cycle. Mayfly spinners usually appear on the water at dusk and can be recognized by their steady flight, long tails and, in most cases, glassy-clear wings.

There seems to be some disagreement among anglers as to the importance of spinners. My experience is that, when the fish are feeding on spinners rather than duns, you really need them. Fish can become very selective and refuse everything but a particular size or shade of spinner.

In most cases, the conversion of the dry fly dun into a spinner is quite simple. Usually the body color is the same. For wings on spinners, I use very pale blue dun hackle fashioned as you will note in the following tying instructions. On smaller flies, I often use a pale gray polypropylene yarn for the wings. The worst thing you can use is cut wings or whole feather wings which will make your fly spin like a propeller during casting.

Tying the Isonychia Spinner

HOOK:	Mustad #94842 or Partridge L3B, size 10
THREAD:	Olive, prewaxed 6/0
TAIL:	Ginger hackle fibers, 2 1/2 hook gaps long, tied splayed
WINGS:	Palest blue dun hackle, 2 hook gaps fiber length
BODY:	Dark reddish-brown fur dubbing
HACKLE:	None
HEAD:	Olive tying thread

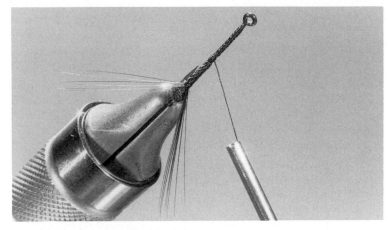

Step 1 Splaying the tail.

Step 2 Attaching the wing hackle.

Step 3 Dividing and splaying the wings.

Step 1: Attach the tying thread on a size 10 hook and wind it back to the bend. Roll a little fur dubbing on the thread and wind a small fur ball. Then wind the tying thread to the middle of the shank and tie in six to eight hackle fibers as a bunch. Be sure they are measured so the tips of the fibers extend 2 1/2 hook gaps beyond the bend when fastened in the middle of the shank.

Now wind toward the rear, holding the fibers bunched together on top of the hook, stopping when you reach a point 1/8″ ahead of the fur ball. Divide the fibers into two equal bunches, one on each side of the fur ball. Wind the thread tight against the fur ball, holding the tail fibers and setting them in a splayed position separated by the fur ball. Make sure that the fibers are sitting parallel with the hook shank. Then apply a little cement. Now wind the thread forward to the middle of the shank where the hackle wing is to be tied in.

Step 2: Select two or three of the palest blue dun hackles you can find and tie them in together in the middle of the shank. For smaller flies, use only two hackles. (For clearer illustration, I am using very dark hackle that shows up better.) Wind the hackle all at once or one at a time, whichever way is easiest for you. It's important that the hackle only occupy 2/3 of the front half of the shank. Tie off the hackle and trim away the surplus.

Step 4 Front view of wings.

Step 3: Divide the hackle fibers above and below the shank into two equal bunches. Gather the fibers from above and below on the near side between your thumb and index finger and pull them out to the near side at a right angle. While holding them with your fingers, take four or five turns of thread directly around the fibers close to the shank. Do the same with the rest of the fibers, setting them as a wing on the far side. The fibers should be well splayed as shown. Apply some cement on the fibers' base and thread windings; then wind the thread back to immediately in front of the tail. (To splay the hackle fibers, you can flatten the thread windings a little with pliers or tweezers when the cement has set a little.)

Step 4: In this front view of the wings, note that they are slanted up ever so slightly.

Step 5: Roll some dubbing on the thread and wind a tapered fur body to directly behind the wings. Now crisscross the dubbing between the wings and take a couple of turns around the shank in front. Tie off the fur, remove the surplus, and wind a small head. Then tie off the thread. Apply some head cement, and your spinner is finished.

Step 5 The finished Isonychia spinner.

Fig. 5.2 Small spinner with poly yarn wings.

On small flies, like the Caenis spinner shown in **Fig. 5.2** sitting on a paper match, you can use a small bunch of poly yarn as the wing. By following the tying instructions for the Isonychia, you will be able to convert any of the dun patterns listed later into spinners. Just lengthen the tails of the standard patterns and use light blue dun hackle for wings.

Isonychia Spinner   79

The Jorgen-Betts Spinner Duns

A few years ago, when I was asked to do a fly tying demonstration at United Fly Tiers in Boston, a young fellow standing next to me asked, "What do you do with all the large hackles you have left on the neck when you have used all the smaller ones?" The question stumped me for a moment, and I thought to myself, "What, indeed, do I do with all the large hackles when I have used the smaller ones?"

Not wanting to appear inept, I quickly said, "Tie flies with them." I knew very well that I now had to prove it.

I took one large grizzly hackle and made an abdomen extension body by reversing the fibers at the tip portion. I set the fibers in tying cement close up against each side of the stem as the late Harry Darbee, legendary Catskill fly designer, had shown me. This was Harry's method of tying his famous two-feather mayfly.

I then cut out the triangle at the tip of the hackle, leaving two fibers to represent the tails. The resulting extension body was 1" long. I tied it on a size 10 up-eyed hook, applied some fur on the shank, wound two large grizzly hackles over the entire shank, and tied them off. I then trimmed off all the hackle fibers underneath, leaving the ones on top to represent the wings. Thus, the Eastern Green Drake was born. It was so simple that even I was surprised when it turned out that this style of fly became the best green drake imitation I'd ever fished with.

Like everything else in flyfishing, if it works, it must be changed. So after John Betts, master of synthetics, devised and perfected the polypropylene abdomen extension body, two of my friends from Boston showed up at my house one day and presented me with the Jorgen-Betts spinner dun. This fly incorporates the Betts abdomen extension body and the Jorgensen wing and thorax.

When I called John Betts to ask his permission to use his wonderful invention, he agreed on the condition that I would send him some flies tied in that style. (By the way, John, there is a waiting list for flies and work I have agreed to do. You are on the list, though, right after Hoagy Carmichael, Lefty Kreh, and about 30 others. Do not despair . . . when this book is finished, back to the tying bench.)

The Jorgen-Betts patterns, to my knowledge, have never been published before, but they are fast becoming a very popular fly during the green drake hatch in the Catskills.

This method can, of course, be used in tying other large mayfly species, as well.

Tying the Eastern Green Drake Dun

HOOK:	Mustad #94842 or Partridge L3B, size 10
THREAD:	Yellow, prewaxed 6/0
TAIL:	Three dark moose mane fibers, length of the body
WINGS:	Two grizzly hackles dyed pale green or one natural grizzly and one pale green wound together.
BODY:	Pale creamish-yellow poly yarn with an olive cast
THORAX:	Gray fur dubbing
HEAD:	Yellow tying thread

NOTE: I use a three-ply polypropylene yarn called Phentex for the abdomen extension on the Jorgen-Betts flies. The formula for the Eastern Green Drake Dun is a mixture of three plies off-white, one ply bright yellow, and 1/3 of a ply dark green. The diameter of the extension for this fly is equal to half of a three-ply skein. If you are using single strand yarn, you will have to separate the strands to come up with the formula. In that case, I would estimate the diameter of the extension to be about 3/32".

Step 1: To prepare the extension you must first mix the poly yarn. This is done with a special wire brush designed for grooming dogs. It has wire "bristles" and can be purchased in your pet supply store. Start by cutting some 5" lengths of the yarn mentioned in the formula above. Place the strands side-by-side on your leg or on a piece of cardboard on the table.

Hold all the yarn bunched together and start brushing the yarn beginning at your fingers and working out toward the ends, as shown in the Step 1b photo. When the fibers start to separate from one another, roll them around lengthwise,

Step 1a Dog grooming brush for mixing poly yarn.

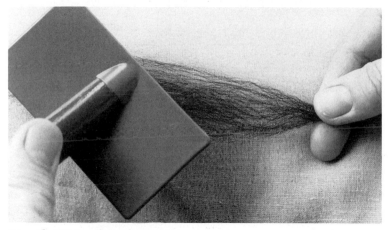

Step 1b Mixing the poly yarn.

Step 2a Heating the poly yarn.

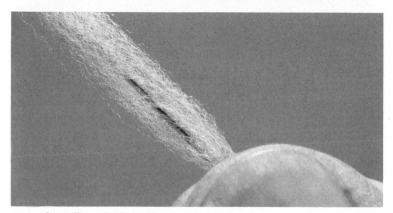

Step 2b Rolling the heated poly yarn end.

mixing them with your fingers. Brush again and continue in this manner until all the colors are thoroughly mixed. Now make an overhand knot in the end to hold the fiber bunch together.

Step 2: Separate a bunch of fibers that when combined are about 3/32″ in diameter. Cut a 2″ length from the bunch and trim one end even. Now insert a sewing needle lengthwise in the middle of the bunch and let it extend about 1/4″ out from the end of the yarn. The needle should be .025″ in diameter. The yarn fibers should be packed as tightly as possible around the needle.

Slowly warm up the tip of the needle with the flame from a lighter. Slowly move the flame up the tip of the needle until the heat begins to melt the end of the yarn, as shown in the Step 2a photo. Let it melt a little. Then quickly drop the lighter, moisten your thumb and index finger, and roll the yarn and needle between them, as shown in the Step 2b photo. (Be sure you moisten your fingers, or you will get a bad burn.)

Step 3 The finished extension tip.

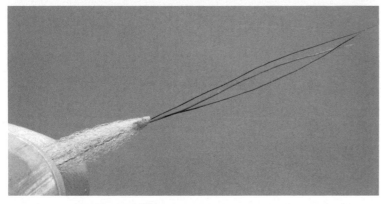

Step 4 Inserting the tail fibers.

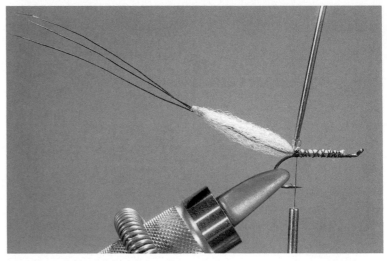

Step 5 Attaching the extension.

Step 3: Remove the needle. The extension tip is now melted together with a hole in the middle of the end for the tails.

Step 4: Insert the butt ends of three dark moose mane fibers in the end of the extension. The tip ends of the moose fibers should extend about 1 1/4″ from the tip of the extension, and the butt ends should extend at least the same length inside so they can be fastened on the shank together with the extension.

Step 5: Place a size 10 hook in the vise and attach the tying thread. Then wind it to a point midway between the barb and the hook point. Tie in the extension with four or five tight turns of thread. The distance between the eye of the hook and the tip of the extension should be 1″. (The distance will vary depending on the species and the size of the fly.) Trim the excess yarn and tail material just short of the eye and wind it down on the shank with tying thread. Now wind the thread back to the tie-in spot. Apply a little cement at the base of the extension, and your fly should look like the one in the photo.

Step 6: Prepare two large hackles with fibers 1″ long and tie them in just slightly ahead of the extension. Wind over the hackle stems, binding them down on the shank. Wind the thread back to the extension and dub some fur on the thread. Then hold the hackle out of the way while taking one or two turns of fur to the left of them, covering the extension's tie-in windings. Continue to wind the fur forward over the shank to the front, making sure to leave enough room for the head.

Step 6 Attaching the hackle and winding the body.

Step 8 Trimming the hackle.

Step 7 Winding the hackle.

Step 9 The finished Jorgen-Betts Eastern Green Drake.

Step 7: Wind the hackles over the fur body and tie them off in front. Trim the surplus and wind a small head before applying some head cement.

Step 8: Trim off the hackle fibers underneath close to the stem, and the front of your fly should look like the one shown in the photo.

Step 9: The finished fly should look like the one shown in the photo.

Step 1 Attaching the extension.

Step 2 The finished Jorgen-Betts Eastern Green Drake Spinner.

Tying the Eastern Green Drake Spinner

The materials list for this spinner, tied in the Jorgen-Betts style, is the same as that of the dun above, except that the extension is made with off-white poly yarn, and the wing is made with one natural grizzly and one very pale blue dun hackle. A slight modification is made when tying in the extension as explained in the following steps.

Step 1: Attach the tying thread and wind it to just above the point of the hook. Prepare the extension as explained in Steps 1 through 4 of the tying instructions for the dun. Tie it in above the hook point. Now separate the yarn from the butt ends of the moose mane fibers and double the yarn tightly back over the extension. Hold it there while taking some close turns of thread 1/16″ toward the rear over the

yarn and the base of the extension. Trim the moose mane butts to just short of the eye and wind the thread over them. Then wind back to a position directly in front of the extension base.

Step 2: Tie in the two hackles and wind the fur underbody, with the first turn of fur covering the windings fastening on the extension. Complete the hackle as you did with the dun, including the hackle trimming on the underside. Divide the hackle fibers on top into two equal bunches and pull them out to the sides. Now grasp the poly yarn end and pull it forward over and between the two bunches of hackle. Tie the yarn down in front of the hackle and trim the surplus. Wind a small head, apply head cement, and the spinner is finished.

Step 1 Attaching the tail.

Step 2 Combing out the deer hair underfur.

The Hair-Wing Dry Fly

The Humpy, also called the Goofus Bug, is one of the most famous western flies. According to Jack Dennis, author of *Western Trout Fly Tying Manual*, (Jackson Hole, Wyoming: Snake River Books, 1974), the Humpy probably originated around Jackson Hole. Inasmuch as it does not represent anything in particular, the Humpy's ability to attract trout, steelhead, and salmon is remarkable.

Today, the Humpy is not only used in the West but has found its way to eastern trout streams, as well, particularly in small sizes. The Humpy can be tied in varying ways—traditional Humpy style, parachute style, hair-wing, and Royal Humpy. It is tied in a full range of sizes from 2 to 22.

For some, it is not an easy fly to tie because the hump back and the wings are made from the same bunch of material. But if you follow the tying instructions I have given and practice a few times, you will soon find the Humpy just as easy to tie as any other dry fly.

Tying the Humpy

HOOK: Mustad #94840 or #7957B, sizes 2 to 22

THREAD:	Black, red, orange, yellow, or green, pre-waxed 3/0 or 6/0
TAIL:	Dark moose body hair
WINGS:	Tips of the natural or bleached cream deer body hair used for body
BODY:	Tying thread with natural or bleached cream deer body hair tied over as shellback
HACKLE:	Brown, or grizzly and brown mixed
HEAD:	Tying thread

Step 1: Place a size 10 hook in the vise and attach the tying thread. Select 10 to 12 stiff moose body hairs and line up the tips. Tie in the tail so it is two hook gaps long with the butt ends reaching to exactly the middle of the shank. (The length is important, as it's used later for a measurement when the body is tied in.) Let the tying thread hang by the bobbin in the middle of the shank.

Step 2: Cut a bunch of natural deer body hair from the skin. The hair should be 1 1/2″ long. I prefer fine-textured hair with well-marked tips from a yearling deer. Comb out the short hair and underfur with a small comb or brush, as shown.

Step 3 Stacking the deer hair.

Step 4 Measuring the deer hair.

Step 5 Attaching the deer hair and forming the underbody.

Step 3: Insert the hair in a hair stacker and tap the stacker on the table to align the tips. Hold the stacker tilted on its side while removing the funnel with the aligned hair.

Step 4: Take the hair out of the stacker by the tips. Since both the body and wings are made of the same bunch of hair, make sure you have enough in the bunch to do the job. After a few disasters, you will soon know how much hair is needed for a particular size fly. Now measure and cut the hair bunch so it is equal to the distance between the eye of the hook and the tip of the tail.

Step 5: Hold the butt ends of the hair exactly in the middle of the shank and tie in. Wind the tying thread over the hair toward the rear, binding it down on top of the shank and the butt ends of the tail. Wind the thread back to the bend and continue to wind back and forth until the hair is completely covered with thread, thus forming the underbody, as shown in the photo.

Step 6 Tying down the deer hair shellback.

Step 7 Setting the deer hair wings.

Step 6: Grasp all the deer hair as a bunch (being careful to leave the moose hair tail) and pull it forward over the body. Hold on to the hair tips and tie the bunch down with thread windings directly in front of the underbody. Make sure all the hair is pulled tight and tied down on top of the shank.

Step 7: Hold the hair tips tight between your fingers on top of the shank. Then wind the thread forward over the hair to the middle of the front half of the shank. Raise the hair tips up and divide them into two equal portions. Apply some crisscross and figure-eight windings in the same manner as when setting the wing on the American March Brown. After setting the wings securely with thread, apply some cement to fasten them permanently.

Step 8: Tie in the hackle and wind it as explained in the American March Brown tying instructions, Steps 15, 16, and 17. Wind a small head, apply cement, and your Humpy is finished.

Step 8 The finished Humpy.

Fig. 5.3 Royal Wulff, upright and divided hair wings.

Fig. 5.4 Royal Humpy, upright wings, parachute hackle.

Other Styles of Hair-Wing Dry Flies

Hair is the most durable material you can use for wings on dry flies. The famed Wulff patterns, originated by Lee Wulff, are examples of typical hair-wing flies. White and

Fig. 5.5 Preparing an upright hair wing for parachute hackle.

natural brown bucktail, calf tail, woodchuck guard hairs, and many other types of hair can be used.

They can be dressed on the hook in the same basic manner as flank feathers . . . upright and divided. (See the Royal Wulff in **Fig. 5.3**.) Unlike flank feathers and other types of wing material, they can also be set upright as a bunch, in which case the hackle can be wound around the base of the wing in parachute style. (See the Royal Humpy in **Fig. 5.4**.) Flies that are dressed in this fashion are very durable and are particularly popular among western anglers.

When tying an upright and undivided hair wing for use with a parachute hackle, a good foundation must be made for the hackle to be wound on. This is done by winding some tying thread a short distance up the base of the wing and then applying some cement to strengthen it (**Fig. 5.5**). Before you can apply such a wing on a Royal Humpy, however, the hair tips that would normally form the wing must be trimmed off close to the tie-down windings. The hair wing can now be tied in and the butt ends trimmed close to the body. I sometimes wind a little red fur over the thread windings before applying the hackle to make a better looking fly.

It is not always possible to even up the tips of the hair in a stacking tool. Therefore, I suggest that you simply line up

Fig. 5.6 Forming a smooth transition.

Fig. 5.7 Side view of Irresistible body.

Fig. 5.8 Top view of Irresistible body.

Fig. 5.9 Front view of Irresistible body.

Deer Hair Bodies

There are some important dry flies with bodies of spun deer body hair, trimmed to shape. While I personally use this type of fly only for Atlantic salmon, there are anglers in the West who frequently use patterns utilizing bodies of spun deer body hair, such as the Irresistible, for trout fishing.

The technique of spinning deer hair is dealt with in great detail in the tying instructions for deer-hair sculpins and bass bugs. Therefore, I shall show only the shape of the body in this chapter and ask you to study the tying instructions in the streamer and bass bug chapters. **Figures 5.7, 5.8,** and **5.9** show the side, top, and front views, respectively. A finished fly is illustrated in **Fig. 5.10**.

the tips the best you can. Hair is often used for both tails and wings and since it is much coarser than feathers, it's important to make a smooth transition between the butt ends in order to make a nice overbody. Tie in the tail first with the butts reaching to the middle of the shank and trim them on a long slant. Trim the butt ends from the wing on a slant in the opposite direction. Wind the tying thread over the ends, and the fly should look like the one in **Fig. 5.6**.

Fig. 5.10 The finished Irresistible tied for Atlantic salmon.

Midges

Midge flies are very popular among dry fly purists, and there are times when they are deadly, even for large brown and rainbow trout. A number of the most popular midge patterns are included in a separate section of the list of selected patterns given at the end of this chapter. My friend Tony Ottomano, who is a midge specialist, insists that certain well-known patterns such as the Adams, Blue Quill, and Black Gnat, tied on size 20 to 28 hooks, will take more fish more often than any other flies.

The tying methods previously explained in this chapter will enable you to tie the midge patterns in the list of selected patterns, all of which I've found effective at one time or another. In addition to these, you may find that the Trico spinner will serve as a midge now and then, as will some of the very small emerger patterns found in the nymph chapter, Chapter 7.

The hook I prefer for these tiny flies is Mustad #94859. It is the same as Mustad #94840 (which has a turned-down eye) except that it has a ringed eye, specifically designed for midges so the eye does not interfere with hooking the fish. It is available in sizes 18 through 28 only.

Selected Dry Fly Patterns

Since this is a book of fly tying techniques rather than a list of hundreds of patterns, I have selected only flies that I use myself and with which I have had great success in fishing around the world. If you have closely followed and practiced the various tying techniques in this chapter, you will be able to tie most of the standard dries and spinners that are listed.

Standard Dry Flies

ADAMS

HOOK:	Mustad #94840 or #7957B, sizes 10 to 20
THREAD:	Black, prewaxed 6/0
TAIL:	Grizzly and brown hackle fibers, mixed
WINGS:	Grizzly hackle tips
BODY:	Muskrat fur dubbing
HACKLE:	Grizzly and brown mixed
HEAD:	Black tying thread

NOTE: In the West the fly is often tied on a Mustad #7957B with a tail of dark moose body hair.

AUSABLE WULFF

HOOK:	Mustad #94840 or #7957B, sizes 6 to 16
THREAD:	Red, prewaxed 6/0
TAIL:	Woodchuck guard hairs
WINGS:	White calf tail, upright and divided
BODY:	Burnt-orange fur dubbing
HACKLE:	Grizzly and brown wound together
HEAD:	Red tying thread

BADGER SPIDER

HOOK:	Mustad #9523, sizes 12 to 18
THREAD:	Black, prewaxed 6/0
TAIL:	Badger hackle fibers
WINGS:	None
BODY:	None
HACKLE:	Badger, oversize
HEAD:	Black tying thread

NOTE: Hackle and tail should be twice as long as normal for the size hook being used. Example: Use hackle and tail appropriate for size 8 fly on a size 12 hook.

BLACK GNAT

HOOK:	Mustad #94840, sizes 12 to 22
THREAD:	Black, prewaxed 6/0
TAIL:	Black hackle fibers
WINGS:	Gray duck wing quill segments
BODY:	Black fur dubbing
HACKLE:	Black
HEAD:	Black tying thread

BLUE DUN

HOOK:	Mustad #94840, sizes 10 to 22
THREAD:	Black, prewaxed 6/0
TAIL:	Blue dun hackle fibers
WINGS:	Gray duck wing quill segments
BODY:	Muskrat fur dubbing
HACKLE:	Blue dun
HEAD:	Black tying thread

BLUE QUILL

HOOK:	Mustad #94840, sizes 10 to 22
THREAD:	Black, prewaxed 6/0
TAIL:	Blue dun hackle fibers
WINGS:	Blue dun hackle tips
BODY:	Blue dun hackle stem, stripped
HACKLE:	Blue dun
HEAD:	Black tying thread

BLUE-WINGED OLIVE (BAETIS)

HOOK:	Mustad #94840, sizes 16 to 24
THREAD:	Olive, prewaxed 6/0
TAIL:	Blue dun hackle fibers
WINGS:	Blue dun hackle tips, dark
BODY:	Olive-brown fur dubbing
HACKLE:	Medium blue dun
HEAD:	Olive tying thread

BLUE-WINGED OLIVE NO-HACKLE

HOOK:	Mustad #94842, sizes 14 to 24
THREAD:	Olive, prewaxed 6/0
TAIL:	Blue dun hackle fibers, tied splayed
WINGS:	Blue-gray duck wing quill segments
BODY:	Yellowish-olive fur dubbing
HACKLE:	None
HEAD:	Olive tying thread

BROWN BIVISIBLE

HOOK:	Mustad #94840, sizes 10 to 18
THREAD:	Black, prewaxed 6/0
TAIL:	Brown hackle fibers
WINGS:	None
BODY:	None
HACKLE:	Brown, covering full length of shank and fronted with a few turns of white
HEAD:	Black tying thread

CAHILL, LIGHT

HOOK:	Mustad #94840, sizes 12 to 22
THREAD:	Primrose, prewaxed 6/0
TAIL:	Light ginger hackle fibers
WINGS:	Wood duck flank feather
BODY:	Cream fox fur dubbing
HACKLE:	Light ginger
HEAD:	Primrose tying thread

CREAM VARIANT

HOOK:	Mustad #94833, sizes 10 to 12
THREAD:	Yellow, prewaxed 6/0
TAIL:	Very stiff cream hackle fibers
WINGS:	None
BODY:	Cream hackle stem, stripped
HACKLE:	Cream rooster neck or saddle hackle
HEAD:	Yellow tying thread

GRAY FOX VARIANT

HOOK:	Mustad #94833, sizes 10 to 14
THREAD:	Yellow, prewaxed 6/0
TAIL:	Ginger hackle fibers, very stiff
WINGS:	None
BODY:	Ginger hackle stem, stripped
HACKLE:	Light ginger, dark ginger, and grizzly wound together
HEAD:	Yellow tying thread

Fig. 5.11 Gray Fox Variant. The late Elsie Darbee was very particular about the proportions on variants. She used size 6 hackles for a size 10 fly, and the very stiff tail had to be the same length as the fibers on the hackle.

GRAY FOX

HOOK:	Mustad #94840, sizes 12 to 14
THREAD:	Yellow, prewaxed 6/0
TAIL:	Ginger hackle fibers
WINGS:	Mallard flank feather
BODY:	Light fawn-colored fox fur dubbing
HACKLE:	Light ginger and grizzly wound together
HEAD:	Yellow tying thread

GRAY WULFF

HOOK:	Mustad #94840 or #7957B, sizes 6 to 16
THREAD:	Black, prewaxed 6/0
TAIL:	Brown bucktail
WINGS:	Brown bucktail
BODY:	Muskrat fur dubbing
HACKLE:	Dark blue dun
HEAD:	Black tying thread

GRIZZLY WULFF

HOOK:	Mustad #94840 or #7957B, sizes 6 to 16
THREAD:	Black, prewaxed 6/0
TAIL:	Brown bucktail
WINGS:	Brown bucktail
BODY:	Yellow floss
HACKLE:	Brown and grizzly wound together
HEAD:	Black tying thread

HENDRICKSON

HOOK:	Mustad #94840, sizes 10 to 18
THREAD:	Black, prewaxed 6/0
TAIL:	Blue dun hackle fibers
WINGS:	Wood duck flank feather
BODY:	Pinkish-cream fox fur dubbing
HACKLE:	Rusty blue dun
HEAD:	Black tying thread

HENDRICKSON NO-HACKLE

HOOK:	Mustad #94840 or Partridge L3B, sizes 10 to 16
THREAD:	Black, prewaxed 6/0
TAIL:	Dark blue dun hackle fibers, tied divided and splayed
WINGS:	Dark gray duck wing quill sections
BODY:	Gray muskrat fur
HACKLE:	None
HEAD:	Black tying thread

HUMPY

HOOK:	Mustad #94840 or #7957B, sizes 2 to 22
THREAD:	Black, red, orange, yellow, or green, prewaxed 3/0 or 6/0
TAIL:	Dark moose body hair
WINGS:	Tips of natural or bleached cream deer body hair used for the body
BODY:	Tying thread with natural or bleached cream deer body hair tied over as shellback
HACKLE:	Brown or grizzly and brown mixed
HEAD:	Tying thread

IRRESISTIBLE

HOOK:	Mustad #94840 or #7957B, sizes 6 to 16
THREAD:	Black, prewaxed 6/0
TAIL:	Brown bucktail
WINGS:	Brown bucktail
BODY:	Deer body hair, spun and trimmed to shape
HACKLE:	Blue dun
HEAD:	Black tying thread

NOTE: See body shape under Deer Hair Bodies, this chapter.

MARCH BROWN, AMERICAN

HOOK:	Mustad #94840, sizes 10 to 12
THREAD:	Orange, prewaxed 6/0
TAIL:	Dark ginger hackle fibers
WINGS:	Well-marked wood duck flank feather
BODY:	Light fawn-colored fox fur
HACKLE:	Grizzly and dark ginger wound together
HEAD:	Orange tying thread

PALE EVENING DUN

HOOK:	Mustad #94840, sizes 14 to 18
THREAD:	White, prewaxed 6/0
TAIL:	Pale blue dun
WINGS:	Pale blue dun hackle tips
BODY:	Pale yellow fur dubbing
HACKLE:	Pale blue dun
HEAD:	White tying thread

QUILL GORDON

HOOK:	Mustad #94840, sizes 12 to 18
THREAD:	Black, prewaxed 6/0
TAIL:	Blue dun hackle fibers
WINGS:	Wood duck flank feather
BODY:	Stripped peacock quill
HACKLE:	Blue dun
HEAD:	Black tying thread

RAT-FACED McDOUGAL

HOOK:	Mustad #94840 or #7957B, sizes 6 to 12
THREAD:	Black, prewaxed 6/0
TAIL:	White calf tail
WINGS:	White calf tail
BODY:	Deer body hair, spun and trimmed to shape

Fig. 5.12 Quill Gordon, a typical sparsely dressed eastern-style dry fly.

HACKLE:	Ginger
HEAD:	Black tying thread

NOTE: For salmon, use Partridge Code 01 dry fly salmon hook. The body shape is the same as that of the Irresistible, shown in the photos in the section on deer hair bodies in this chapter.

RED QUILL

HOOK:	Mustad #94840, sizes 12 to 18
THREAD:	Black, prewaxed 6/0
TAIL:	Blue dun hackle fibers
WINGS:	Wood duck flank feather
BODY:	Dark brown hackle stem, stripped
HACKLE:	Blue dun
HEAD:	Black tying thread

RENEGADE

HOOK:	Mustad #94840 or #7957B, sizes 4 to 18
THREAD:	Black, prewaxed 6/0 or 3/0 Monocord

Fig. 5.13 Renegade, a very important western fly.

TAIL:	None
TAG:	A small segment of gold tinsel
BODY:	Three or four strands of peacock herl
HACKLE:	Brown hackle rear, white hackle front
HEAD:	Black tying thread

ROYAL COACHMAN

HOOK:	Mustad #94840, sizes 10 to 20
THREAD:	Black, prewaxed 6/0
TAIL:	Golden pheasant tippet
WINGS:	White wing quill strips
BODY:	Peacock herl with red floss center segment
HACKLE:	Coachman brown (dark mahogany brown)
HEAD:	Black tying thread

ROYAL HUMPY

HOOK:	Mustad #94840 or #7957B, sizes 6 to 16
THREAD:	Red, prewaxed 6/0 or 3/0 Monocord
TAIL:	Dark moose body hair
WINGS:	White calf tail
BODY:	Red tying thread with natural deer body hair tied over as a shellback

HACKLE:	Brown, tied heavy on larger flies
HEAD:	Red tying thread

NOTE: A photo of the Royal Humpy appears in the section on hair wings in this chapter.

ROYAL WULFF

HOOK:	Mustad #94840 or #7957B, sizes 2 to 16
THREAD:	Black, prewaxed 6/0 or 3/0 Monocord
TAIL:	White or brown calf tail
WINGS:	White or brown calf tail
BODY:	Peacock herl segments fore and aft with red floss center
HACKLE:	Dark reddish brown
HEAD:	Black tying thread

SMALL DUN VARIANT

HOOK:	Mustad #94838, sizes 14 to 18
THREAD:	Olive, prewaxed 6/0
TAIL:	Blue dun hackle fibers, stiff
WINGS:	None
BODY:	Yellowish-olive fur dubbing
HACKLE:	Blue dun, oversize; for a size 14 hook, size 10 hackle
HEAD:	Olive tying thread

SPIRIT OF PITTSFORD MILLS

HOOK:	Mustad #94840, sizes 12 to 16
THREAD:	Yellow, prewaxed 6/0
TAIL:	Ginger hackle fibers
WINGS:	Light-grizzly hackle tips
BODY:	Grayish-white duck down dubbing, palmered with trimmed ginger hackle
HACKLE:	Light ginger
HEAD:	Yellow tying thread

SPRUCE FLY

HOOK:	Mustad #94840 or #7957B, sizes 8 to 24
THREAD:	Black, prewaxed 6/0 or 3/0 Monocord
TAIL:	Dark moose body hair or badger hackle fibers
WINGS:	Badger hackle tips
BODY:	Rear half red floss, front half peacock herl
HACKLE:	Badger
HEAD:	Black tying thread

WESTERN GREEN DRAKE
HOOK: Mustad #94840, sizes 8 to 14
THREAD: Olive, prewaxed 6/0
TAIL: Brownish moose body hair or light brown bucktail
WINGS: Well-marked natural deer body hair
BODY: Olive-brown fur dubbing
HACKLE: Grizzly and brown wound together
HEAD: Olive tying thread

WHITE MILLER
HOOK: Mustad #94840, sizes 8 to 14
THREAD: White, prewaxed 6/0
TAIL: White hackle fibers
WINGS: White hackle tips
BODY: White fur dubbing
HACKLE: White
HEAD: White tying thread

WHITE WULFF
HOOK: Mustad #94840 or #7957B, sizes 6 to 16
THREAD: White, prewaxed 6/0
TAIL: White calf tail
WINGS: White calf tail
BODY: Cream fur dubbing or wool
HACKLE: Cream badger
HEAD: White tying thread

Midge Patterns

BADGER MIDGE
HOOK: Mustad #94859, sizes 22 to 28
THREAD: Black, prewaxed 6/0
TAIL: None
WINGS: None
BODY: Peacock quill, stripped
HACKLE: Badger
HEAD: Black tying thread

BLACK GNAT
HOOK: Mustad #94859, sizes 22 to 28
THREAD: Black, prewaxed 6/0
TAIL: Black hackle fibers

WINGS: Black wing quill sections
BODY: Peacock quill, stripped
HACKLE: Black
HEAD: Black tying thread

BLACK HERL MIDGE
HOOK: Mustad #94859, sizes 22 to 28
THREAD: Black, prewaxed 6/0
TAIL: Black hackle fibers
WINGS: None
BODY: Black ostrich herl
HACKLE: None
HEAD: Black tying thread

BLACK MIDGE
HOOK: Mustad #94859, sizes 22 to 28
THREAD: Black, prewaxed 6/0
TAIL: Black hackle fibers
WINGS: None
BODY: Black tying thread or fur dubbing
HACKLE: Black
HEAD: Black tying thread

BROWN MIDGE
HOOK: Mustad #94859, sizes 22 to 28
THREAD: Brown, prewaxed 6/0
TAIL: Brown hackle fibers
WINGS: None
BODY: One strand of cock pheasant tail fiber
HACKLE: Brown
HEAD: Brown tying thread

CREAM MIDGE
HOOK: Mustad #94859, sizes 22 to 28
THREAD: White, prewaxed 6/0
TAIL: Cream hackle fibers
WINGS: None
BODY: Cream fur dubbing
HACKLE: Cream or light ginger
HEAD: White tying thread

DUN MIDGE
HOOK: Mustad #94859, sizes 22 to 28
THREAD: Gray, prewaxed 6/0

TAIL: Blue dun hackle fibers
WINGS: None
BODY: Muskrat fur dubbing
HACKLE: Blue dun
HEAD: Gray tying thread

GRAY HERL MIDGE
HOOK: Mustad #94859, sizes 22 to 28
THREAD: Gray, prewaxed 6/0
TAIL: Blue dun hackle fibers
WINGS: None
BODY: Natural gray ostrich herl
HACKLE: None
HEAD: Gray tying thread

GREEN MIDGE
HOOK: Mustad #94859, sizes 22 to 28
THREAD: Olive, prewaxed 6/0
TAIL: Pale olive hackle fibers
WINGS: None
BODY: Olive hackle stem, stripped
HACKLE: Light olive
HEAD: Olive tying thread

LIGHT OLIVE MIDGE
HOOK: Mustad #94859, sizes 22 to 28
THREAD: Olive, prewaxed 6/0
TAIL: Blue dun hackle fibers
WINGS: Blue dun hackle tips
BODY: Light olive-brown fur dubbing
HACKLE: Blue dun
HEAD: Olive tying thread

MOSQUITO
HOOK: Mustad #94859, sizes 22 to 28
THREAD: Black, prewaxed 6/0
TAIL: Grizzly hackle fibers
WINGS: Grizzly hackle tips
BODY: Light and dark moose mane, wound together
HACKLE: Grizzly
HEAD: Black tying thread

ROYAL MIDGE
HOOK: Mustad #94859, sizes 22 to 28
THREAD: Black, prewaxed 6/0
TAIL: None
WINGS: Fine-textured tan deer body hair
BODY: Peacock herl, with red floss center band
HACKLE: None
HEAD: Black tying thread

Jorgensen's Cut-Wing Parachute Duns

BLUE-WINGED OLIVE CUT-WING
HOOK: Mustad #94842 or Partridge L3B, sizes 16 to 20
THREAD: Olive, prewaxed 6/0
TAIL: Blue dun hackle fibers, tied up at 45-degree angle
WINGS: Dark blue dun hen body feather, trimmed to shape
BODY: Yellowish olive-brown fur dubbing
HACKLE: Cream badger, tied parachute style
HEAD: Olive tying thread

GOLDEN DRAKE CUT-WING
HOOK: Mustad #94842 or Partridge L3B, sizes 10 to 12
THREAD: Yellow, prewaxed 6/0
TAIL: Pale yellow hackle fibers, tied up at 45-degree angle
WINGS: Creamish-yellow hackle, trimmed to shape
BODY: Creamish-yellow fur dubbing
HACKLE: Pale ginger, tied parachute style
HEAD: Yellow tying thread
NOTE: Wing cut from the webby portion of a saddle hackle dyed yellow.

GRAY FOX CUT-WING
HOOK: Mustad #94842 or Partridge L3B, sizes 12 to 14
THREAD: Orange, prewaxed 6/0
TAIL: Ginger hackle fibers, tied up at 45-degree angle
WINGS: Gray partridge body feather, trimmed to shape
BODY: Creamish-tan fur dubbing
HACKLE: Grizzly and light ginger, tied parachute style
HEAD: Orange tying thread

HENDRICKSON (MALE) CUT-WING
HOOK:	Mustad #94842 or Partridge L3B, size 14
THREAD:	Black, prewaxed 6/0
TAIL:	Blue dun hackle fibers, tied up at 45-degree angle
WINGS:	Dark blue dun hen body feather, trimmed to shape
BODY:	Rusty-brown fur dubbing
HACKLE:	Blue dun, tied parachute style
HEAD:	Black tying thread

HENDRICKSON (FEMALE) CUT-WING
HOOK:	Mustad #94842 or Partridge L3B, size 12
THREAD:	Black, prewaxed 6/0
TAIL:	Blue dun hackle fibers, tied up at 45-degree angle
WINGS:	Dark blue dun hen body feather, trimmed to shape
BODY:	Pinkish-gray fur dubbing
HACKLE:	Blue dun, tied parachute style
HEAD:	Black tying thread

ISONYCHIA CUT-WING
HOOK:	Mustad #94842 or Partridge L3B, size 10
THREAD:	Olive, prewaxed 6/0
TAIL:	Dark ginger hackle fibers or moose hair, tied up at 45-degree angle
WINGS:	Two dark blue dun hen or rooster body feathers, trimmed to shape
BODY:	Dark reddish-brown fur dubbing
HACKLE:	Dark ginger rooster hackle, tied parachute
HEAD:	Olive tying thread

LIGHT CAHILL CUT-WING
HOOK:	Mustad #94842 or Partridge L3B, size 14
THREAD:	Yellow, prewaxed 6/0
TAIL:	Pale ginger hackle fibers, tied up at 45-degree angle
WINGS:	Gray partridge body feather dyed pale yellow, trimmed to shape
HACKLE:	Ginger, tied parachute style
HEAD:	Yellow tying thread

MARCH BROWN CUT-WING
HOOK:	Mustad #94842 or Partridge L3B, sizes 10 to 12
THREAD:	Orange, prewaxed 6/0
TAIL:	Dark ginger hackle fibers, tied up at 45-degree angle
WINGS:	Brown partridge body feather, trimmed to shape
BODY:	Grayish-amber fur dubbing
HACKLE:	Brown and grizzly, tied parachute style
HEAD:	Orange tying thread

SULPHUR DUN CUT-WING
HOOK:	Mustad #94842 or Partridge L3B, sizes 16 to 18
THREAD:	Yellow, prewaxed 6/0
TAIL:	Light ginger hackle fibers, tied up at 45-degree angle
WINGS:	Light blue dun hen body feather, trimmed to shape
BODY:	Sulphur-yellow fur dubbing
HACKLE:	Very light blue dun, tied parachute style
HEAD:	Yellow tying thread

Fur Spinners

The following are standard patterns modified into fur spinners by the author.

BLUE-WINGED OLIVE SPINNER
HOOK:	Mustad #94842 or Partridge L3B, sizes 14 to 22
THREAD:	Olive, prewaxed 6/0
TAIL:	Four to six blue dun hackle fibers (length, 2 1/2 hook gaps), divided and splayed
WINGS:	Palest blue dun hackle (fiber length, 2 hook gaps), tied spent
BODY:	Olive-brown fur dubbing
HACKLE:	None
HEAD:	Olive tying thread

NOTE: On the smaller sizes, use poly yarn for wings. It should be same color as hackle and fastened with crisscross windings.

GRAY FOX SPINNER
HOOK:	Mustad #94842 or Partridge L3B, sizes 12 to 14
THREAD:	Orange, prewaxed 6/0

TAIL: Four to six ginger hackle fibers (length, 2 1/2 hook gaps), divided and splayed
WINGS: Palest blue dun and grizzly hackles (fiber length, 2 hook gaps), tied spent
BODY: Creamish-tan fur dubbing
HACKLE: None
HEAD: Orange tying thread

HENDRICKSON (MALE) SPINNER
HOOK: Mustad #94842 or Partridge L3B, size 14
THREAD: Black, prewaxed 6/0
TAIL: Four to six blue dun hackle fibers (length, 2 1/2 hook gaps), divided and splayed
WINGS: Palest blue dun hackle (fiber length, 2 hook gaps), tied spent
BODY: Reddish-brown fur dubbing
HACKLE: None
HEAD: Black tying thread

HENDRICKSON (FEMALE) SPINNER
HOOK: Mustad #94842 or Partridge L3B, size 12
THREAD: Black, prewaxed 6/0
TAIL: Four to six blue dun hackle fibers (length, 2 1/2 hook gaps), divided and splayed
WINGS: Palest blue dun hackle (fiber length, 2 hook gaps), tied spent
BODY: Pinkish-gray fur dubbing
HACKLE: None
HEAD: Black tying thread

ISONYCHIA SPINNER
HOOK: Mustad #94842 or Partridge L3B, size 10
THREAD: Olive, prewaxed 6/0
TAIL: Ginger hackle fibers (length, 2 1/2 hook gaps), divided and splayed
WINGS: Palest blue dun hackle (fiber length, 2 hook gaps), tied spent
BODY: Dark reddish-brown fur dubbing
HACKLE: None
HEAD: Olive tying thread

LIGHT CAHILL SPINNER
HOOK: Mustad #94842 or Partridge L3B, sizes 12 to 14
THREAD: Yellow, prewaxed 6/0

TAIL: Four to six light ginger hackle fibers (length, 2 1/2 hook gaps), divided and splayed
WINGS: Palest blue dun hackle (fiber length, 2 hook gaps), tied spent
BODY: Cream fur dubbing
HACKLE: None
HEAD: Yellow tying thread

LITTLE RUSTY SPINNER
HOOK: Mustad #94842 or Partridge L3B, sizes 16 to 22
THREAD: Black, prewaxed 6/0
TAIL: Four to six dark blue dun hackle fibers (length, 2 1/2 hook gaps), divided and splayed
WINGS: Palest blue dun hackle (fiber length, 2 hook gaps), tied spent
BODY: Rusty-brown fur dubbing
HACKLE: None
HEAD: Black tying thread
NOTE: On the smaller sizes, use poly yarn for wings. It should be the same color as hackle wings and fastened with crisscross windings.

MARCH BROWN SPINNER
HOOK: Mustad #94842 or Partridge L3B, sizes 10 to 12
THREAD: Orange, prewaxed 6/0
TAIL: Four to six ginger hackle fibers (length, 2 1/2 hook gaps), divided and splayed
WINGS: Palest blue dun and grizzly hackles (fiber length, 2 hook gaps), tied spent
BODY: Creamish-tan fur dubbing
HACKLE: None
HEAD: Orange tying thread

POTAMANTHUS (GOLDEN DRAKE) SPINNER
HOOK: Mustad #94842 or Partridge L3B, sizes 10 to 12
THREAD: Yellow, prewaxed 6/0
TAIL: Four to six pale yellow hackle fibers (length, 2 1/2 hook gaps), divided and splayed
WINGS: Palest yellow hackle (fiber length, 2 hook gaps), tied spent
BODY: Creamish-yellow fur dubbing
HACKLE: None
HEAD: Yellow tying thread

QUILL GORDON SPINNER

HOOK: Mustad #94842 or Partridge L3B, sizes 12 to 14
THREAD: Black, prewaxed 6/0
TAIL: Four to six pale blue dun hackle fibers (length, 2 1/2 hook gaps), divided and splayed
WINGS: Palest blue dun hackle (fiber length, 2 hook gaps), tied spent
BODY: Yellowish-brown fur dubbing
HACKLE: None
HEAD: Black tying thread

SULPHUR SPINNER

HOOK: Mustad #94842 or Partridge L3B, sizes 16 to 18
THREAD: Yellow, prewaxed 6/0
TAIL: Four to six pale blue dun hackle fibers (length, 2 1/2 hook gaps), divided and splayed
WINGS: Palest blue dun hackle (fiber length, 2 hook gaps), tied spent
BODY: Sulphur-yellow fur dubbing
HACKLE: None
HEAD: Yellow tying thread

WHITE FLY SPINNER

HOOK: Mustad #94842 or Partridge L3B, size 14
THREAD: White, prewaxed 6/0
TAIL: Four to six white hackle fibers (length, 2 1/2 hook gaps), divided and splayed
WINGS: White hackle (fiber length, 2 hook gaps), tied spent
BODY: White fur dubbing
HACKLE: None
HEAD: White tying thread

Jorgen-Betts Spinner Duns

The patterns listed below were created by the author and follow the style described earlier in this chapter.

BLUE-WINGED OLIVE DUN, JORGEN-BETTS STYLE

HOOK: Mustad #94842 or Partridge L3B, size 18
THREAD: Olive, prewaxed 6/0
TAIL: Three dark dun-colored Microfibetts (body length)
WINGS: Dark blue dun hackles (fibers body length)
BODY: Olive-brown poly yarn extension, 3/4 ply diameter; total body length 5/16" (9mm)
THORAX: Gray fur dubbing
HEAD: Olive tying thread
NOTE: Extension formula—3 plies olive, 1/2 ply brown

BLUE-WINGED OLIVE SPINNER, JORGEN-BETTS STYLE

HOOK: Mustad #94842 or Partridge L3B, size 18
THREAD: Olive, prewaxed 6/0
TAIL: Three dark dun-colored Microfibetts (body length)
WINGS: Palest blue dun hackles (fibers body length)
BODY: Olive-brown poly yarn extension, 3/4 ply diameter; total body length 5/16" (9mm)
THORAX: Gray fur dubbing
HEAD: Olive tying thread
NOTE: Extension formula—3 plies olive, 1/2 ply brown

EASTERN GREEN DRAKE DUN, JORGEN-BETTS STYLE

HOOK: Mustad #94842 or Partridge L3B, size 10
THREAD: Yellow, prewaxed 6/0
TAIL: Three dark moose mane fibers (body length)
WINGS: Two grizzly hackles dyed pale green or one natural grizzly and one pale green wound together
BODY: Pale creamish-yellow poly yarn extension with an olive cast, 1 1/2 ply diameter; total body length 1" (25mm)
THORAX: Gray fur dubbing
HEAD: Yellow tying thread
NOTE: Extension formula—3 plies off-white, 1 ply bright yellow, 1/3 ply dark green

EASTERN GREEN DRAKE SPINNER, JORGEN-BETTS STYLE

HOOK: Mustad #94842 or Partridge L3B, size 10
THREAD: Yellow, prewaxed 6/0
TAIL: Three dark moose mane fibers (body length)
WINGS: One natural grizzly and one very pale blue dun hackle wound together

BODY: Pale creamish-yellow poly yarn extension with an olive cast, 1 1/2 ply diameter; total body length 1″ (25mm)
THORAX: Gray fur dubbing
HEAD: Yellow tying thread
NOTE: Extension formula—4 plies off-white

POTAMANTHUS DUN (GOLDEN DRAKE), JORGEN-BETTS STYLE
HOOK: Mustad #94842 or Partridge L3B, size 12
THREAD: Yellow, prewaxed 6/0
TAIL: Three pale wood duck flank feather fibers (body length)
WINGS: Pale ginger hackles (fibers body length)
BODY: Creamish-yellow poly yarn extension, 1 1/2 ply diameter; total body length 5/8″ (16mm)
THORAX: Gray fur dubbing
HEAD: Yellow tying thread
NOTE: Extension formula—1 ply cream, 1 ply yellow

POTAMANTHUS SPINNER (GOLDEN DRAKE), JORGEN-BETTS STYLE
HOOK: Mustad #94842 or Partridge L3B, size 12
THREAD: Yellow, prewaxed 6/0
TAIL: Three pale wood duck flank feather fibers (body length)
WINGS: Pale ginger and blue dun hackles (fibers body length)
BODY: Creamish-yellow poly yarn extension, 1 1/2 ply diameter; total body length 5/8″ (16mm)
THORAX: Gray fur dubbing
HEAD: Yellow tying thread
NOTE: Extension formula—1 ply cream, 1 ply yellow

HENRICKSON DUN, JORGEN-BETTS STYLE
HOOK: Mustad #94842 or Partridge L3B, size 14
THREAD: Tan, prewaxed 6/0
TAIL: Three dun-colored Microfibetts (1 1/2 body length)
WINGS: Rusty blue dun hackles (fibers body length)
BODY: Creamish-pink poly yarn extension, 1 ply
THORAX: Gray fur dubbing
HEAD: Tan tying thread
NOTE: Extension formula—3 plies cream, 1 ply pink

HEXAGENIA DUN, JORGEN-BETTS STYLE
HOOK: Mustad #94842 or Partridge L3B, size 8
THREAD: Olive, prewaxed 6/0
TAIL: Two brown moose mane fibers (body length)
WINGS: Three or four dark blue dun hackles (fibers body length)
BODY: Yellowish-brown poly yarn extension, 2 ply diameter; total body length 1 1/4″ (32mm)
THORAX: Gray fur dubbing
HEAD: Olive tying thread
NOTE: Extension formula—3 plies brown and 1 ply yellow

HEXAGENIA SPINNER, JORGEN-BETTS STYLE
HOOK: Mustad #94842 or Partridge L3B, size 8
THREAD: Olive, prewaxed 6/0
TAIL: Two brown moose mane fibers (body length)
WINGS: Three or four palest blue dun hackles (fibers body length)
BODY: Yellowish-brown poly yarn extension, 2 ply diameter; total body length 1 1/4″ (32mm)
THORAX: Gray fur dubbing
HEAD: Olive tying thread
NOTE: Extension formula—3 plies brown and 1 ply yellow

MARCH BROWN DUN, JORGEN-BETTS STYLE
HOOK: Mustad #94842 or Partridge L3B, size 12
THREAD: Orange, prewaxed 6/0
TAIL: Two wood duck flank feather fibers, 3/4″ long
WINGS: One grizzly and one brown hackle (fibers body length)
BODY: Yellowish-tan poly yarn extension, 1 1/2 ply diameter; total body length 9/16″ (15mm)
THORAX: Gray fur dubbing
HEAD: Orange tying thread
NOTE: Extension formula—1 ply cream, 1 ply yellow, 2 plies medium brown

MARCH BROWN SPINNER, JORGEN-BETTS STYLE
HOOK: Mustad #94842 or Partridge L3B, size 12
THREAD: Orange, prewaxed 6/0
TAIL: Two wood duck flank feather fibers, 3/4″ long
WINGS: One pale blue dun and one pale grizzly hackle (fibers body length)

BODY: Yellowish-tan poly yarn extension, 1 1/2 ply diameter; total body length 9/16″ (15mm)
THORAX: Gray fur dubbing
HEAD: Orange tying thread
NOTE: Extension formula—1 ply cream, 1 ply yellow, 2 plies medium brown

SLATE DRAKE DUN (ISONYCHIA), JORGEN-BETTS STYLE
HOOK: Mustad #94842 or Partridge L3B, size 12
THREAD: Black, prewaxed 6/0
TAIL: Two pale brown moose mane fibers (body length)
WINGS: Dark blue dun hackles (fibers body length)
BODY: Dark reddish-brown poly yarn extension, 1 1/2 ply diameter; total body length 5/8″ (16mm)
THORAX: Gray fur dubbing
HEAD: Black tying thread
NOTE: Extension formula—4 plies dark brown, 1 ply black, 1 ply red

SLATE DRAKE SPINNER (ISONYCHIA), JORGEN-BETTS STYLE
HOOK: Mustad #94842 or Partridge L3B, size 12
THREAD: Black, prewaxed 6/0
TAIL: Two pale brown moose mane fibers (body length)
WINGS: Palest blue dun hackles (fibers body length)
BODY: Dark reddish-brown poly yarn extension, 1 1/2 ply diameter; total body length 5/8″ (16mm)
THORAX: Gray fur dubbing
HEAD: Black tying thread
NOTE: Extension formula—4 plies dark brown, 1 ply black, 1 ply red

SULPHUR DUN, JORGEN-BETTS STYLE
HOOK: Mustad #94842 or Partridge L3B, size 18
THREAD: Orange, prewaxed 6/0
TAIL: Three light dun Microfibetts (body length)
WINGS: Light blue dun hackles (fibers body length)
BODY: Sulphur-yellow poly yarn extension, 1/2 ply diameter; total body length 5/16″ (9mm)

THORAX: Gray fur dubbing
HEAD: Orange tying thread
NOTE: Extension formula—3 plies yellow, 1 ply red

SULPHUR SPINNER, JORGEN-BETTS STYLE
HOOK: Mustad #94842 or Partridge L3B, size 18
THREAD: Orange, prewaxed 6/0
TAIL: Three light dun Microfibetts (body length)
WINGS: Palest blue dun hackles (fibers body length)
BODY: Sulphur-yellow poly yarn extension, 1/2 ply diameter; total body length 5/16″ (9mm)
THORAX: Gray fur dubbing
HEAD: Orange tying thread
NOTE: Extension formula—3 plies yellow, 1 ply red

WESTERN GREEN DRAKE DUN, JORGEN-BETTS STYLE
HOOK: Mustad #94842 or Partridge L3B, size 12
THREAD: Olive, prewaxed 6/0
TAIL: Three brown moose mane fibers (body length)
WINGS: Dark blue dun hackles (fibers body length)
BODY: Olive-brown poly yarn extension, 1 1/2 ply diameter; total body length 5/8″ (16mm)
THORAX: Gray fur dubbing
HEAD: Olive tying thread
NOTE: Extension formula—3 plies olive, 1/2 ply brown, 1/2 ply black

WESTERN GREEN DRAKE SPINNER, JORGEN-BETTS STYLE
HOOK: Mustad #94842 or Partridge L3B, size 12
THREAD: Olive, prewaxed 6/0
TAIL: Three brown moose mane fibers (body length)
WINGS: Palest blue dun hackles (fibers body length)
BODY: Olive-brown poly yarn extension, 1 1/2 ply diameter; total body length 5/8″ (16mm)
THORAX: Gray fur dubbing
HEAD: Olive tying thread
NOTE: Extension formula—3 plies olive, 1/2 ply brown, 1/2 ply black

Chapter 6
Wet Flies

I have yet to meet an angler who didn't have a favorite wet fly pattern. Those who have studied the behavior of stream insects have found that several mayfly species leave their nymphal stage sooner in the life cycle than other species. The dun (dry fly) emerges while the nymph is still on the bottom or on its way to the surface. When this occurs, wet flies are extremely effective. However, many wet flies represent other insects as well. For instance, caddis pupae and diving caddis adults depositing eggs are imitated by wet fly patterns.

When tying a wet fly, you can use the same basic instructions given in the Beginner's Tying Practice, Chapter 4, and other instructions given for tying dry flies in Chapter 5. Wet fly proportions are nearly the same as for dry flies, except that the tail, if any, and the hackle (or beard, as it is also called), should be 2 hook gaps long unless otherwise described in the dressings. Wings should lay low and reach back even with the hook bend or, if you wish, they may be just slightly longer.

If you ask a dozen fly tiers what hook to use for wet flies,

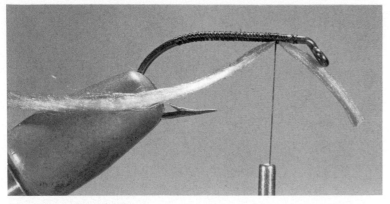

Step 1 Attaching the floss.

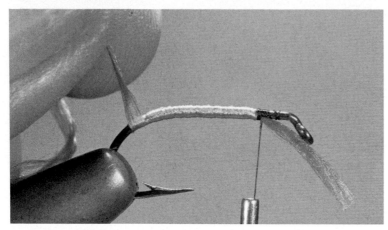

Step 2 Winding the floss body.

you would probably get half a dozen different answers. After trying them all, I have found that the regular length Mustad #3906 with a sproat bend is, at least for me, the one best suited to this type of fly.

The Soft-Hackle Wet Fly

A soft-hackle wet fly is very simple to tie, yet it incorporates most of the techniques used for tying all types of wet flies. It should be noted that the body, which in most cases is

made with silk or rayon floss, should be wound over a shank that is covered completely with the same color tying thread as the color floss being used. If not, the shank will show when the floss is wet.

Grouse and partridge hackle are often used for wet fly hackle. Since it is not always possible to obtain this hackle with fibers short enough for smaller flies such as sizes 12 and 14, you must pull the fibers from the stem and tie them in as a bunch. You should distribute them evenly around the shank with your fingers, rather than winding the hackle in the usual manner.

Tying the Partridge and Orange

HOOK:	Mustad #3906 or Partridge K12ST, sizes 6 to 14
THREAD:	Orange, prewaxed 6/0
BODY:	Orange floss
THORAX:	Dark brown hare's ear fur dubbing covering front 1/3 of body
HACKLE:	Brown partridge body feather with fibers reaching to the end of the body
HEAD:	Orange tying thread

Step 1: Place a size 6 hook in the vise and cover the shank with orange tying thread. Cut a 6″ length of narrow floss and fasten it on the shank with three or four tight turns of thread about 1/8″ from the eye, as shown.

Step 2: Wind the floss on the shank over and away from you. This is done by taking it over the shank with your left hand, then grasping it with your right and taking it under. Grasp it again with your left hand, take it over, and continue in this manner with each turn side by side down the shank until you reach a point above the barb.

Step 3: Continue to wind the floss on the shank as explained in Step 2, but this time wind forward over the first layer to the position where you first tied it in. Make sure the shank is completely covered. Tie off the floss with several turns of tying thread and trim the excess floss ends close to the thread

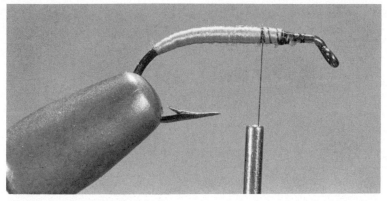

Step 3 Finishing the floss body.

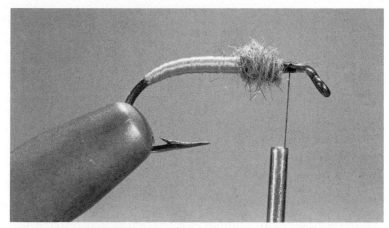

Step 4 Dubbing the thorax.

windings. Now wind the thread back to a position 1/3 of the body length from the eye. Let the thread hang by the weight of the bobbin, and you are ready to apply the thorax.

Step 4: Roll a small amount of fur dubbing on the tying thread and wind it on the front 1/3 of the body. Tie it off 1/8" from the eye, and the thorax is finished. If you have excess fur on the thread, remove it before tying off. If you have too little fur on the thread, you can always apply more as you wind it on the hook. Let the thread hang midway between the front of the thorax and the eye of the hook, and you are ready for the next step.

Step 5: Select a brown partridge feather with fibers long enough to reach from the front of the thorax back to the end of the body. Hold it by the tip and stroke it down with your fingers until the fibers stand out at right angles. Pull off the soft fibers and fuzz from the stem. Prepare the tip portion by trimming the fibers with your scissors, leaving some short stumps about 1/4" up each side. The prepared feather should now look like the one shown in the photo, with about 1/2" of usable fibers remaining on the stem.

Step 5 Preparing the partridge hackle.

Step 6 Attaching the hackle.

Step 7 Securing the hackle.

Step 6: Hold the feather as shown with the dull underside up. Fasten it on the shank by the tip with a couple of tight turns of thread. It should now sit as shown, with the feather projecting forward over the eye.

Step 7: After completing Step 6, grasp the feather and hold it back over the body toward the rear. Take a few windings of thread over the stem by which it was first tied in, binding it down so the hackle sits directly in front of the thorax with a little clear stem between the hook and the lower fibers. This tie-in procedure will double-secure the hackle in place so it will not be pulled off when being wound. Now wind the thread forward to a position close to the eye and let it hang.

Step 8 Winding the partridge hackle.

Step 9 The finished Partridge and Orange soft-hackle wet fly.

Step 8: Using your hackle pliers, hold the hackle above the hook. With the fingers of your left hand, double the hackle fibers back so it looks as if they are all coming from one side of the stem. While holding the fibers in that position, start winding the hackle over and away from you. When you have started the first turn, you can let go of the fibers as they are now trapped against the hook shank.

Step 9: After completing the first turn of the hackle, come all the way around and again hold it above the hook. Double the next bunch of fibers back and continue in that manner until you have applied three or four turns of hackle, one turn directly in front of the other. Tie off the hackle and cut the surplus stem. Hold the hackle fibers back toward the rear with your fingers while winding the head. Tie off the thread and apply some cement on the windings. This completes the soft-hackle wet fly.

The Quill-Wing Wet Fly

What an Adams is to the dry fly purist, the Gold-Ribbed Hare's Ear is to the wet fly angler. This is one fly I would not want to be without on opening day of the trout season. In April, when the river is high and cold, a wet fly fished deep and slow is deadly. The fur dubbing with all its guard hairs somehow makes the fly look very buggy and delicious.

From a technical point of view, the instructions that follow teach you several important techniques that are used not only for these simple wet flies, but also for some of the more complicated salmon, steelhead, and saltwater flies. Among the techniques is how to apply the ribbing, but perhaps the most important is how to set the wing. While I prefer primary wing feathers (pointers) for dry flies, I prefer secondary flight feathers for wet fly wings. These quill strips have less curvature and make a better looking wing. When you order wing

Step 1 Attaching the tail and ribbing.

Step 2 Finishing the body.

quills from your supplier, it's best if you buy a whole left and right wing so you have a good selection of feathers. Better yet, if you have a duck hunter as a friend, ask him to save the wings, for then you are sure to get wings that come from the same bird.

Tying the Gold-Ribbed Hare's Ear

HOOK:	Mustad #3906, #3906B, or Partridge K12ST, sizes 6 to 14
THREAD:	Black, prewaxed 6/0
TAIL:	Brown hen hackle fibers
WINGS:	Gray duck wing quill segments (secondary feathers)
BODY:	Grayish-brown hare's ear fur dubbing, ribbed with narrow gold tinsel
HACKLE:	None; pick out fur dubbing in front for legs
HEAD:	Black tying thread

Step 1: Attach the tying thread on a size 8 hook and tie in a small bunch of hen hackle fibers for the tail. They should be two hook gaps long. Now take a 4″ piece of narrow flat or oval gold tinsel and tie it in under the shank directly above the barb where the tail was tied in. Roll some hare's ear fur on the tying thread so it forms a neatly tapered piece of dubbing 2″ long as shown.

Step 2: Wind the dubbing on the shank over and away from you, moving toward the front. Tie it off 1/16″ from the eye. Try to make a nice tapered body. Now grasp the tinsel and spiral it over the dubbed body to the front and tie it off. Cut the surplus, and the body of the fly is finished.

Step 3 Picking out the legs.

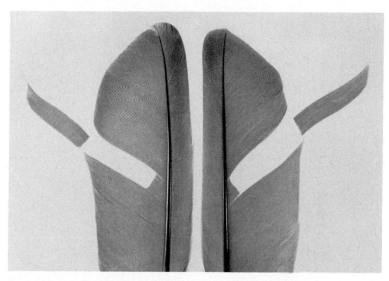

Step 4 Preparing the quill wings.

Step 3: Since the fly has no hackle, you should pick out the fur in front underneath the body with a dubbing needle to represent the legs. Study the photo to determine the correct amount of fur to be picked out.

Step 4: Select a left and a right secondary wing feather of the same size, shade, and texture. Set the pins on your wing divider so the distance between them is equal to about 2/3 the hook gap. (For complete information on the use of the wing divider, see the instructions for tying the Royal Coachman in Chapter 5.) Separate a quill section from each feather stem. The section from the left feather is for the right wing (near wing for a right-handed tier), and the right section is for the far wing.

Step 5: Hold the quill sections with the concave sides together and the tips even. They should reach back to above the hook bend. At the spot where the tying thread is hanging, the quills should sit a little on the side of the shank, NOT on top. In that way, the wings will sit with a nice low profile.

Step 5 Measuring the wings.

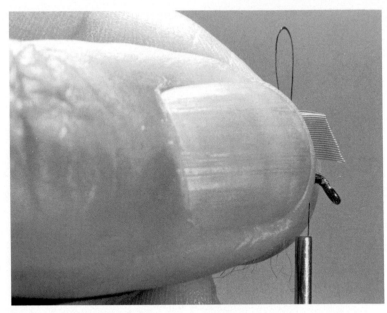

Step 6 Attaching the wings.

Step 7 Judging the wing position.

Step 6: Now, without moving the wings, grasp them with the other hand and hold them firmly in place. Take the tying thread up between the near wing and your thumb and hold it there while taking the thread over the wing and down on the far side between the wing and your index finger, thus forming a slack loop as shown. Come all the way around under the shank and up on the near side between the wing and your thumb. This results in a complete loop. Hold the wings firmly while pulling the loop tight with an upward pull. Repeat this procedure a couple of times.

Step 7: Move your fingers back and check the position of the wing. It should sit as shown in the photo. If it does, hold the wings and take a couple of extra turns of thread so they are securely fastened on the shank. If not, do them over until you get the hang of it. Apply a little penetrating cement on the thread windings.

Step 8 The finished Gold-Ribbed Hare's Ear.

Step 8: Trim the butt ends from the wing and wind a small head. Finish off with a whip finish and cut the thread. Apply some cement on the head, and your fly is finished.

The Flank-Feather Wing Wet Fly

Many of the better-known wet flies are dressed with flank feather wings. The fibers sitting low over the body in a bunch seem to give a little more "life" to the fly than the quill wings do. Early in the season, when the rivers and streams are high, discolored, and cold, I fish a Cahill as a dropper with great success. My notes from past years are clearly in favor of the darker Cahill, not only for trout but for bluegills and other panfish as well.

Some fly tiers, even veterans with years of experience, have trouble setting the wing in a low profile. The trouble, I've noticed, is that they place the wing on top of the shank where the front of the body will prevent the wing from laying flat. Consequently, it sits half-way up in the air and interferes with the fly's performance. In fact, it often causes the fly to spin during casting and ruin the leader.

If you remember to taper the body a little in front and let the wing fibers drape down a little on each side of the shank when tying them in, the problem is solved, as the following instructions will clearly illustrate.

Tying the Dark Cahill

HOOK:	Mustad #3906, #3906B, or Partridge K12ST, sizes 6 to 14
THREAD:	Black, prewaxed 6/0
TAIL:	Small bunch of wood duck flank feather fibers, 2 hook gaps long
WINGS:	Wood duck flank feather fibers on the stem, bunched
BODY:	Muskrat fur dubbing
HACKLE:	Brown hen hackle, wound as a collar and tied under as a beard
HEAD:	Black tying thread

NOTE: On some wet flies the hackle is first wound, then divided on top and the fibers tied down on the sides of the shank. This type of hackle is then referred to as a "beard" rather than a hackle. Sometimes it is also called "legs".

Step 1 Preparing to make the beard.

Step 2 Forming the beard.

Step 1: Tie in the tail, dub the body, and wind the hackle as explained in earlier instructions.

Step 2: Divide the hackle fibers on top of the shank and hold them down on each side while winding the thread toward the rear over the base of the fibers. This forms the "beard" and leaves space for tying the wing. Let the tying thread hang by the bobbin about 1/8" from the eye (less for smaller hooks).

Step 3 Measuring the flank-feather wing.

Step 4 Attaching the wing.

Step 3: Select a well-marked flank feather and pull off the fuzz and fibers at the butt end, leaving a feather equal to 1 1/2 times the finished wing length. Bunch the fibers between your fingers and hold them flat over the body with the tip ends reaching to the bend or slightly past. Make sure the fibers drape down on each side of the shank.

Step 4: Fasten the wing on the shank using the slack loop technique explained in Steps 6 and 7 for the quill wings on the Gold-Ribbed Hare's Ear.

Step 5: Trim the butt ends from the wing and wind a small head. Finish off with a whip finish and cut the thread. Apply some cement on the head, and your Dark Cahill is finished.

Hair-Winged Wet Flies

Some of the flies listed under the following Selected Wet Fly Patterns are dressed with wings of hair instead of feather. Wings of that type are attached like the flank-feather wing, with the hair tips aligned by holding the bunch out at a 90-degree angle from the skin before cutting it off. If you

Step 5 The finished Dark Cahill.

use a hair stacker to align the hair, the wing will look like a paint brush. Clean out the underfur and pull out any long, unwanted fibers. Trim them to the finished wing length and apply a little cement on the butt ends before tying them in.

Selected Wet Fly Patterns

ALDER
HOOK:	Mustad #3906, #3906B, or Partridge K12ST, sizes 6 to 16
THREAD:	Black, prewaxed 6/0
TAIL:	None
WINGS:	Dark mottled-brown turkey quill sections
BODY:	Peacock herl
HACKLE:	Black hen hackle fibers
HEAD:	Black tying thread

BLACK GNAT
HOOK:	Mustad #3906, #3906B, or Partridge K12ST, sizes 6 to 16
THREAD:	Black, prewaxed 6/0
TAIL:	None
WINGS:	Gray goose or duck quill sections
BODY:	Black chenille
HACKLE:	Black hen hackle fibers
HEAD:	Black tying thread

BLUE DUN
HOOK:	Mustad #3906, #3906B, or Partridge K12ST, sizes 6 to 14
THREAD:	Black, prewaxed 6/0
TAIL:	Blue dun hen hackle fibers
WINGS:	Blue-gray duck quill sections
BODY:	Muskrat fur dubbing
HACKLE:	Blue dun hen hackle
HEAD:	Black tying thread

COACHMAN
HOOK:	Mustad #3906, #3906B, or Partridge K12ST, sizes 6 to 16
THREAD:	Black, prewaxed 6/0
TAIL:	None; instead, wind a small gold tag at the hook bend
WINGS:	White duck wing quill sections
BODY:	Peacock herl
HACKLE:	Reddish-brown hen hackle
HEAD:	Black tying thread

NOTE: The Leadwing Coachman is the same as the Coachman except that it is tied with a dark gray wing.

DARK CAHILL
HOOK:	Mustad #3906, #3906B, or Partridge K12ST, sizes 6 to 14
THREAD:	Black, prewaxed 6/0
TAIL:	Small bunch of wood duck flank feather fibers, 2 hook gaps long
WINGS:	Wood duck flank feather fibers on the stem, bunched
BODY:	Muskrat fur dubbing
HACKLE:	Brown hen hackle, wound as a collar and tied under as a beard
HEAD:	Black tying thread

GOLD-RIBBED HARE'S EAR
HOOK:	Mustad #3906, #3906B, or Partridge K12ST, sizes 6 to 14
THREAD:	Black, prewaxed 6/0
TAIL:	Brown hen hackle fibers
WINGS:	Gray duck wing quill segments (secondary feathers)
BODY:	Grayish-brown hare's ear fur dubbing, ribbed with narrow gold tinsel
HACKLE:	None; pick out fur dubbing in front for legs
HEAD:	Black tying thread

GREENWELL'S GLORY
HOOK:	Mustad #3906, #3906B, or Partridge K12ST, sizes 6 to 14
THREAD:	Black, prewaxed 6/0
TAIL:	None; instead, wind a small gold tag at the hook bend
WINGS:	Dark gray goose or duck quill sections
BODY:	Green floss ribbed with flat gold tinsel
HACKLE:	Dark brown furnace hen hackle
HEAD:	Black tying thread

GRIZZLY KING
HOOK:	Mustad #3906, #3906B, or Partridge K12ST, sizes 6 to 16
THREAD:	Black, prewaxed 6/0
TAIL:	Narrow goose quill section dyed red
WINGS:	Gray mallard flank feather fibers
BODY:	Green floss ribbed with flat gold tinsel
HACKLE:	Cream badger hen hackle
HEAD:	Black tying thread

HENDRICKSON, DARK

HOOK: Mustad #3906, #3906B, or Partridge K12ST, sizes 6 to 16
THREAD: Olive, prewaxed 6/0
TAIL: Small bunch of wood duck flank feather fibers
WINGS: Wood duck flank feather fibers
BODY: Grayish-brown fur dubbing or medium brown Seal-Ex (#111)
HACKLE: Blue dun hen hackle
HEAD: Olive tying thread

LIGHT CAHILL

HOOK: Mustad #3906, #3906B, or Partridge K12ST, sizes 6 to 16
THREAD: Yellow, prewaxed 6/0
TAIL: Light ginger hen hackle fibers
WINGS: Wood duck flank feather fibers
BODY: Cream fox fur dubbing or yellowish-cream Seal-Ex (#117)
HACKLE: Light ginger hen hackle
HEAD: Yellow tying thread

MARCH BROWN, AMERICAN

HOOK: Mustad #3906, #3906B, or Partridge K12ST, sizes 6 to 16
THREAD: Orange, prewaxed 6/0
TAIL: Brown hen hackle fibers
WINGS: Dark mottled turkey quill sections
BODY: Brown fur dubbing or Seal-Ex (#111), ribbed with flat gold tinsel
HACKLE: Brown and grizzly hen hackle, wound together
HEAD: Orange tying thread

MARRYATT, LITTLE

HOOK: Mustad #3906, sizes 14 to 16
THREAD: Yellow, prewaxed 6/0
TAIL: Pale ginger hen hackle fibers
WINGS: Pale duck wing quill sections
BODY: Yellowish-tan fur dubbing
HACKLE: Pale ginger hen hackle
HEAD: Yellow tying thread

McGINTY

HOOK: Mustad #3906, #3906B, or Partridge K12ST, sizes 6 to 14
THREAD: Black, prewaxed 6/0
TAIL: Red hackle fibers with short teal flank feather section over
WINGS: White-tipped secondary mallard wing quill sections or none
BODY: Alternate bands of yellow and black chenille
HACKLE: Reddish-brown hen hackle
HEAD: Black tying thread

MONTREAL

HOOK: Mustad #3906, #3906B, or Partridge K12ST, sizes 6 to 14
THREAD: Black, prewaxed 6/0
TAIL: Red hen hackle fibers
WINGS: Brown mottled turkey wing quill sections
BODY: Claret floss ribbed with flat gold tinsel
HACKLE: Claret hen hackle
HEAD: Black tying thread

ORANGE FISH HAWK

HOOK: Mustad #3906, #3906B, or Partridge K12ST, sizes 6 to 16
THREAD: Orange, prewaxed 6/0
TAIL: None
WINGS: None
BODY: Orange wool yarn or Seal-Ex (#120), ribbed with gold tinsel
HACKLE: Soft badger hen hackle
HEAD: Orange tying thread

PARMACHENE BELLE

HOOK: Mustad #3906, #3906B, or Partridge K12ST, sizes 6 to 12
THREAD: Black, prewaxed 6/0
TAIL: Red and white hackle fibers, mixed
WINGS: White duck quill with narrow, red duck quill section on the side, in middle of wing
BODY: Yellow wool ribbed with flat gold tinsel
HACKLE: Red and white hen hackle, wound together
HEAD: Black tying thread

PARTRIDGE AND GREEN SOFT-HACKLE

HOOK:	Mustad #3906 or Partridge K12ST, sizes 6 to 14
THREAD:	Green, prewaxed 6/0
TAIL:	None
WINGS:	None
BODY:	Green floss
HACKLE:	Gray partridge body hackle
HEAD:	Green tying thread

PARTRIDGE AND ORANGE SOFT-HACKLE

HOOK:	Mustad #3906 or Partridge K12ST, sizes 6 to 14
THREAD:	Orange, prewaxed 6/0
TAIL:	None
WINGS:	None
BODY:	Orange floss
THORAX:	Dark brown hare's ear fur dubbing covering front 1/3 of body
HACKLE:	Brown partridge body feather with fibers reaching to the end of the body
HEAD:	Orange tying thread

PHEASANT TAIL SOFT-HACKLE

HOOK:	Mustad #3906 or Partridge K12ST, sizes 6 to 14
THREAD:	Brown, prewaxed 6/0
TAIL:	Three cock pheasant center tail fibers
WINGS:	None
BODY:	Four or five long fibers from cock pheasant center tail, wound together and ribbed with fine copper wire
HACKLE:	Brown or gray partridge body feather
HEAD:	Brown tying thread

PICKET PIN

HOOK:	Mustad #3906B or #9671 2X long
THREAD:	Black, prewaxed 6/0
TAIL:	Brown hen hackle fibers
WINGS:	White-tipped squirrel tail
BODY:	Peacock herl palmered with brown hackle
HACKLE:	Brown hen hackle
HEAD:	Peacock herl segment wound in front of wing

NOTE: Palmer hackle is tied in at the bend and spiraled forward over the body.

PROFESSOR

HOOK:	Mustad #3906, #3906B, or Partridge K12ST, sizes 6 to 14
THREAD:	Black, prewaxed 6/0
TAIL:	Red hackle fibers
WINGS:	Gray mallard flank feather fibers
BODY:	Yellow floss ribbed with flat gold tinsel
HACKLE:	Dark ginger hen hackle
HEAD:	Black tying thread

QUILL GORDON

HOOK:	Mustad #3906 or #3906B, sizes 8 to 14
THREAD:	Black, prewaxed 6/0
TAIL:	Blue dun hen hackle fibers
WINGS:	Wood duck flank feather fibers
BODY:	Grayish-brown fur dubbing
HACKLE:	Blue dun hen hackle
HEAD:	Black tying thread

RIO GRANDE KING

HOOK:	Mustad #3906B or Partridge K12ST, sizes 6 to 14
THREAD:	Black, prewaxed 6/0
TAIL:	Yellow hackle fibers
WINGS:	White duck quill sections
BODY:	Black chenille
HACKLE:	Brown or yellow hen hackle
HEAD:	Black tying thread

ROYAL COACHMAN

HOOK:	Mustad #3906B, sizes 6 to 14
THREAD:	Black, prewaxed 6/0
TAIL:	Golden pheasant tippet fibers
WINGS:	White duck quill sections
BODY:	Peacock herl with red floss center segment
HACKLE:	Coachman brown (dark mahogany brown) hen hackle
HEAD:	Black tying thread

Fig. 6.1 The Wooly Worm.

TUPS INDISPENSABLE SOFT-HACKLE

HOOK: Mustad #3906, #3906B, or Partridge K12ST, sizes 6 to 14
THREAD: Yellow, prewaxed 6/0
TAIL: Small bunch of blue dun hen hackle fibers
WINGS: None
BODY: Yellow floss, rear 2/3 of shank
THORAX: Light pink fur dubbing
HACKLE: Blue dun hen hackle
HEAD: Yellow tying thread

WICKHAM'S FANCY

HOOK: Mustad #3906, # 3906B, or Partridge K12ST, sizes 6 to 14
THREAD: Black, prewaxed 6/0
TAIL: Brown hen hackle fibers
WINGS: Gray duck quill sections
BODY: Flat gold tinsel palmered with brown hackle
HACKLE: Brown hen hackle
HEAD: Black tying thread

NOTE: Palmer hackle is tied in at the bend and spiraled forward over the body.

WOOLY WORM

HOOK: Mustad #9671 2X long, sizes 2 to 12
THREAD: Red, prewaxed 6/0 or 3/0 Monocord for large flies
TAIL: Short red wool butt
WINGS: None
BODY: Chenille
HACKLE: Grizzly saddle hackle, palmered
HEAD: Red tying thread

NOTE: The body can be made with any regular or fluorescent color of chenille; black, red, yellow, orange, and green are popular colors. Instructions for working with chenille and palmer hackle can be found in the section on tying the Wooly Bugger in the streamer chapter, Chapter 11.

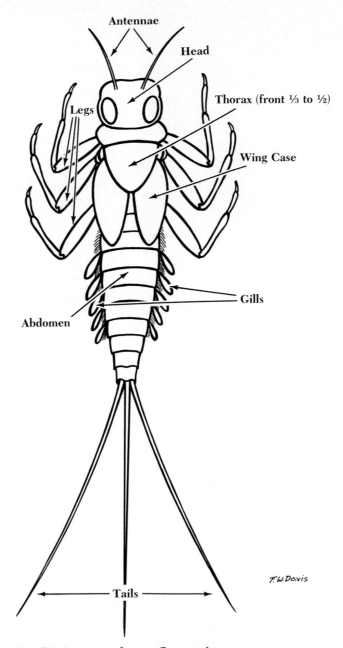

Fig. 7.1 Anatomy of a mayfly nymph.

Chapter 7
Mayfly Nymphs and Emergers

To be successful in trout fishing, there are several important things you must learn. You must, for instance, be able to read the water and determine where the fish are holding and feeding. Then, you must identify the insects upon which the fish are feeding, if they are feeding.

When you are learning to tie your own flies, there are other important matters, aside from those of fishing, you must also attend to. Not the least of them is deciding which flies to tie. When you were buying your flies, I am sure you noticed the hundreds of nymph patterns and styles on display in your supplier's cases. If I tell you that most of them are not needed, I will probably get in trouble, but nevertheless, that's a fact.

In order to get matters into perspective, I suggest you divide nymph patterns into three major groups (traditional, imitator, and simulator) and later, if you wish, subdivide those into smaller groups for your own use. In this way, you can come up with a short list of nymphs that are of particular importance in the area you are fishing. It is vital, however, that you learn to dress several styles of nymphs to become a well-trained fly tier.

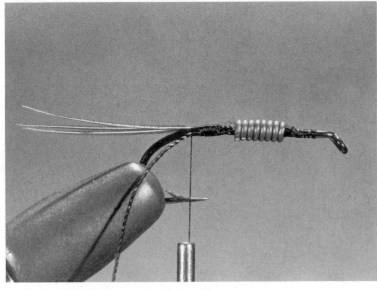

Step 1 Attaching the tail, ribbing, and weight.

The Traditional Nymph

While adult mayflies of all species are almost identical in appearance, except for color and size, mayfly nymphs vary widely. They appear in many different shapes, forms, colors, and sizes.

Traditional nymph patterns of the past, almost without exception, used color and size as their principal distinguishing features. This may have limited their effectiveness as representatives for specific nymphs.

Within the group of traditional nymphs, you will find patterns that were designed to imitate certain immature stages of important mayflies, a task which, in my opinion, they do not perform very well. Also, you will find simulator nymphs, referred to in some circles as searching nymphs, which do not imitate any specific insect but look interesting and edible to fish.

Before you engage in practicing the tying steps for any of the nymphs in this chapter, I suggest that you familiarize yourself thoroughly with the beginner's tying practice in Chapter 4. You may also find it helpful to refer to procedures found in the wet fly chapter, Chapter 6. With that knowledge, and with the instructions that follow for tying traditional nymphs, you will be able to tie most of the simulator patterns as well.

To help you understand the characteristics of the mayfly nymph, I have included a drawing showing the anatomy of the nymph (**Fig. 7.1**). Careful study of this illustration will help you determine proportions and correct use of materials.

Tying the American March Brown

HOOK:	Mustad #3906 or #3906B, sizes 10 to 14
THREAD:	Olive, prewaxed 6/0
TAIL:	Three fibers from cock pheasant center tail
BODY:	Amber seal's fur mixed with small amount of tan fox fur or pale amber Seal-Ex dubbing (#104)
RIBBING:	Brown tying thread, size 3/0 or A
LEGS:	Brown partridge or grizzly hen hackle dyed tan
WING CASE:	Quill section from short side of a cock pheasant tail feather
HEAD:	Olive tying thread

NOTE: This pattern also serves as a representative for the Cahill nymph when dressed on a size 14 hook and the Gray Fox nymph when dressed on size 12. All three insects belong to the *Stenonema* group.

Step 1: Attach the tying thread and wind it on the shank to the bend. Tie in three tail fibers that are as long as one hook length; then tie in the ribbing thread under the shank at the same spot. If you want the nymph to be weighted, you should wrap some .025″ lead wire on the middle 1/3 of the shank before going any further.

Step 2 Dubbing the tapered abdomen.

Step 3 Attaching the wing case and hackle.

Step 2: Dub some fur on the thread and form a tapered dubbing. Apply a little cement on the shank and wind on the dubbing to form a tapered abdomen. Tie it off in the middle of the shank and trim the surplus fur. Next, spiral the ribbing forward over the body and tie it off in front. Cut the surplus ribbing and let the tying thread hang at the tie-off spot.

Step 3: For the wing case, cut a section from the tail feather mentioned in the material list. It should be at least 1″ long and wide enough, so when doubled lengthwise, it's as wide as the front of the body. Fasten it in front of the body with the long end projecting toward the rear. Prepare a hackle with fibers that are 1 1/2 hook gaps long and tie it in by the tip at the same spot as the wing case feather.

Step 4: Dub some fur on the front body portion. Spiral the hackle over it to the front and tie it off. Trim the surplus and make sure there is a little room in front for tying down the wing case feather.

Step 4 Winding the hackle.

American March Brown   121

Step 5 The finished traditional American March Brown.

Step 5: Divide the top hackle fibers evenly to each side before folding the wing feather strip forward over the front body portion and tying it off. Trim away the surplus and wind a small head with tying thread before applying a whip finish and cutting the thread. Apply some cement on the head and wing case, and your traditional nymph is finished.

The Imitator Nymph

The discovery of new materials and techniques and the development of fly tying skills make it possible to treat each nymphal form individually, with special attention to the features that characterize the insect the fly was dressed to imitate.

Entomologists will tell you that there are four main groups of mayfly nymphs of particular interest to the angler and fly tier—clingers, burrowers, crawlers (or sprawlers), and swimmers (or climbers). Characteristics of the burrowers and swimmers are explained in the imitator patterns given here. The American March Brown, described above, is a clinger. The Caenis, listed at the end of the chapter in Selected Mayfly Nymph Patterns, is a crawler.

Step 1 Bending the hook.

Tying the Hexagenia Nymph

Description of the natural: Burrower. Very long, slender, and oval in cross section, with shovel-like legs and large tusk-like gill projections on each side of the abdomen. It's one of the largest mayfly nymphs in America.

HOOK:	Mustad #9575 6X long, sizes 2 to 4
THREAD:	Olive, prewaxed 6/0
TAIL:	Three light tannish-gray mini ostrich herl tips, 1 1/2 hook gaps long
ABDOMEN:	Light golden-brown Seal-Ex dubbing (#103) with narrow strip of well-marked teal flank feather, dyed tan, on top
RIBBING:	Fine oval gold tinsel or wire
GILLS:	Dubbing material picked out rather long on each side of the abdomen
THORAX, LEGS:	Well-marked guard hairs with underfur from the back of a brown rabbit, natural color
WING CASE:	Purplish-brown quill section, 1/3 body length
HEAD:	Olive tying thread

Step 1: Bend the front 1/3 of the hook shank at an angle as shown. Then attach the tying thread at the eye and cover the shank to the bend. Tie in three ostrich mini herl tips at the bend.

Step 2 Preparing the abdomen back.

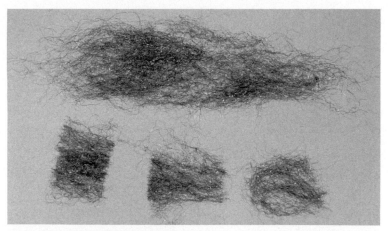

Step 4 Preparing the dubbing.

Step 3 Attaching the ribbing and back.

Step 5 Dubbing the body.

Step 2: Prepare a strip of teal flank feather about 1/8″ wide and spray it with Tuffilm or clear Krylon and stroke it into shape. It should be tapered down toward the tip end as shown.

Step 3: Tie in a 4″ length of ribbing under the shank in the same place as the tie-in spot for the tail. Then tie in the prepared teal strip on top at the same spot so it projects toward the rear with the underside up.

Step 4: Draw out a layer of Seal-Ex dubbing (top) and cut it into 1/2″ chunks. Since Seal-Ex is long-strand dubbing designed for making tapered bodies, it is best to cut it up and tease it with your fingers or mix it in a fur blender so it can be picked out later for gills.

Step 5: Roll the dubbing on the tying thread. Apply some cement on the shank and wind a tapered, rather tight, cigar-shaped body on the shank and tie it off in front, close to the upward bend. Remove the surplus dubbing.

Step 6 Attaching the back and ribbing.

Step 8 Tying down the wing case.

Step 7 Forming the thorax.

Step 6: Fold the teal strip forward over the body and tie it down in front; then spiral the tinsel or wire ribbing forward over the body, tying down the teal in the process. Tie off the ribbing tinsel in front and trim the surplus ends of both materials before applying some cement along the top of the abdomen.

Step 7: Tie in a 1/8″ wide wing case feather strip treated with Tuffilm or Krylon. Then apply the thorax and leg section using a spinning loop. Form a 1 1/2″ long loop of thread using a spring-loaded dubbing twister. Cut fur from the skin with guard hairs long enough to cover the front shank portion. The length of the guard hairs should be about 1 1/2 hook gaps.

With the loop open, insert the fur layer. Close the loop. Spread out the fur, leaving the fur longer to the left of the loop. Spin the fun into a chenille by turning the dubbing twister. Hold the fur above the hook and moisten it with saliva while stroking the fur back so it appears to be coming from one side of the loop. Wind the fur in front of the body, stroking it back with each turn. Tie off the fur in front and cut the surplus. (This process is explained in detail in Chapter 8 for tying the caddis pupae, Steps 6 through 11.)

Step 8: Divide the fur and guard hairs on top of the thorax and pull it out to each side to represent legs. Fold the wing case feather strip forward over the top and tie it down in front. Tie off the thread with a whip finish and cut it. Trim the surplus feather so a little is left to imitate the head. Apply some cement on the thread windings.

Step 9 The finished imitator Hexagenia.

Step 9: Pick out the dubbing on each side of the front 2/3 of the abdomen with your dubbing needle to represent the gills. They should be rather long and heavy for this particular fly. I sometimes trim the fur and guard hair under the thorax if it's too heavy, but that's a matter of preference. You can now apply some cement on top of the wing case and along the underside of the abdomen, and your nymph is finished.

Swimming and Rising Imitator Nymphs

The fish get a much better look at a nymph than they do a dry fly, particularly if you are fishing the sides and slower tailwater of a fast run. For that reason, I think, it's important not only to come as close to the natural as possible in shape and size, but also to pay a great deal of attention to the artificial's behavior and movement when it's being fished.

Hook manufacturers are very much aware of this and are now making hooks that are shaped to facilitate this endeavor. One such hook is the Tiemco TMC 400, made in Japan. It's curved in such a way that when lead weight is applied on the front curve, the fly will swim right side up in an erratic swimming motion as the rod tip is moved up and down rapidly.

If lead is placed on the curve in the rear portion of the shank, the fly must be tied upside-down, as the weight will turn the hook and cause it to ride with the point up. If you let a nymph tied in this manner drift with little or no movement of the rod tip until the line straightens out below you, the fly will rise to the surface like a natural emerging nymph.

Tying the Swimming Isonychia Nymph

Description of the natural: Swimmer. The nymph is long and slim with small plate-like gills along each side of the abdomen. It's very agile in its underwater habitat and is easily recognized by a pale white stripe down the middle of the top of the abdomen. It crawls up on rocks along the shore to hatch, where anglers can determine what color and size is needed for a particular area.

HOOK:	Tiemco TMC 400, sizes 8 to 10
THREAD:	Brown, prewaxed 6/0
TAIL:	Three cock pheasant center tail fibers
WEIGHT:	Lead wire (.030″) on front shank curve
ABDOMEN:	Isonychia Seal-Ex dubbing, dark purplish-brown (#101)
RIBBING:	Fine oval gold or brass tinsel
BACK:	Dark brown wing quill strip and white cotton thread
GILLS:	Dubbing picked out, short
THORAX:	Same as abdomen
LEGS:	Brown partridge dyed olive
WING CASE:	Dark brown wing quill strip and white cotton thread
HEAD:	Brown tying thread

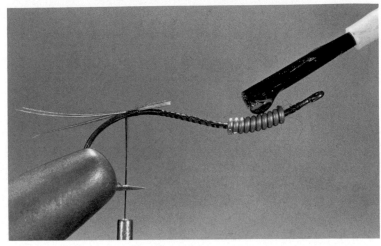

Step 1 Attaching the tail and weight.

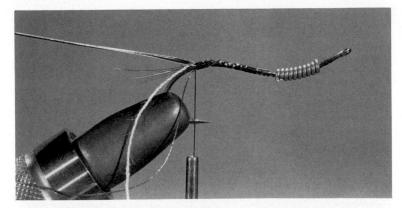

Step 2 Attaching the ribbing and back.

Step 3 Preparing the dubbing.

Step 1: Attach the tying thread in front and wind back to above the barb. Tie in three tail fibers that are about one hook gap long and let the thread hang at the tie-in spot. Next, wrap some lead wire on the front curve of the shank, leaving a little room open in front. Trim the ends of the lead and apply a little cement.

Step 2: Tie in a 4″ length of the ribbing material under the shank and an equal length of white cotton thread on top. Then fasten a 1/8″ wide dark brown quill strip that is 1 1/2 hook lengths long on top of the cotton thread and wind down the ends of the material on the shank. Let the thread hang at the tie-in spot.

Step 3: Draw out a layer of Seal-Ex dubbing that is slightly tapered. Roll a point in the tapered end and tie it in on top of the shank as shown.

Step 4 Forming the abdomen.

Step 5 Preparing the leg feather.

Step 6 Attaching the leg feather.

Step 4: Hold the dubbing and tying thread together and wind them on the shank to form a cigar-shaped body. Tie them off on the first couple of lead wraps. Remove the surplus dubbing and fold the brown quill section forward over the top and tie it off in front of the dubbed body portion. Do not trim the surplus— it's used for the wing case later.

Now pull the white cotton thread forward over the middle of the quill and tie it off, leaving the end long enough for use on the wing case. Spiral the ribbing tinsel forward over the body, binding down the feather and white thread in the process, and tie it off at the same spot as the other materials. Trim the surplus tinsel, and make sure the white cotton thread is centered to form the stripe. Now apply a little cement on top of the body, and your fly should look like the one shown in the photo.

Step 5: Select a brown partridge feather with fibers about 1 1/2 hook gaps long near the tip. Hold the feather by the tip and stroke down the stem with your fingers until the fibers stand out at a right angle. Prepare the tip portion by trimming the fibers with your scissors, leaving some short stumps about 1/4″ up each side of the stem. Pull off the fibers from the butt end so there is a 1/4″ portion of stem with fibers across from each other, which when tied in will represent the legs.

Step 6: Cover the lead wraps with tying thread and tie in the feather leg section, underside up, with a short distance of bare stem between the first fibers and the body.

Step 7 The finished imitator Swimming Isonychia Nymph.

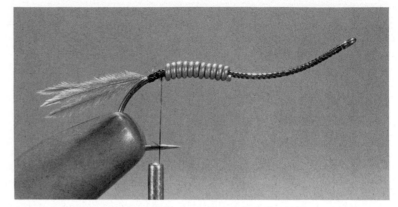

Step 1 Attaching the weight.

Step 7: Dub some fur on the thorax portion and tie the leg section down over the top; then tie it down in front. Apply a little cement along the stem. Take the wing case and white cotton thread over the thorax and tie it down in front. Trim the surplus material and wind the head before applying a whip finish and cutting the thread. Make sure the white stripe is straight and in the middle of the wing case before applying cement to it and to the head. Now pick out the dubbing a little on each side of the abdomen with your dubbing needle to represent the gills. The picked out dubbing on this particular nymph should be trimmed so it attains the shape shown, and the Isonychia nymph is finished.

Tying the Rising Eastern Green Drake

Description of the natural: Burrower. This large, beautiful mayfly nymph is almost identical to the large Hexagenia nymph described earlier. It's slightly smaller and somewhat lighter in color.

HOOK:	Tiemco TMC 400, size 6
THREAD:	Brown, prewaxed 6/0
TAIL:	Three light tannish-gray mini ostrich herl tips, 1/3 body length
ABDOMEN:	Pale amber Seal-Ex dubbing (#104), with narrow strip of well-marked mallard flank feather, dyed tan, on top
RIBBING:	Fine oval gold or brass tinsel
GILLS:	Dubbing material picked out heavily on each side of abdomen
THORAX, LEGS:	Well-marked guard hairs with underfur from the back of a brown rabbit
WING CASE:	Brown wing quill section, 1/3 body length
HEAD:	Brown tying thread

Step 1: The "rising" nymph is tied upside-down on the hook, which causes the fly to rise to the surface without erratic swimming action. This, as I explained earlier, is accomplished by applying the lead weight to the rear curve of the shank, as shown.

Step 2 The finished Eastern Green Drake.

Step 2: The Eastern Green Drake tied upside-down. The techniques for tying this fly are similar to those used in tying the Isonychia except the legs are created by picking out the guard hairs in the thorax dubbing material.

The Mayfly Emerger

When nymphs reach the surface of the water to hatch, there are times when the adults have difficulty in escaping the nymphal skin or for other reasons are unable to leave the surface immediately. Thus, they find themselves floating and struggling for a long time on the surface— a circumstance which permits trout to feed on them in a leisurely and often splashy manner without expending too much energy. For that reason, an emerger-type artificial is needed to get the full benefit of the hatch.

For all practical purposes, an emerger is half nymph and half dun (the first stage of the adult). It should be dressed on a light hook and should float with the abdomen portion submerged for best results. All the nymphs in this chapter can be converted to emergers by adding a half-developed wing made of closed-cell Beamoc Foam (described in Chapter 3) that is tinted to a shade that matches the wings on mature adults. The important factor is to choose the amount of foam that will allow the fly to float at the prescribed angle. Emergers can also be dressed with or without parachute hackle.

Tying the Hexagenia Emerger

HOOK:	Tiemco TMC 200, sizes 4 to 6
THREAD:	Olive, prewaxed 6/0
TAIL:	Three light tannish-gray mini ostrich herl tips, 1 1/2 hook gaps long
ABDOMEN:	Light golden-brown Seal-Ex dubbing (#103), with a narrow strip of well-marked teal flank feather, dyed tan, on top
RIBBING:	Fine oval gold tinsel or wire
GILLS:	Dubbing material picked out long on each side of abdomen
WINGS:	White mini-cell Beamoc Foam strip, 1/8″ square, tinted gray and looped one hook gap high
THORAX:	Rough tan hare's ear dubbing
LEGS:	Grizzly hackle dyed tan and wound parachute style (optional)
HEAD:	Olive tying thread

Step 1 Attaching the foam.

Step 3 Attaching the hackle.

Step 2 Forming the foam loop.

Step 1: Dress the tail and abdomen in the same manner as explained for dressing the standard Hexagenia nymph. The abdomen on this fly should occupy the rear 2/3 of the shank. Tie in a 1″ length of foam in front of the body as shown in the photo. It's best to tint it before tying it in.

Step 2: Form a loop one hook gap high with the foam and tie it down on the shank. Trim the surplus and cover the end with tying thread. Take several turns of thread directly around the base of the foam structure and let the thread hang in front of the abdomen. Apply a little cement on the windings.

Step 3: Prepare a dry fly hackle and tie it in at the base of the foam wing so it projects toward the rear with the good side up. Fasten it securely; then apply the hare's ear dubbing on the thorax portion in front. Try to end up the dubbing so the thread is hanging right in front of the wing.

Step 4 The finished Hexagenia Emerger.

Step 4: Wind the hackle parachute-style around the base of the foam wing and tie it off on the wing structure. (See Chapter 5 on dry flies for instructions on tying parachute-style hackle.) Apply some cement on the windings and also on top of the hackle close to the wing for extra strength, and your emerger is finished.

Selected Mayfly Nymph Patterns

The following list of patterns is by no means a complete list of all nymphs that are known to be effective for trout fishing. I have included a mixture of traditional, imitator, and simulator patterns which, at one time or another, have taken good fish in areas I most frequently fish. Emergers to me are very important, and nearly all the patterns I use can be converted by following the tying instructions given earlier.

Also, although I find Seal-Ex dubbing to be the best material to use whenever it's called for in the materials list, you can use any of the coarser furs like fox, bear, or woodchuck. However, they somehow lack the translucency of Seal-Ex.

BAETIS NYMPH (TRADITIONAL)
HOOK: Mustad #94840, size 20, or Mustad #3906B, sizes 16 to 18

THREAD: Olive, prewaxed 6/0
TAIL: Three wood duck flank feather fibers, 1/2 body length
ABDOMEN: Olive-brown fur dubbing
THORAX, LEGS: Medium brown hare's ear dubbing, picked out for legs
WING CASE: Dark grayish-brown wing quill section
HEAD: Olive tying thread

BLUE-WINGED OLIVE NYMPH (TRADITIONAL)
HOOK: Mustad #3906 or #3906B, sizes 14 to 16
THREAD: Black, prewaxed 6/0
TAIL: Three wood duck flank feather fibers, 2/3 body length
ABDOMEN: Dark brownish-olive fur dubbing or Seal-Ex (#109), picked out lightly for gills
THORAX, LEGS: Olive-brown hare's ear dubbing, picked out for legs
WING CASE: Black wing quill section
HEAD: Black tying thread

BREADCRUST (SIMULATOR)
HOOK: Mustad #3906, sizes 8 to 18
THREAD: Black, prewaxed 6/0
BODY: Hot orange Seal-Ex dubbing (#120), heavy and tapered
RIBBING: Dark brown Larva Lace or heavy tying thread for small flies
HACKLE: Grizzly hen hackle
HEAD: Black tying thread

CAENIS NYMPH (TRADITIONAL)

HOOK: Mustad #3906, size 18
THREAD: Olive, prewaxed 6/0
TAIL: Three brown fibers from cock pheasant center tail, 1/2 body length
ABDOMEN: Grayish-brown fur dubbing
THORAX, LEGS: Grayish-brown hare's ear dubbing, picked out for legs
WING CASE: Dark gray wing quill section
HEAD: Olive tying thread

CASUAL DRESS (SIMULATOR)

HOOK: Mustad #9672 3X long, sizes 4 to 10
THREAD: Black, prewaxed 6/0
TAIL: Muskrat guard hairs with underfur
BODY: Muskrat fur dubbing
COLLAR: Muskrat guard hairs with underfur, spun in loop
HEAD: Black ostrich herl and black tying thread

DARK NYMPH (TRADITIONAL/SIMULATOR)

HOOK: Mustad #3906 or #3906B, sizes 8 to 18
THREAD: Black, prewaxed 6/0
TAIL: Dark brown hackle fibers
BODY: Reddish-brown fur or Isonychia Seal-Ex dubbing (#101)
RIBBING: Oval gold tinsel
HACKLE: Soft furnace hen hackle
WING CASE: Dark gray duck wing quill section
HEAD: Black tying thread

DUN VARIANT NYMPH (TRADITIONAL/SIMULATOR)

HOOK: Mustad #3906, sizes 10 to 14
THREAD: Olive, prewaxed 6/0
TAIL: Three short sections of peacock herl
BODY: Bronze peacock herl or Isonychia Seal-Ex dubbing (#101)
COLLAR: Grouse body feather
HEAD: Olive tying thread

EASTERN GREEN DRAKE (IMITATOR)

HOOK: Tiemco TMC 400, size 6
THREAD: Brown, prewaxed 6/0
TAIL: Three light tannish-gray mini ostrich herl tips, 1/3 body length
ABDOMEN: Pale amber Seal-Ex dubbing (#104), with narrow strip of well-marked mallard flank feather, dyed tan, on top
RIBBING: Fine oval gold or brass tinsel
GILLS: Dubbing material picked out heavily on each side of abdomen
THORAX, LEGS: Well-marked guard hairs with underfur from the back of a natural brown rabbit
WING CASE: Brown wing quill section, 1/3 body length
HEAD: Brown tying thread

EPHORON NYMPH (BURROWER— SIMULATOR)

Description of the natural: A rather small nymph for a burrower. The abdomen is slim and oval to round in shape. Artificials are fished only as emergers floating in the surface film. They are used from late afternoon to right before dark.

HOOK: Mustad #38941 3X long, sizes 12 to 14
THREAD: Gray, prewaxed 6/0
TAIL: Three soft white wing quill fibers, 1/3 body length
ABDOMEN: Creamish-white Seal-Ex dubbing (#115) or dirty white fur dubbing
RIBBING: Fine oval gold tinsel
GILLS: Dubbing material, picked out heavily on each side of abdomen
WINGS: White mini-cell Beamoc Foam strip, 1/8" square, one hook gap high
THORAX: White fur with cut-up guard hairs (white hare's ear dubbing)
LEGS: White hackle tied parachute style
HEAD: Gray tying thread

FLEDERMAUS (SIMULATOR)

HOOK: Mustad #9672 3X long, sizes 1 to 14
THREAD: Black, prewaxed 6/0

BODY:	Muskrat fur dubbing
WINGS:	Gray squirrel tail, one body length
HEAD:	Black tying thread

GOLD-RIBBED HARE'S EAR (SIMULATOR)

HOOK:	Mustad #3906B, sizes 8 to 18
THREAD:	Black, prewaxed 6/0
TAIL:	Soft brown hen neck hackle fibers
ABDOMEN:	Tan hare's ear dubbing
RIBBING:	Oval gold tinsel
THORAX, LEGS:	Rough brown hare's ear dubbing, picked out for legs
WING CASE:	Dark gray duck wing quill section
HEAD:	Black tying thread

HENDRICKSON NYMPH (TRADITIONAL)

HOOK:	Mustad #3906 or #3906B, sizes 10 to 18
THREAD:	Olive, prewaxed 6/0
TAIL:	Small bunch of wood duck flank feather fibers
BODY:	Grayish-brown fur or light golden-brown Seal-Ex dubbing (#103)
RIBBING:	Fine oval gold tinsel or wire
HACKLE:	Brown partridge
WING CASE:	Gray duck wing quill section
HEAD:	Olive tying thread

HEXAGENIA NYMPH (IMITATOR)

HOOK:	Mustad #9575 6X long, sizes 2 to 4
THREAD:	Olive, prewaxed 6/0
TAIL:	Three light tannish-gray mini ostrich herl tips, 1 1/2 hook gaps long
ABDOMEN:	Light golden-brown Seal-Ex dubbing (#103), with narrow strip of well-marked teal flank feather, dyed tan, on top
RIBBING:	Fine oval gold tinsel or wire
GILLS:	Dubbing material picked out rather long on each side of the abdomen
THORAX, LEGS:	Well-marked guard hairs with underfur from the back of a brown rabbit
WING CASE:	Purplish-brown quill section, 1/3 body length
HEAD:	Olive tying thread

ISONYCHIA NYMPH (IMITATOR)

HOOK:	Tiemco TMC 400, sizes 8 to 10
THREAD:	Brown, prewaxed 6/0
TAIL:	Three cock pheasant center tail fibers
WEIGHT:	Lead wire (.030″) on front shank curve
ABDOMEN:	Isonychia Seal-Ex dubbing, dark purplish-brown (#101)
BACK:	Dark brown wing quill strip and white cotton thread
RIBBING:	Fine oval gold or brass tinsel
GILLS:	Dubbing picked out, short
THORAX:	Same as abdomen
LEGS:	Brown partridge dyed olive
WING CASE:	Dark brown wing quill strip and white cotton thread
HEAD:	Brown tying thread

LEPTOPHLEBIA NYMPH (CRAWLER— IMITATOR)

Description of the natural: This small, dark brown nymph is active all through the day from late April through early June. It can be used as an all-purpose nymph by both eastern and western anglers.

HOOK:	Mustad #38941 3X long, sizes 12 to 14
THREAD:	Brown, prewaxed 6/0
TAIL:	Three brown cock pheasant center tail fibers, body length
ABDOMEN:	Dark brown Seal-Ex dubbing (#110)
RIBBING:	Fine oval gold tinsel or wire
GILLS:	Dubbing material, picked out heavily on each side of abdomen
THORAX:	Dark gray hare's ear dubbing
LEGS:	Brown partridge tied in as a section
WING CASE:	Blackish-brown wing quill section
HEAD:	Brown tying thread

LIGHT NYMPH (TRADITIONAL/SIMULATOR)

HOOK:	Mustad #3906 or #3906B, sizes 8 to 18
THREAD:	Black, prewaxed 6/0
TAIL:	Small bunch of wood duck flank feather fibers
BODY:	Cream fur or yellowish-cream Seal-Ex dubbing (#117)
RIBBING:	Oval gold tinsel
HACKLE:	Gray partridge
WING CASE:	Gray duck wing quill section
HEAD:	Black tying thread

LITTLE BLUE DUN NYMPH (TRADITIONAL/SIMULATOR)

HOOK:	Mustad #3906B, sizes 16 to 18
THREAD:	Brown, prewaxed 6/0
TAIL:	Three wood duck flank feather fibers, 1/2 body length
ABDOMEN:	Light golden-brown Seal-Ex dubbing (#103)
RIBBING:	Brown tying thread
GILLS:	Dubbing material, picked out each side of abdomen
THORAX, LEGS:	Tan hare's ear dubbing, picked out for legs
WING CASE:	Dark grayish-brown wing quill section
HEAD:	Brown tying thread

MARCH BROWN NYMPH (TRADITIONAL)

HOOK:	Mustad #3906 or #3906B, sizes 10 to 14
THREAD:	Olive, prewaxed 6/0
TAIL:	Three cock pheasant center tail fibers
BODY:	Amber seal's fur mixed with small amount of tan fox fur or pale amber Seal-Ex dubbing (#104)
RIBBING:	Brown tying thread, size 3/0 or A
LEGS:	Brown partridge or grizzly hen hackle dyed tan
WING CASE:	Quill section from short side of a cock pheasant tail feather
HEAD:	Olive tying thread

MEDIUM NYMPH (TRADITIONAL/SIMULATOR)

HOOK:	Mustad #3906 or #3906B, sizes 8 to 18
THREAD:	Black, prewaxed 6/0
TAIL:	Three cock pheasant center tail fibers
BODY:	Hare's ear fur dubbing
RIBBING:	Oval gold tinsel
HACKLE:	Brown partridge
WING CASE:	Gray duck wing quill section
HEAD:	Black tying thread

MUSKRAT NYMPH (SIMULATOR)

HOOK:	Mustad #9671 2X long, sizes 8 to 18
THREAD:	Black, prewaxed 6/0
BODY:	Muskrat fur dubbing, tapered
THROAT:	Speckled guinea fowl fibers
HEAD:	Black ostrich herl

PHEASANT TAIL NYMPH (SIMULATOR)

HOOK:	Mustad #3906, sizes 12 to 18
THREAD:	Dark brown, prewaxed 6/0
TAIL:	Four or five cock pheasant center tail fibers
BODY:	Long ends from tail fibers twisted with tying thread
RIBBING:	Copper wire
WING CASE:	Remainder of body material wound as thorax and folded over as wing
HEAD:	Dark brown tying thread

POTAMANTHUS NYMPH (CRAWLER— IMITATOR)

Description of natural: This is another nymph with rather long tusk-like gills and an oval body that is heavily marked on top of the abdomen. It's the nymph of Art Flick's famous Cream Variant dry fly.

HOOK:	Mustad #38941 3X long or Tiemco TMC 400, size 10
THREAD:	Brown, prewaxed 6/0
TAIL:	Three light brown cock pheasant center tail fibers, 1/3 body length
ABDOMEN:	Light golden-brown Seal-Ex dubbing (#103), with narrow strip of well-marked mallard flank feather, dyed tan, on top
RIBBING:	Fine oval gold tinsel or wire
GILLS:	Dubbing material, picked out long on each side of abdomen
THORAX, LEGS:	Well-marked guard hairs with underfur from the back of a brown rabbit, natural and sparse; guard hairs 1/2 body length
WING CASE:	Reddish-brown wing quill section, 1/3 body length
HEAD:	Brown tying thread

QUILL GORDON NYMPH

HOOK:	Mustad #3906 or #3906B, sizes 8 to 14
THREAD:	Black, prewaxed 6/0
TAIL:	Blue dun hen hackle fibers
WINGS:	Wood duck flank feather fibers
BODY:	Grayish-brown fur dubbing
HACKLE:	Blue dun hen hackle
HEAD:	Black tying thread

SULPHUR NYMPH (CRAWLER— IMITATOR)

Description of natural: Nymphs belonging to the crawling group move around slowly in all types of water. The abdomen is fairly round, and the nymph has thin, feeble legs. It is well known to anglers in both the East and the West.

HOOK: Mustad #3906B, sizes 14 to 16
THREAD: Brown, prewaxed 6/0
TAIL: Three pale tan cock pheasant center tail fibers, 1/2 body length
ABDOMEN: Pale amber Seal-Ex dubbing (#104), with goose biot, dyed medium brown, on top
RIBBING   Fine gold wire
GILLS: Dubbing material, picked out lightly on each side of abdomen
THORAX: Tan hare's ear dubbing
LEGS: Brown partridge feather segment
WING CASE: Brown wing quill section
HEAD: Brown tying thread

TELLECO NYMPH (SIMULATOR)

HOOK: Mustad #3906B, sizes 8 to 16
THREAD: Black, prewaxed 6/0
TAIL: Brown hackle fibers
BODY: Yellow floss
RIBBING: One strand of peacock herl
BACK: Two or three peacock herls
HACKLE: Soft brown hen hackle
HEAD: Black tying thread

ZUG BUG (SIMULATOR)

HOOK: Mustad #9671 2X long, sizes 6 to 16
THREAD: Black, prewaxed 6/0
TAIL: Three short peacock sword fibers
BODY: Peacock herl
RIBBING: Oval gold tinsel
WING CASE: Mallard flank feather section tied flat by stem and trimmed to 1/3 body length
HACKLE: Soft brown hen hackle
HEAD: Black tying thread

Crustaceans

Crustaceans are not, of course, relatives of mayflies. However, I chose to include a couple of crustacean imitations in this chapter because the patterns are nymph-like. **Fig. 7.2** shows the Cress Bug (left) and the Freshwater Shrimp.

Fig. 7.2 Cress Bug, left, and Freshwater Shrimp patterns.

CRESS BUG (SOWBUG SIMULATOR)

HOOK: Mustad #3906, sizes 16 to 18
THREAD: Olive, prewaxed 6/0
BODY: Gray rabbit fur with guard hairs dyed medium olive, spun in a loop "chenille style," then wound and trimmed on top, bottom, and sides to a very flat, oval-shaped body
HEAD: Olive tying thread

FRESHWATER SHRIMP (YELLOW SCUD SIMULATOR)

HOOK: Partridge K4A, sizes 16 to 18
THREAD: Olive, prewaxed 6/0
BODY: Yellowish-olive rabbit fur with guard hairs spun in a loop "chenille style," then wound and trimmed on top and both sides, leaving the fur and guard hair a hook gap long on the underside to represent the legs
HEAD: Olive tying thread

NOTE: Try to pick the fur and guard hair to correct length. For best results, you should avoid trimming the legs.

Chapter 8
Caddisflies

If you have studied the chapter dealing with mayflies and have learned the basic tying procedures, you should have no trouble dressing the caddisflies in their various stages.

In their underwater habitat the caddisflies differ from mayflies and stoneflies in both appearance and development. After hatching from the egg, they appear as worm-like larvae that, upon completion of growth, change into the pupal stage and remain as such for a couple of weeks longer, depending on the species. The pupae then rise to the surface and emerge as winged adults.

Some caddis larvae are often referred to as caddis worms and they move about freely on the stream bottom, while others build a protective case of underwater fragments such as leaves, small sticks, or fine sand.

For the fly tier, then, it's important to be able to dress all three caddisfly stages, the larva, the pupa, and the adult.

The Caddis Larva

The little caddis larvae have the appearance of slim cylin-

Step 1 Attaching the Larva Lace.

Step 2 Winding the floss body.

drical worms and are quite simple to dress. I have not given any entomological classification to the artificials I use, as they merely represent a few of a long list of species with which I have successfully fished throughout the United States and elsewhere.

Tying the Green Caddis Larva

HOOK:	Mustad #3906 or #3906B, sizes 8 to 18
THREAD:	Dark brown, prewaxed 6/0
BODY:	Bright fluorescent green floss with overlay of narrow peacock herl and overwound with clear Larva Lace
THORAX:	Brownish-black Seal-Ex dubbing (#102) on front 1/4 of body
LEGS:	Thorax dubbing, picked out from underside
HEAD:	Dark brown tying thread

NOTE: The peacock herl overlay that runs along the top of the floss body imitates the slightly darker shade found on

top of the natural and also exposes some of the flues from the herl, giving a little fuzz to the top of the body. When cutting the herl at the end of the body after the Larva Lace is wound, leave some fuzz there as well.

Step 1: Place a size 10 hook in the vise so most of the bend is exposed. Attach the tying thread and tie in a 3″ length of clear Larva Lace 1/8″ from the eye; then wind the thread back and down to the middle of the hook bend, binding the Larva Lace down on the shank in the process. Now wind the thread forward on the shank to 1/8″ from the eye.

Step 2: Tie in a single strand of floss and wind it on the shank to the middle of the bend with close turns. Then wind it back over the first layer to the tie-in position and tie it off. Trim the surplus floss and tie in a narrow strand of peacock herl on top of the shank with the long end pointing toward the rear. Narrow herl is found near the peacock eye.

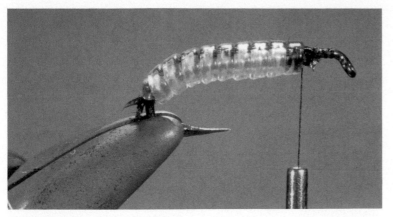

Step 3 Winding the Larva Lace.

Step 4 The finished Green Caddis Larva.

Step 3: Hold the herl along the top of the floss underbody and wind over it with the first turns of Larva Lace to hold the herl in position. Now wind the Larva Lace forward over the body with close side-by-side turns, making sure the herl is kept on top of the floss. Tie it off in front. Trim both herl and Lace. For the size fly we are tying, you should have at least a 1/8″ space between the front of the body and the eye of the hook.

Step 4: Wind a very small amount of Seal-Ex dubbing on the space in front and tie it off. Whip finish the head and cut the thread before applying some clear cement on the windings. Pick out a small amount of dubbing under the thorax for legs, and the fly is finished.

Additional Larva Patterns

I have found the green and white caddis larva in size 10 to be the most effective for me. There are, however, other colors that might work better in your area. The only thing you need change is the color of the floss underbody; all the rest is the same on all patterns. The following colors are some of the most productive for me.

Olive Caddis Larva: Light or medium olive floss

White Caddis Larva: White floss

Orange Caddis Larva: Bright orange floss

Yellow Caddis Larva: Bright yellow floss

The Caddis Pupa

Good imitations of caddis pupae are rare indeed, and until a few years ago no attempt had been made to create a series of artificials designed specifically to represent the many species of caddis. Nevertheless, anglers successfully overcame this handicap by using traditional wet flies of the same general color and size as those of the migrating pupae. This fact seems to prove my own theory that many of the wet flies designed by pioneering fly anglers were not meant to imitate a drowned mayfly but, rather, imitated the caddis pupae.

The biggest challenge that faces the fly tier when imitating the naturals is to incorporate the glistening sheen of the silvery air bubbles trapped within the translucent pupal skin. Other fly tying writers have come up with some excellent artificials that work very well, but there is always room for new ideas, new materials, and new tying methods.

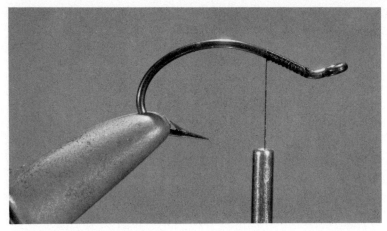

Step 1 Attaching the thread.

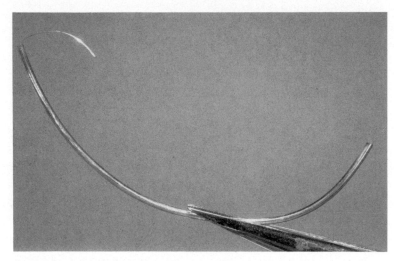

Step 2 Preparing the Larva Lace.

Seal-Ex dubbing and Larva Lace lend themselves very well to this type of work because they create a natural sheen and are very translucent in water. I no longer use wing cases on my pupae, and I have found that it makes very little difference.

Instructions for tying the Dark Brown Caddis Pupa are given below. This pupa is a general representative of a variety of brown pupae found in many sizes throughout the United States and elsewhere. Additional pupa patterns are given in the section on Selected Caddis Patterns at the end of this chapter.

Tying the Dark Brown Caddis Pupa

HOOK: Partridge Yorkshire sedge hook K2B, sizes 8 to 16

THREAD: Brown, prewaxed 6/0

BODY: Medium brown Seal-Ex dubbing (#111) overwound with silver wire inside clear Larva Lace tinted pale brown with waterproof marking pen

THORAX,
LEGS: Well-marked guard hairs with underfur from the back of a brown rabbit

HEAD: Brown tying thread

NOTE: For the thorax and legs on very small flies, I use the neck portion of an Australian opossum instead of rabbit. At the same time, the Seal-Ex dubbing is replaced by finer animal fur of the same general shade dressed in a segmented fashion without the Larva Lace.

Step 1: Place a size 10 hook in the vise with most of the bend exposed. Attach the tying thread in front and let it hang at a position that is about 1/4 of the body length from the eye. (On a size 10 hook, it's a little more than 1/8".)

Step 2: Prepare a 3" length of clear Larva Lace by tinting it with a brown waterproof marking pen. Now insert some very fine silver wire through the hollow lace, exposing it a little at each end as shown.

Step 3 Attaching the Larva Lace and dubbing.

Step 4 Winding the dubbing.

Step 3: Trim the wire even at one end of the Lace and tie it in, starting 1/4 of the body length from the eye. Wind the thread back and down to the middle of the bend, binding the Larva Lace down on the shank in the process. Prepare a narrow, tapered layer of Seal-Ex dubbing as long as the Larva Lace and roll a point in the end with a little saliva. Tie in the dubbing by the pointed end midway down on the bend. Your fly should now look like the one shown.

Step 4: Spiral the dubbing lightly around the thread in a counterclockwise direction. Hold the dubbing and the thread together and wind the body. Release the dubbing now and then while winding it or it will be too tight. The tapered body should be rather slim, bearing in mind that the Larva Lace is wound over it later. Tie off the dubbing 1/4 the body length from the eye and trim the surplus.

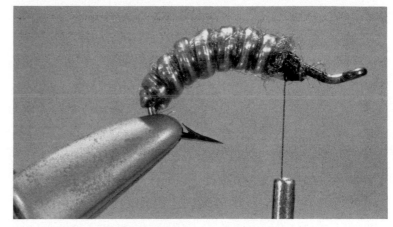

Step 5 Winding the Larva Lace.

Step 5: Wind the Larva Lace forward over the body with tight turns, leaving only a small area between each turn to expose the dubbing a little. Tie off the Lace in front and cut the surplus. Make sure there is still at least 1/4 of the body length between the front of the body and the hook eye.

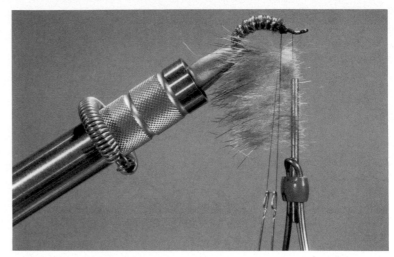

Step 8 Inserting the fur.

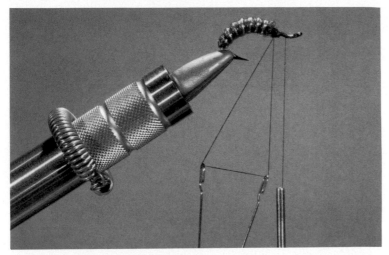

Step 6 Forming a spinning loop.

Step 7 Cutting the leg and thorax fur.

Step 6: With the thread hanging directly in front of the body, form a 1 1/2″ long spinning loop using a spring-loaded dubbing twister or another favorite tool that allows you to keep the loop open.

Step 7: Cut the fur for the leg and thorax from the skin. It should be long enough for the guard hairs to project beyond the bend a little when wound on the hook. Make sure the fur and guard hairs are not mixed up but are kept in a layer just as they come from the skin. Otherwise, the technique will not work.

Step 8: With the spinning loop open, insert the fur layer. Close the loop. Spread out the fur so it occupies about 3/4″ for the size 10 fly we are tying. With the loop thread as a guideline, it should be noted that the fur bunch is much longer to the left in the loop, and that the guard hairs in this case reach to a little beyond the bend. That section becomes the legs. The fur to the right of the loop becomes the thorax. Its length should be equal to about 1/4 of the body length.

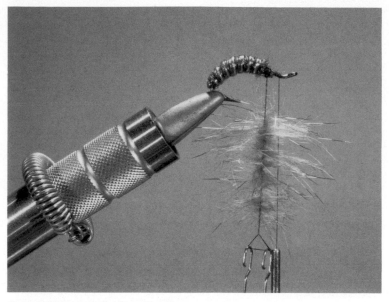

Step 9 Spinning the fur chenille.

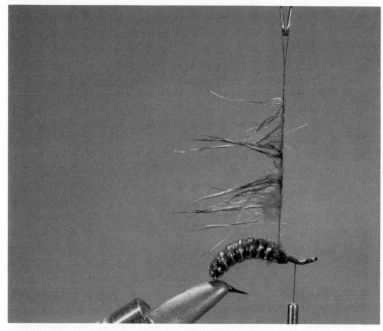

Step 10 Preparing to wind the fur chenille.

Step 11 The finished Dark Brown Caddis Pupa.

Step 9: Spin a fur chenille by turning the dubbing twister in a clockwise direction. Do not moisten the fur layer before making the chenille.

Step 10: Hold the fur chenille up above the hook by the twister and moisten it a little with saliva while stroking all the fur and guard hair back so it appears to be coming from one side of the loop only.

Step 11: Wind the fur in front of the body like a wet fly hackle, stroking it back after each turn. Three or four turns will do. Tie off and cut the surplus before winding a small head and applying some clear cement. If the leg and thorax appear to be too heavy, you can trim a little off. I usually just trim some off the top, leaving enough guard hairs to imitate the horns, and I add a little cement on top in front, stroking the hairs down so they sit flat over the body. This finishes the pupa.

Step 1 Preparing to add the wings.

Step 2 Selecting and preparing the wing feathers.

Emerger and Stillborn Caddis

There are times when the fish are splashing and jumping around near the surface to catch their prey, but no matter what you offer, there are no takers. This is very frustrating to say the least, and puzzled me for several seasons. After examining the stomach contents of a 12″ brown trout I caught behind my house, I think I found the answer. The stomach contained a variety of insects, among them some half-developed caddis; sort of a cross between a pupa and an adult. I realized then that caddis, much like mayflies, also have a so-called emerger or stillborn stage where the adult doesn't quite make it out of its protective skin.

To imitate the emerger or stillborn, I use the basic pupa pattern. But since it's fished on or near the surface, I leave out the Larva Lace and change the dubbing to a mixture of rabbit fur and Seal-Ex. To mix this, cut the Seal-Ex into 1/2″ lengths and put it in a fur blender with natural rabbit fur and guard hairs taken from the back of a brown rabbit. I dub the body on a Mustad dry fly hook (#94838) or a light wet fly hook (#3906). As a final touch, I add a pair of wings that are cut from solid chicken or rooster body feathers in a blue-gray shade. You can attach the wings in any position, but the two positions I prefer are splayed above the body or slanting down and out a little to each side.

As an example for converting the Dark Brown Caddis Pupa into an emerger or stillborn, you can use the following instructions.

Tying the Dark Brown Caddis Emerger

HOOK:	Mustad #94838 or #3906, sizes 8 to 16
THREAD:	Dark brown, prewaxed 6/0
BODY:	Rabbit fur with guard hairs and medium brown Seal-Ex dubbing (#111) cut into 1/2″ lengths and mixed in a fur blender
THORAX, LEGS:	Well-marked guard hairs and underfur from the back of a brown rabbit
WINGS:	Two solid blue-gray chicken or rooster body feathers trimmed to shape
HEAD:	Dark brown tying thread

Step 1: Dub a fur body on the hook you have selected. Since the dubbing is now shorter and blended, you should use the ordinary roll dubbing method, applying a little at a time on the thread and overlapping each application to get a tapered dubbing. Add the thorax and leg section as explained in the instructions for the pupa and trim off the fur on top.

Step 3 The finished Dark Brown Caddis Emerger.

Step 2: Select two medium-sized body feathers and strip the fibers off one side of each feather as shown. They should be stripped from opposite sides of the stem to make a left and a right wing. Trim them to a narrow shape with your nail clippers or scissors as shown. They should be long enough to reach at least to the bend of the hook when tied in.

Step 3: Tie in a wing on each side of the body with the good side out and the stem as the lower edge. Wind a small head and whip finish before cutting the thread. Apply some clear head cement, and the emerger is finished.

Caddis Dry Flies

For many years the caddisflies, or sedges as they are often called, were not considered to be of any major interest to the angler except in their aquatic stages. They have, of course, been around all the time, and I have the feeling that some of the old traditional dries like the Quill Gordon, Light Cahill, and the Adams are taken by fish that somehow mistake them for caddis.

Step 1 Winding the body.

Adult caddisflies can be dressed in a variety of styles. The first of these we will tie is the hair-wing style, consisting of a bunch of fine deer body hair dressed in a down-wing fashion, with the wing laying low and parallel with the fur body. The tips of the wing extend beyond the bend of the hook and aid the fly in floating much like the tail does on a traditional dry fly. The hackle is applied in the conventional dry-fly style after the wing has been secured and is then trimmed on the lower side as explained in the following instructions. The same wing style is used on a parachute pattern of recent vintage. Both patterns are considered to be of eastern origin and are quite sparsely dressed.

Tying the Hair-Wing Caddis

HOOK:	Mustad #94833 or #94840, sizes 10 to 18
THREAD:	Brown, prewaxed 6/0
BODY:	Dark olive fur dubbing
WINGS:	Fine-textured, well-marked natural deer body hair
HACKLE:	Medium brown
HEAD:	Brown tying thread

Step 1: Attach the tying thread and wind it to the bend, covering the shank in the process. Now apply a rather thin tapered fur body as explained in the dry fly chapter, Chapter

Step 2 Cutting the deer body hair.

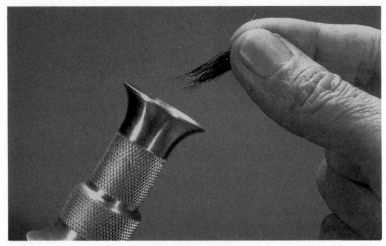

Step 3a Inserting the hair into the stacker.

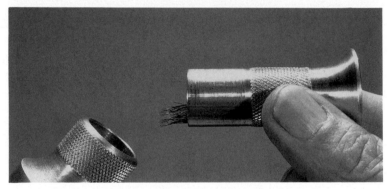

Step 3b Removing the stacked hair.

5, under Tying the American March Brown, Steps 10-12. It should cover 2/3 of the shank.

Step 2: Select a piece of deer body skin with fine, well-marked hair. (When buying hair for this type of work, it's best to ask for early deer with hair 3/4″ to 1 3/4″ in length which will flare very little when tied in.) Gather a small bunch of hair between your fingers and cut it close to the skin with your heavy scissors.

Step 3: Remove the underfur and fuzz with a comb. Insert the hair in your hair stacker tips first as shown in the Step 3a photo. Bang it on the table a few times to align the hair tips and remove the hair as shown in the Step 3b photo.

Step 4: Remove the hair from the stacker by the tips. Hold it on top of the shank with the tips extending a full body length beyond the hook bend. Then fasten it 1/3 of the shank length from the eye with a couple of loose turns of thread to hold it in place. Now press the hair down a little on each side of the shank and fasten it securely. Trim the butt ends and apply some clear penetrating cement. Make sure the wing is sitting flat and unflared.

Step 4 Attaching the wing.

Step 5 Winding the hackle.

Step 6 The finished Hair-Wing Caddis.

Step 5: Select two good brown dry fly hackles. They should be measured, tied in, and wound in the same manner as regular dry fly hackle. Tie them off, cut the surplus, and wind a small head before finishing the fly with a whip finish and some clear cement. NOTE: I suggest that you study hackle selection and how to wind hackle in the dry fly chapter, Chapter 5, under tying the American March Brown, Steps 13-17.

Step 6: When a caddis dry fly is being fished, it should sit very low on the water like the natural insect, and for this reason we break the unwritten rule of fly tying— we trim the hackle. It should be trimmed with great care so it will not ruin the balance and overall attractiveness of the fly. The hackle is trimmed horizontally underneath the body so the fibers on the bottom are one hook gap long and the fibers on the sides and top are full length. The finished fly should look like the one shown.

Step 1 Applying the body and wing.

Step 2 Preparing the hackle base.

Tying the Hair-Wing Caddis Parachute Style

In tying this pattern, you can use the same instructions and materials list as for the regular pattern. The main difference, then, is the hackle application. Aside from representing an adult caddis, this pattern also works well when fished as an adult stonefly. It can be tied in any size and color.

Step 1: Dub a slim, tapered fur body that covers 2/3 of the shank; then cut a small bunch of fine, well-marked deer body hair that is twice as long as the hook and clean out the underfur and fuzz. Even up the tips in a hair stacker and tie them in on top of the shank in front of the fur body with the tips extending a full body length past the bend. If the hair is flared too much, you can wind the thread back a few loose turns to hold the fibers closer together. Fasten the wing securely and apply a little cement on the windings, as shown.

Step 2: Gather the butt ends of the wing hair between your fingers and hold them back while taking several turns of thread close in front of them. Continue by winding four or five turns of thread up on the base of the butt ends to build a foundation on which the hackle is to be wound. Apply a little cement on all the windings and make sure the butt ends are standing up at a 90-degree angle to the hook shank.

Step 3 Attaching the hackle.

Step 4 Winding the hackle.

Step 3: Prepare a dry fly hackle as explained in the dry fly chapter, Chapter 5, under Tying the American March Brown. Tie it in on top of the hook behind the wing butts so it sits flat and projects toward the rear. Wind over the hackle stem in front and let the tying thread hang directly up against the butt-end structure. Before you proceed, I suggest you hold the wing hair out of the way by doubling a piece of paper over the wing and clamping a pair of hackle pliers to the ends, thus forming a loop with the paper. You can now wind the hackle without trapping any of the wing fibers.

Step 4: Wind the hackle on the wing butts horizontally in a clockwise direction. Make sure that each succeeding turn is beneath the previous one. Four or five turns should be enough. When the last turn is completed, hold the remainder of the hackle toward you on the near side while taking the tying thread over the hackle stem. Then wind the thread in a clockwise direction around the wing butts between the lowest turn of hackle and the body. Take several turns of thread in that fashion, thus securing the hackle stem.

Step 5 The finished Hair-Wing Caddis Parachute Style.

Step 5: Wind a small head. Then tie off the thread close to the hook eye with a half-hitch tool. Cut the thread and trim away the surplus hackle. Carefully trim the hair butts above the hackle, leaving some small flared stumps. Apply some clear cement and let it soak in among the hackle windings. Now cement the tie-off windings on the shank, and your fly is finished.

Step 1 Attaching the hackle.

Tying the Tan Elk Hair Caddis

The Elk Hair Caddis was designed for fishing western rivers with heavier currents. This, of course, does not mean that it cannot be fished all over, but quite frankly, the more sparsely dressed flies work a little better on the slower, more placid eastern and midwestern streams.

HOOK: Mustad #94840, sizes 10 to 20
THREAD: Tan, prewaxed 6/0
BODY: Hare's ear dubbing, light
WINGS: Fine elk body hair, tan
HACKLE: Furnace, tied palmer
HEAD: Tan tying thread

Step 1: Place the hook in the vise and dub a slim tapered hare's ear body covering 3/4 of the shank. Then tie in the body hackle in front. The fibers on the hackle should be 1 1/2 hook gaps long. Fasten it securely with the good side toward the front; then spiral the thread back to the bend and let it hang.

Plate 1: DRY FLIES (left to right, top to bottom)
  Adams—Gray Fox Variant—Hendrickson No-Hackle—Humpy—March Brown
  Quill Gordon—Renegade—Royal Coachman—Isonychia Cut-Wing Parachute—Isonychia Spinner
  Green Drake Jorgen-Betts Spinner—Bird's Stonefly—Joe's Hopper
  Improved Sofa Pillow—Little Brown Stonefly—Hair-Wing Caddis—Hair-Wing Caddis Parachute—Elk Hair Caddis
  Letort Cricket—Beamoc Beetle—Beamoc Mini-Beetle—Beamoc Ant—Flying Beamoc Ant—Letort Hopper

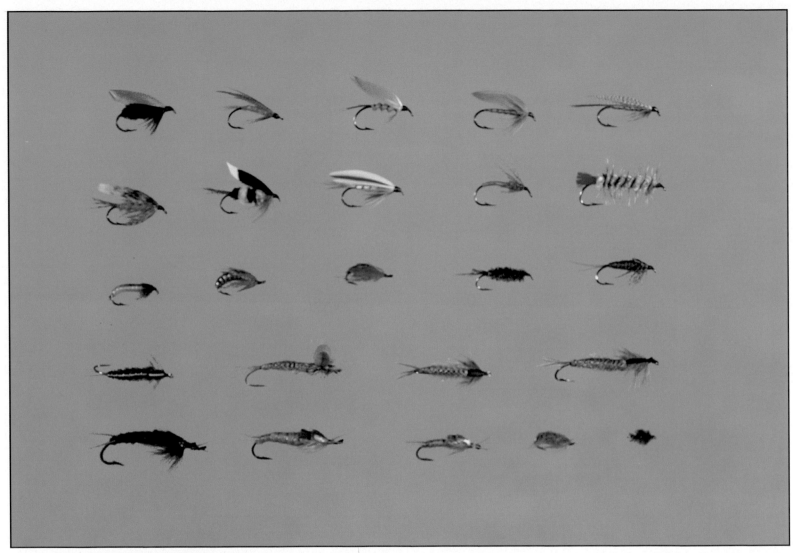

Plate 2: WET FLIES (left to right, top to bottom)
  Black Gnat—Dark Cahill—Gold-Ribbed Hare's Ear—Greenwell's Glory—Professor
  March Brown—McGinty—Parmachene Bell—Partridge and Orange Soft Hackle—Wooly Worm
  Green Caddis Larva—Dark Brown Caddis Pupa—Caddis Emerger—Insult Nymph—March Brown Nymph
  Swimming Isonychia Nymph—Hexagenia Emerger—Green Drake Nymph—Hexagenia Nymph
  Large Black Stonefly Nymph—Golden Stonefly Nymph—Perla Stonefly Creeper—Freshwater Shrimp—Cress Bug

Plate 3: STREAMERS (left to right, top to bottom)
   Olive Zonker—Matuka—Black Ghost
   Wooly Bugger—Matuka Sculpin—Muddler Minnow
   Gray Ghost—Black Nose Dace—Mickey Finn

Plate 4: SALMON FLIES (left to right, top to bottom)
  Lady Joan—Green Butt—Crossfield (low-water)—Cosseboom
  Blue Rat—Green Highlander (converted)—Jock Scott (converted)—Orange Blossom

STEELHEAD FLIES
  Glo-Bug Egg Fly—Fall Favorite—Skunk—Golden Demon
  October Caddis—Grease Liner—Babine Special—Purple Peril

Plate 5: SALTWATER FLIES (left to right, top to bottom)
   Brown and White Bendback—Dirty Water Tarpon Fly—Crazy Charlie
   Lefty's Deceiver
   Keys Tarpon Fly (Yellow and Orange)—Strawberry Blonde

Plate 6: CORK AND HAIR BUGS (left to right, top to bottom)
   Weedless Hammerhead—Deer Hair Bug
   Cork-Bodied Popper—Hammerhead Baitfish Imitation

Step 2 Winding the hackle.

Step 3 Attching the wing.

Step 2: Grasp the hackle with your hackle pliers and take one complete turn of hackle before spiraling it back over the body palmer-style. Tie it off at the bend with several tight turns of thread. While still maintaining tension on the thread, wind it through the hackle to the front of the first turn. Trim the surplus hackle tip at the rear. Make sure that you still have 1/4 of the shank length left in front for the wing.

Step 3: Cut a small bunch of fine-textured tan elk hair and clean out the fuzz and underfur. Even up the tips in a hair stacker and tie the bunch in on top of the shank with the tips reaching to the hook bend. Fasten it securely with some additional thread windings before applying a whip finish and cutting the thread.

Step 4: Trim the hair butts as shown in the photo. Then apply some clear cement on the thread windings both in the front and in the rear where the hackle was tied off, and the Tan Elk Hair Caddis is finished.

Step 4 The finished Elk Hair Caddis.

Selected Caddis Patterns

Caddis Pupa Patterns

Like the brown pupa described in the tying instructions, the following patterns should be considered as general representatives of a variety of insects in the shades mentioned in each dressing. They can be tied in many different sizes to match the ones found in your favorite stream.

CINNAMON SEDGE PUPA

HOOK: Partridge sedge hook K2B, sizes 8 to 12
THREAD: Brown, prewaxed 6/0
BODY: Brown Seal-Ex dubbing (#123) overwound with silver wire inside clear Larva Lace tinted pale brown with waterproof marking pen
THORAX, LEGS: Well-marked guard hairs with underfur from the back of a brown rabbit
HEAD: Brown tying thread

GRAY CADDIS PUPA

HOOK: Partridge sedge hook K2B, sizes 10 to 16
THREAD: Brown, prewaxed 6/0
BODY: Creamish-white Seal-Ex dubbing (#115) overwound with silver wire inside clear Larva Lace
THORAX, LEGS: Well-marked guard hairs with underfur from the back of a brown rabbit
HEAD: Brown tying thread

GREEN CADDIS PUPA

HOOK: Partridge sedge hook K2B, sizes 8 to 16
THREAD: Brown, prewaxed 6/0
BODY: Grass-green Seal-Ex dubbing (#112) overwound with silver wire inside clear Larva Lace tinted pale green with waterproof marking pen
THORAX, LEGS: Well-marked guard hairs with underfur from the back of a brown rabbit
HEAD: Brown tying thread

OLIVE CADDIS PUPA

HOOK: Partridge sedge hook K2B, sizes 10 to 14
THREAD: Brown, prewaxed 6/0
BODY: Pale olive Seal-Ex dubbing (#108) overwound with silver wire inside clear Larva Lace tinted pale olive with waterproof marking pen
THORAX, LEGS: Well-marked guard hairs with underfur from the back of a brown rabbit
HEAD: Brown tying thread

REDDISH-BROWN PUPA (LARGE)

HOOK: Partridge sedge hook K2B, sizes 4 to 6
THREAD: Brown, prewaxed 6/0
BODY: Isonychia Seal-Ex dubbing (#101) overwound with silver wire inside clear Larva Lace tinted brown with waterproof marking pen
THORAX, LEGS: Well-marked guard hairs with underfur from the back of a brown rabbit
HEAD: Brown tying thread

YELLOW CADDIS PUPA

HOOK: Partridge sedge hook K2B, sizes 10 to 14
THREAD: Brown, prewaxed 6/0
BODY: Yellowish-cream Seal-Ex dubbing (#117) overwound with silver wire inside clear Larva Lace tinted yellow with waterproof marking pen
THORAX, LEGS: Well-marked guard hairs with underfur from the back of a brown rabbit
HEAD: Brown tying thread

Caddis Dry Fly Patterns

Caddis hair-wing patterns in the following color combinations can be dressed with either regular or parachute-style hackle. The list is by no means inclusive, and there are many other colors and sizes you may find better suited for fishing in your area. I suggest that you collect some live specimens to determine your special needs.

BODY	WING	HACKLE	HOOK SIZES
Dark gray	Tannish-gray	Light blue dun	10 to 16
Dark olive	Medium brown	Medium brown	10 to 16
Light green	Tan	Light ginger	10 to 16
Brown	Brown	Brown	12 to 18
Dark green	Brown	Ginger	12 to 18
Light olive	Tan	Ginger	12 to 18
Dirty cream	Dark gray	Light blue dun	10 to 16
Pale olive	Cream	Cream	14 to 22

BROWN ELK HAIR CADDIS

HOOK: Mustad #94840, sizes 8 to 20
THREAD: Tan, prewaxed 6/0
BODY: Olive hare's ear dubbing
WINGS: Fine-textured elk body hair, dyed brown
HACKLE: Brown, palmered
HEAD: Tan tying thread
NOTE: This artificial can also be dressed with a wing of natural dun-gray deer body hair instead of brown elk.

ORANGE ELK HAIR CADDIS

HOOK: Mustad #94840, sizes 10 to 16, or Mustad #9671 2X long, sizes 4 to 8
THREAD: Orange, prewaxed 6/0 for small flies, 3/0 Monocord for large flies
BODY: Orange fur dubbing or wool
WINGS: Brown elk hair or natural brown bucktail
HACKLE: Furnace neck or saddle hackle, palmered
HEAD: Orange tying thread
NOTE: This fly can also be dressed with a yellow body.

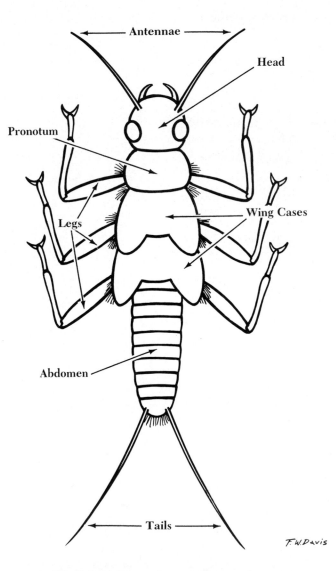

Fig. 9.1 Anatomy of a stonefly nymph.

Chapter 9
Stoneflies

Both stonefly nymphs and adults are among the most effective artificials I have ever used on a trout stream. Like caddisflies, they can be fished throughout the season anywhere in the country.

I do not mean to imply that particular species do not have a certain time of hatching, but their long growth periods (as long as three years for some) makes at least the nymph ever present. They are found crawling among rocks in the stream beds of swift rivers where oxygen sufficient for their existence is generated.

When the nymphs are ready to hatch, they migrate to shallow areas and crawl up on rocks or debris where their skin splits open and the adult insect emerges. If you are walking along the rocky banks of a stream early in the morning and notice the empty skins on stones, it is an indication that a hatch is in progress or has just taken place. At such times you can pick an artificial that closely matches the empty skins in size and color. The color of the living nymph will be much darker than the empty skin, and it's a good idea to try to collect a nymph before deciding on the color of the artificial you will use.

Step 1 Securing the weight.

The Stonefly Nymph

Stonefly nymphs are generally flat throughout their bodies and have long, segmented abdomens with two tails at the posterior end. They are easily distinguished from other nymphs because of their two beautifully marked wing cases. The mayfly has only one. In addition, there is a third segment in front of the wing cases called the pronotum, which will help in identification but which you can ignore if the fly is dressed just for fishing. The nymph has two antennae in front that are 1/5 to 1/2 as long as the nymph's body.

The first and foremost consideration before starting to dress the nymph is to evaluate its dimensions, and this is perhaps more important for stoneflies than for any other insects because of their unique structure. The drawing of the stonefly nymph included here will help you determine correct proportions as you tie (**Fig. 9.1**). Study the drawing before you begin to tie the nymph.

Aside from having two distinct wing cases, there is one more important factor that makes stoneflies different from other nymphs. They have a smooth outer shell without hairy filaments, as opposed to the mayfly with its breathing gills along each side of the abdomen. My methods of tying the stonefly nymph may differ from others you have seen, but if you follow the instructions carefully, you will be able to tie a very nice, simple, and effective artificial.

Tying the Large Black Stonefly Nymph

I have chosen this large nymph for the tying instructions to give you the best possible visual details. The entomological name for this large nymph is *Pteronarcys dorsata*, and the species is found in both eastern and western rivers. It is one of the largest and most impressive stoneflies in the country.

According to anglers who have followed *P. dorsata* activities, the hatching period starts in May and lasts well into the summer months. The nymph is best fished in the early morning hours when they migrate to the shallow areas of the river to hatch. This pattern can also be used as a representative pattern for other black stoneflies when dressed in smaller sizes.

HOOK:	Partridge CS10, Bartleet salmon hook or Mustad #38941 3X long, sizes 2 to 6
THREAD:	Black, prewaxed 6/0
UNDERBODY:	Lead wire (.025″), secured on either side of the shank
TAIL:	Brownish-black goose biots, 1/3 body length
BODY:	Brownish-black Seal-Ex dubbing (#102)
RIBBING:	Dark brown or black Larva Lace or 1/32″ Swannundaze
WING CASES:	Two folds of black Swiss straw, a little wider than front of body
LEGS:	Guard hairs with underfur from the back of a rabbit, dyed black
ANTENNAE:	Brownish-black goose biots, 1/5 body length (optional)
HEAD:	Black tying thread and small remainder of front wing case.

Step 1: Place a size 4 hook in the vise (a Bartleet hook is used in the photos) and cover the entire shank with tying

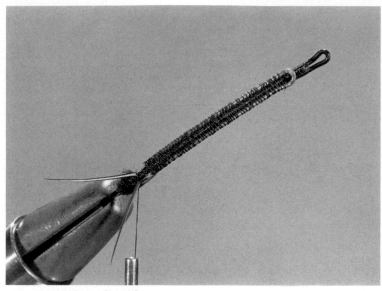

Step 2 Attaching the tail.

Step 3 Preparing the dubbing and ribbing.

thread from the eye to a point above the hook barb. Double a short length of lead wire to the shape of a hairpin and cut it to a length that will reach from above the hook point to 1/8″ from the eye. Tie it in on the shank with the loop forward toward the eye and the lead running along each side of the hook.

Use a pair of pliers to flatten the loop and adjust the lead to follow the contour of the shank. Now roll a very small amount of Seal-Ex dubbing on the thread and form a small fur ball directly above the hook barb. Before you proceed to the next step, apply some cement on the lead and thread windings.

Step 2: For the tail, tie in the biots splayed as shown. They should be as long as 1/3 the body length. Fasten them directly on each side of the shank between the lead wire and the fur ball. Wind the tying thread up against the fur ball to splay the biots and let the tying thread hang by the weight of the bobbin.

Step 3: Wind the tying thread to the middle and tie in the ribbing under the shank. Wind the thread back to directly in front of the fur ball, binding the ribbing down under the shank in the process. Draw out a 3″ tapered layer of Seal-Ex dubbing and roll a point in the end using a little saliva. Tie in the pointed end under the shank in front of the fur ball with a couple of turns of thread as shown.

Large Black Stonefly Nymph   157

Step 4 Winding the dubbing and ribbing.

Step 5 Attaching the antennae.

Step 6 Attaching the wing case.

Step 4: Spiral the dubbing lightly around the thread in a counterclockwise direction. Hold the dubbing and the tying thread together and wind the body, applying it in a direction over and away from you, making sure to start directly in front of the fur ball to make a smooth transition. Release the dubbing now and then while winding it on the shank, or it will twist too much and give you a segmented body, which is nice, but not for this fly.

Tie off the dubbing 1/3 of the body length from the eye and trim the surplus. Don't make the body too fat. Now wind the ribbing forward in fairly close spirals and tie it off in front of the body. Cut the surplus and let the thread hang at the tie-off spot. Make sure that there is space equal to at least 1/3 of the body length between the front of the body and the hook eye where the wing cases and leg section are to be applied.

Step 5: If you want the fly to have antennae, you should tie them in now as shown. They should sit in an open V shape and be equal to 1/5 the body length.

Step 6: Select a 3″ length of black Swiss straw. This material is always very wrinkled and must be unravelled and refolded so it's a little wider than the front of the body. When that's done, tie it in flat directly in front of the body with the long end projecting toward the rear. Trim the surplus in front and apply a very sparse amount of Seal-Ex dubbing to cover the tie-in windings.

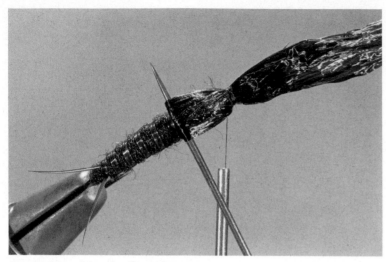

Step 7 Measuring the first wing case.

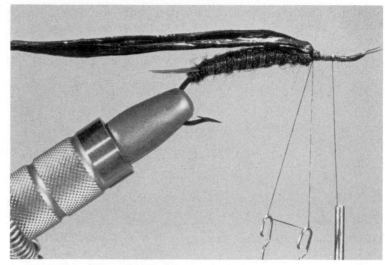

Step 8 Forming the spinning loop.

Step 7: Measuring the correct length of the first wing case is very important. To do so, hold the Swiss straw flat on top of the dubbed body and let it project toward the rear. Place your dubbing needle on top of the wing material, as shown, at a position that is 1/3 of the dubbed body length from the front of the body. Hold it there while doubling the material forward over the needle to form the wing case. Tie it down directly in front of the dubbed body and wind a small thread segment that is about 1/32″ wide, binding the straw down on the shank. This is necessary in order to tie down the other wing case later.

Step 8: Pull the remainder of the wing case material back over the body toward the rear and tie it down in front of the first wing case with a few thread windings. Then form a spinning loop 1 1/2″ long which will be used for the leg section. Forming the leg section is done in the same manner as explained in Steps 6-10 for tying the caddis pupa in Chapter 8.

Step 9: Cut the fur and insert it in the spinning loop. Of course, the color and length of the fur used varies. For the size stonefly nymph we are tying, the fur and guard hairs to

Step 9 Applying the legs.

the left in the loop should reach to about the middle of the body (Step 8 for the caddis pupa). Spin a fur chenille, and while holding it above the hook, moisten the fur and stroke it back (Steps 9 and 10 for the caddis pupa). Then wind the fur section in front of the wing case and tie it off a short distance from the eye. Separate the fur on top and pull it down to each side of the body. Your fly should now look like the one shown.

Large Black Stonefly Nymph   159

Step 10 The finished Large Black Stonefly Nymph.

Step 11 Side view of the finished fly.

Step 10: Place your dubbing needle on the wing case material at a point even with the middle of the first wing case. Fold the material forward over the needle and tie it down in front of the fur leg section. Add some additional thread windings and tie off with a whip finish. Trim the surplus wing case material close to the tie-off windings but leave enough to represent the head. The Large Black Stonefly Nymph is now finished.

Step 11: Side view of the finished nymph.

The Adult Stonefly

Large adult stonefly artificials such as Bird's Stonefly and the Improved Sofa Pillow are among the most important flies for fishing our western rivers. In the East, however, adult stoneflies are smaller and of less importance. In fact, I cannot recall that I have needed more than two, the Little Yellow and the Little Brown Stonefly, both of which I have often successfully imitated by using a hair-wing caddis.

The patterns I have included in this chapter are fairly simple and can be dressed by using the tying instructions given for the adult caddisflies. The most important pattern, at least for me, is Bird's Stonefly, which is a bit more complicated than the rest. However, by closely following the instructions given here, it can be learned by anyone who can dress an ordinary dry fly.

Tying Bird's Stonefly

HOOK:	Mustad #9672 3X long or #9671 2X long, sizes 4 to 10
THREAD:	Orange, prewaxed 6/0
TAIL:	Two stripped hackle stems dyed or tinted brown
BODY:	Orange floss or Seal-Ex dubbing (#120)
RIBBING:	Two furnace saddle hackles, trimmed
WINGS:	Natural brown bucktail or fox squirrel tail
HACKLE:	Three or four furnace saddle hackles
ANTENNAE:	Two stripped hackle stems dyed or tinted brown
HEAD:	Orange tying thread

NOTE: This fly can also be dressed with a yellow body and ginger hackle to represent the large golden stonefly of the West.

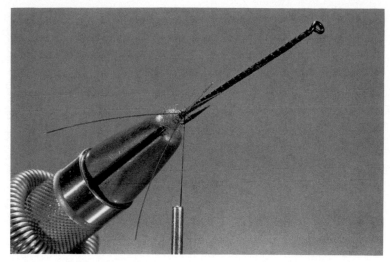

Step 1 Attaching the tail.

Step 2 Attaching the ribbing hackle.

Step 3 Preparing the dubbing.

Step 1: Place a size 6 hook in the vise and attach the tying thread. Wind it to the bend and dub a small fur ball. Then tie in the tail hackle stems in a slightly splayed position. Their length should equal 2/3 of the shank length.

Step 2: Select two long furnace saddle hackles and trim the fibers so they are a hook gap long on each side of the stem. Prepare and tie in the hackles just slightly forward of the fur ball in the same manner as you would a dry fly hackle. Fasten them securely with windings over the stems and let the tying thread hang directly in front of the fur ball.

Step 3: Prepare a thin layer of Seal-Ex dubbing by rolling a point in the end with a little saliva and tie it in on the shank directly in front of the fur ball.

Step 4 Winding the trimming the ribbing hackle.

Step 6 Winding the front hackle.

Step 5 Attaching the wing.

from the eye and trim the surplus. Now spiral the hackles forward over the body with close turns and tie them off in front of the body. Trim away the surplus hackle, and the fly should look like the one shown in the photo. Make sure there is at least 1/3 of the shank length clear in front of the body.

Step 5: Cut a bunch of bucktail and clean out the fuzz and underfur. Even up the tips as much as you can without using a hair stacker and tie it on the shank in front. The tips of the wing should not exceed the length of the tails. Trim the butt ends and wind some thread over the remainder to completely cover the butts before applying some clear cement.

Step 6: Tie in and wind three or four hackles in front, dry fly style, forming a heavy hackling. The hackle fibers should be 1 1/2 hook gaps long. Cut off the surplus hackle and wind a good-sized head in front with tying thread. Tie in the two antennae, as long as the tails, on top of the head. Finish off with a whip finish and cut the thread.

Step 4: Twist the dubbing lightly around the tying thread and wind a thin tapered body on the shank, taking the first turn of dubbing to the left of the hackle stems to blend with the fur ball. Tie off the dubbing 1/3 of the shank length back

Step 7: Trim the hackle fibers short on top and bottom as shown, and the Bird's Stonefly is finished.

Selected Stonefly Patterns

There are many stonefly nymphs which may be effective locally. The ones listed here imitate the most commonly found nymphs across the country. For the stonefly adults, I have selected the most popular dry fly patterns. Size and color should be adjusted to match insects you find in your area.

Stonefly Nymph Patterns

BROWN STONEFLY NYMPH
Perhaps the most important among the various representatives of brown nymphs is the Large Western Salmon Fly Nymph. The dark brown pattern can be fished all season in some western rivers, even though the hatching time, depending to some degree on the area being fished, usually starts at the end of April. The hatch gradually occurs later as you move eastward.

There are, of course, other nymphs in the medium to dark brown range that might be of some importance when dressed in smaller sizes.

HOOK:	Partridge CS10, Bartleet salmon hook, sizes 2 to 6, or Mustad #38941 3X long, sizes 6 to 12
THREAD:	Tan or brown, prewaxed 6/0
UNDERBODY:	Lead wire (.025″to .015″) secured on either side of the shank (optional on smaller flies)
TAIL:	Goose biots dyed medium or dark brown, 1/3 body length
BODY:	Seal-Ex dubbing, medium brown (#111) or dark brown (#110)
RIBBING:	Brown Larva Lace or 1/32″ Swannundaze (button-hole silk or Kevlar thread for smaller flies)
WING CASES:	Two folds of fiery brown Swiss straw a little wider than front of body
LEGS:	Guard hairs with underfur from the back of a rabbit, dyed medium to dark brown
ANTENNAE:	Two medium to dark brown goose biots, 1/5 body length (optional)
HEAD:	Tan or brown tying thread and small remainder of front wing case

Step 7 The finished Bird's Stonefly.

EARLY BLACK STONEFLY NYMPH
This small nymph is very important to both eastern and western anglers who don't mind cold weather and icy line guides. In the East, it can provide good fishing from shortly after New Year's to early spring. The western angler who finds these nymphs in mountain streams will discover they become important somewhat later than in the East.

HOOK:	Mustad #38941 3X long, sizes 12 to 14
THREAD:	Black, prewaxed 6/0
UNDERBODY:	None
TAIL:	Cock pheasant center tail fibers dyed black, 1/3 body length
BODY:	Black Seal-Ex dubbing (#118)
RIBBING:	Brown Kevlar thread
WING CASES:	Two folds of black Swiss straw a little wider than front of body
LEGS:	Hare's ear dubbing dyed black and wound in place of usual fur
ANTENNAE:	Two black hackle fibers, one body length
HEAD:	Black tying thread and small remainder of front wing case

GOLDEN STONEFLY NYMPH

This large, handsome stonefly is found in fast western rivers, where it can grow to a length of over 40mm. Artificials, however, are rarely dressed any larger than size 2 (approximately 35mm). The hatch takes place in June and July, depending on locale, and many anglers consider this fly one of the most important to have for western fishing. In the East there is a fly of equal importance called the Perla Stonefly Creeper. It's identical in color but somewhat smaller and is dressed on sizes 4 to 10 3X long hooks, using the same material as the Golden Stone.

HOOK:	Partridge CS10, Bartleet salmon hook, sizes 2 to 6
THREAD:	Tan, prewaxed 6/0
UNDERBODY:	Lead wire (.025″) secured on either side of the shank
TAIL:	Two goose biots dyed golden-tan, 1/3 body length
BODY:	Golden-amber Seal-Ex dubbing (#114)
RIBBING:	Pale tan Larva Lace or 1/32″ Swannundaze
WING CASES:	Golden-tan or copper-colored Swiss straw a little wider than front of body
LEGS:	Guard hairs with underfur from the back of a rabbit, dyed amber
ANTENNAE:	Two goose biots dyed golden-tan, 1/5 body length (optional)
HEAD:	Tan tying thread and small remainder from the front wing case

YELLOW STONEFLY NYMPH

These insects are found in eastern and western rivers all summer long where they hatch in late afternoon and early evening. Unlike many of the stoneflies, at least in the East, the adult is very important to those who enjoy dry fly fishing.

HOOK:	Mustad #38941 3X long, sizes 10 to 12
THREAD:	Pale yellow, prewaxed 6/0
UNDERBODY:	None
TAIL:	Two fine pale yellow wing quill fibers, 1/2 as long as the body
BODY:	Yellowish-cream Seal-Ex dubbing (#117)
RIBBING:	Tan 3/0 Monocord or fine strand of rayon floss
WING CASES:	Two folds of cream Swiss straw a little wider than front of body
LEGS:	Pale creamy-gray hare's ear dubbing wound in place of usual fur

Fig. 9.2 The Improved Sofa Pillow.

ANTENNAE:	Two pale yellow hackle fibers, 1/2 as long as body
HEAD:	Pale yellow tying thread and small remainder from front wing case

NOTE: The body on this and other small stonefly nymphs can be made with a segmented effect without using ribbing by twisting the dubbing into a tapered "rope" before it's wound on the shank.

Adult Stonefly Patterns

GOLDEN STONEFLY ADULT

HOOK:	Mustad #9672 3X long, sizes 4 to 10
THREAD:	Yellow, prewaxed 6/0
TAIL:	Two stripped hackle stems dyed or tinted brown
BODY:	Yellow floss or Seal-Ex dubbing (#119)
RIBBING:	Two ginger saddle hackles, trimmed
WINGS:	Natural brown bucktail or fox squirrel tail
HACKLE:	Three or four ginger saddle hackles
ANTENNAE:	Two stripped hackle stems dyed or tinted brown
HEAD:	Yellow tying thread

IMPROVED SOFA PILLOW

HOOK: Mustad #9672 3X long or #9671 2X long, sizes 4 to 10
THREAD: Brown, prewaxed 6/0
TAIL: Fine, natural tan elk hair
BODY: Orange wool or Seal-Ex dubbing (#120), fairly thin
RIBBING: Brown hackle, palmered and untrimmed
WINGS: Natural dun elk hair or brown bucktail
HACKLE: Three brown hackles dressed dry fly style, untrimmed
HEAD: Brown tying thread
NOTE: To tie this fly, shown in **Fig. 9.2**, you can use the instructions for tying the caddis hair-wing patterns.

LITTLE BROWN STONEFLY, ADULT

HOOK: Mustad #9671 2X long, sizes 10 to 14
THREAD: Brown, prewaxed 6/0
TAIL: Small bunch of stiff brown hackle fibers
BODY: Medium brown fur dubbing
RIBBING: Dark brown tying thread
WINGS: Well-marked dun-colored deer body hair, tied flat
HACKLE: Grizzly, dry fly style
HEAD: Brown tying thread
NOTE: You can also use dun-colored poly yarn or grizzly hackle tips for the wings.

LITTLE YELLOW STONEFLY, ADULT

HOOK: Mustad #9671 2X long, sizes 12 to 16
THREAD: Yellow, prewaxed 6/0
TAIL: Grizzly hackle fibers dyed pale yellow
REAR HACKLE: Grizzly dyed pale yellow
BODY: Chartreuse fur dubbing
RIBBING: Tan tying thread
FRONT
HACKLE: Grizzly dyed pale yellow
HEAD: Yellow tying thread
NOTE: This is a fore-and-aft pattern. The rear hackle is wound at the bend and the other in front in the usual manner.

Chapter 10
Terrestrials

The small creatures hopping in and out of your picnic basket and generally being a nuisance to your comfort during warm summer days also provide a considerable portion of the fish's diet.

Angling historians will tell you that there is little doubt that serious terrestrial fishing started in Pennsylvania. The limestone streams around Carlisle and Chambersburg wind slowly through pastures and meadows, and the famed Letort Spring Creek and others were the testing grounds for many successes and failures. In the warmth of the summer when most of the significant mayfly hatches are over, an abundance of crickets, hoppers, ants, and beetles appears in the meadows.

Charles K. Fox and the late Vincent Marinaro, two of America's leading authorities on terrestrials and their imitations, have shared their early experiences with fellow anglers, and it is they who are largely responsible for the extended dry-fly season we all enjoy.

Most terrestrials are easy to tie, and the materials used in their dressings are simple and uncomplicated. I suggest that you collect some specimens from the area you intend to fish to determine the correct color and size for your artificials.

Step 1 Dubbing the body.

Step 2 Preparing the underwing feather.

The Letort Hopper

Like most other terrestrials in this chapter, the Letort Hopper was developed in the "cradle" of terrestrial fishing, the Letort Spring Creek. However, it was neither Charley nor Vince who created this fine artificial. Rather, it was Ed Shenk who, in this writer's opinion, is one of America's finest short-rod anglers. If I were to re-name the Letort Hopper today, I would probably call it something like "Shenk's All-Round Hopper." I have fished this fine fly from coast to coast and in some foreign countries and have never found a fish who could refuse it when hoppers were around.

Tying the Letort Hopper

HOOK: Mustad #94831 2X long, sizes 8 to 14
THREAD: Yellow, 3/0 Monocord
BODY: Yellowish-tan fur dubbing
WINGS: Brown-mottled turkey wing quill section, lacquered and set flat, over which is natural deer body hair or dyed light golden-brown elk hair

HEAD: Hair from wing butts trimmed
NOTE: Mottled turkey wing is getting scarce and can be substituted for with a back feather from the cock pheasant, as shown in the tying instructions.

Step 1: Place a size 10 hook in the vise and dub a fur body in the usual dry fly style. (See Tying the American March Brown in the dry fly chapter, Chapter 5.) It should be fairly heavy and extend from the hook bend in the rear to 1/8" from the eye. Taper the front a little so the wing will lie flat.

Step 2: For a size 10 fly, cut a section 5/16" wide from a wing quill that has been sprayed with Krylon or Tuffilm. Trim the end to a right angle and round the corners a little with your scissors as shown to the left in the photo. If you cannot get brown-mottled turkey wings (shown on left), use a feather from a cock ring-necked pheasant (middle). Prepare that feather, as shown to the right, by applying some heavy tying cement and stroking it into shape. Trim the end a little and round the corners.

Step 3 Attaching the underwing.

Step 3: Tie in the feather on top of the hook so it lies flat along the body, reaching to just past the end of it. Trim off the surplus feather in front and let the thread hang at the tie-in position.

Step 4: Cut a small bunch of natural deer body hair that is about 2″ long. Comb out the fuzz and short hair and align the tips in a hair stacker. (See instructions for tying the Humpy in Chapter 5, Steps 2 and 3). Hold the hair on top of the hook with the tips reaching to the hook bend. Hold it with your fingers at the tie-in spot. Cut the hair so only 1/2″ of hair butts extend out in front of your fingers.

Now take two loose turns of thread around the hair and pull it tight so the butt ends flare out but the hair between your fingers stays on top, unflared. Spiral some tight turns of thread through the hair butts to the front without winding down any hair. Tie off the thread in front with a whip finish before cutting it. Your fly should now look like the one in the photo.

Step 5: Trim the fibers flat on the bottom, close to the shank. Then gather the ones on top in a bunch and trim the ends, leaving 1/8″ to form the head as shown. Now trim the sides of the head as shown in Step 6.

Step 4 Attaching the deer hair wing.

Step 5 Trimming the head.

Step 6 The finished Letort Hopper, top view.

Step 6: Top view of the finished hopper.

The Letort Cricket

The cricket (**Fig. 10.1**) is tied in exactly the same manner as the hopper but is completely black and generally much smaller, sizes 14 and 16 being the most popular. Black fur dubbing, black deer or elk body hair, and a section of black crow wing quill makes up the dressing.

While fishing during the summer, I have found that the same hopper-type of fly, dressed on size 16 and 18 hooks in all green, all yellow, and even all white, will take fish when nothing else works— at least in the East. In the West, crickets may be tied on somewhat larger hooks.

Fig. 10.1 The Letort Cricket.

Joe's Hopper

Joe's Hopper is one of the best terrestrial patterns we have, and I recommend that you learn to tie this famous fly. While it was originated in Michigan, its claim to fame stems not from there but from the West where anglers use it in large sizes when grasshoppers are present in the meadows along their rivers.

Tying Joe's Hopper

HOOK:	Mustad #9672 3X long, sizes 4 to 6
THREAD:	Black, prewaxed 6/0
TAIL:	Red hackle fibers
BODY:	Yellow chenille or wool
RIBBING:	Brown saddle hackle, trimmed on sides only
WINGS:	Brown-mottled turkey wing segments
HACKLE:	Brown and grizzly wound together
HEAD:	Black tying thread

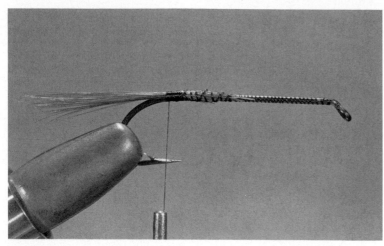

Step 1 Attaching the tail.

Step 2 Forming the chenille loop.

Step 1: Attach the tying thread and tie in a bunch of stiff red hackle fibers. The tail should be 1 1/2 hook gaps long.

Step 2: Wind the thread to the middle of the shank. On top of the hook, tie in a 4″ length of chenille that is 1/8″ in diameter. Hold it toward the rear and wind the thread back to the bend, binding the chenille down on top of the shank in the process. Form a small loop above the tail with the chenille and tie it down at the bend.

Step 3: Prepare a brown saddle hackle with fibers 1 1/2 hook gaps long. Tie it in at the bend. Then grasp the chenille and wind a body to the middle of the shank and tie it off. Trim the surplus material, and your fly should look like the one in the photo.

Step 3 Winding the body.

Step 4 Palmering the body hackle.

Step 5 Attaching the far wing.

Step 6 Attaching the near wing.

Step 4: Wind the hackle forward over the body, palmer style and fairly heavy. Tie it off in front of the body and trim the surplus. After winding it, you should trim the fibers off on the sides so the wings can be tied in close to the body.

Step 5: Cut a quill segment from a left and a right turkey wing feather that have been sprayed with Krylon or Tuffilm. They should be one hook gap wide. Tie in the quill segment on the far side first with the good side out and the tip curving up. The wing should reach back to the tip of the tail with the lower edge of the feather even with the underside of the chenille body.

Step 6: Tie in the near-wing segment and make sure the finished wing sits close to the body as shown. Trim the surplus feather and wind over the ends before applying some cement to the windings.

Step 7 The finished Joe's Hopper.

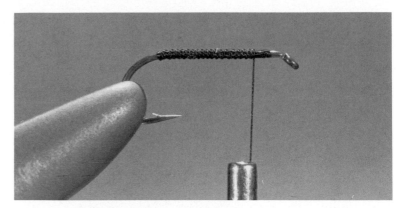

Step 1 Attaching the thread.

Step 7: Tie in and wind one grizzly and one brown hackle, dry fly style. Trim the surplus and wind a small head before applying a whip finish and cutting the thread. Apply some cement on the windings, and the Joe's Hopper is finished.

Beamoc Ants and Beetles

The most serious side-effect of fly tying addiction is an uncontrollable urge to find new materials and tying techniques. In fact, everything is useful until proven otherwise. For that reason it didn't surprise me much when Floyd Frankie, one of my fishing friends, came to my house and showed me some ants and beetles he had made with material extracted from the sole of an old beach shoe. Needless to say, they were very interesting.

I had long been dissatisfied with beetles that got torn up because they were made of deer body hair and ants with fur bodies that floated poorly, if at all.

There are many types of foam you can purchase from your material supplier, but none are well-suited for these flies—they are all too soft. After a long search I found a closed-cell foam that has the texture and quality needed. I simply call

it Beamoc Foam (after my local T.U. chapter, the Beamoc Chapter), and it is available in black and white. (See the materials chapter, Chapter 3, for information on how to order.)

Tying the Beamoc Ant

HOOK: Mustad #94840, sizes 16 to 18
THREAD: Black, prewaxed 6/0
BODY: Two black Beamoc Foam pieces, 1/4″ long and 1/8″ wide, teardrop shape
LEGS: Black, 3/0 Monocord, cut to size
NOTE: The foam can be cut to shape with your scissors from the 1/8″ sheet or stamped out with the tools described in the tying instructions. A red ant can be dressed by using white foam that is tinted reddish-brown after cutting.

Step 1: Place a size 16 hook in the vise and attach the tying thread. Cover the entire shank with thread and let it hang 1/16″ from the eye.

Step 2 Preparing the foam pieces.

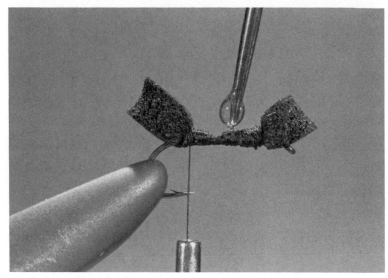

Step 3 Attaching the foam body.

Step 2: Prepare the two foam pieces by trimming to shape with either scissors or cutting tools. The cutting tools illustrated are made from brass tubing purchased in a hobby shop. The smallest is for ants and need not be altered— the teardrop shape you see is the way it comes. The large one is for beetle bodies and is made from a 3/8″ round brass tube flattened into a teardrop shape with pliers. The ends of both tools must be sharpened before use. They work like cookie cutters.

Step 3: Tie in the front body piece first. When tied in, the body lump should be about 1/16″ long and project a little out over the hook eye. Wind the remaining foam completely down on the shank. Then take the thread to the bend and tie in the rear body portion. It should be slightly longer than the front one, about 3/16″. Make sure both pieces are aligned on top of the shank. Now add a little penetrating cement on the tie-in windings, and your fly should look like the one in the photo.

Step 4 Attaching the thread legs.

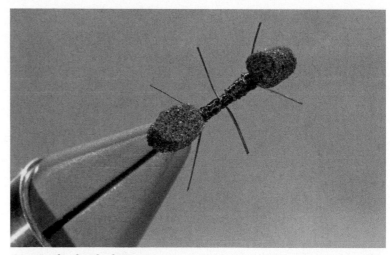

Step 5 The finished Beamoc Ant.

Fig. 10.2 The Beamoc Flying Ant.

Step 4: Prepare three 2″ lengths of 3/0 Monocord and tie them in on the shank with crisscross windings as illustrated. Set the front and rear legs angled as shown and the middle legs at right angles to the body.

Step 5: Apply a whip finish and cut the tying thread before applying some cement to all the thread windings. For a size 16 ant, each leg should now be trimmed so it is 3/16″ long, and the ant is finished.

The Flying Ant

In my experience, trout can be selective when feeding on ants. There are times when flying ants are blown into the water, and the fish will not touch a wingless artificial.

The Beamoc Ant can easily be converted to a flying ant by adding two medium blue dun or grizzly hackle tips, tied on in front of the rear body portion as shown in **Fig. 10.2**. They should be 2/3 of the total body length.

Step 1 Attaching the foam.

Step 3 Finishing the foam body.

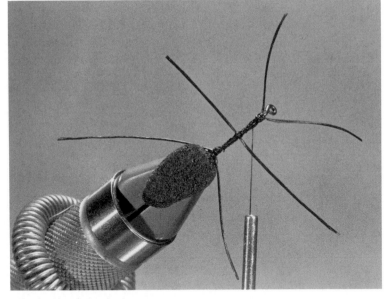

Step 2 Attaching the legs.

Tying the Beamoc Beetle

HOOK: Mustad #94840, sizes 12 to 14
THREAD: Black, prewaxed 6/0
BODY: Beamoc Foam piece, 1/8″ thick, 1/2″ long,

and 1/4″ wide, trimmed or stamped to tear-drop shape
LEGS: Black Kevlar thread

Step 1: Attach your tying thread to a size 14 hook. Cover the shank and wind the thread slightly down the bend. Cut the foam piece. (See Step 2, above, for tying the ant.) Tie it in by the heavy end, making sure it's positioned so it will sit flat when folded forward over the shank later. The foam should now sit as shown in the photo. Apply some penetrating cement on the tie-in windings.

Step 2: Cut three 2″ lengths of Kevlar thread and tie them in on the shank with crisscross windings as illustrated in the photo. Make sure the front legs are sitting close to the eye. The front and rear legs sit at slight angles as shown, and the middle ones sit at right angles. Let the tying thread hang by the bobbin 1/8″ from the eye and apply cement to all thread windings.

Step 3: Fold the foam body forward over the hook with the tip lined up with the eye. Hold it there while tying it down in front with several tight turns of thread. Tie off with a whip finish and cut the thread. Apply some cement on all thread windings and the underside of the body.

Step 4 The finished Beamoc Beetle, top view.

Fig. 10.3 The Mini-Beetle.

Fig. 10.4 The Leafhopper.

Step 4: Trim the six legs so they are 1/8″ long, and your Beamoc Beetle is finished.

The Mini-Beetle

There are times when very small beetles are on the water, and the fish are feeding on them. To imitate those, you can use the foam piece for the ant, but it should be sliced down to a thickness of 1/16″. The legs are then made with 3/0 Monocord, and the flies are dressed on size 18 and 20 hooks, as shown in **Fig. 10.3**. If colors other than black are needed, you can use white foam tinted to the proper color with a waterproof marking pen.

The Leafhopper

The most famous of all the artificials created to imitate the small leafhoppers found along the banks of our meadow streams is the Jassid.

It was originated in 1949 by the late Vincent Marinaro of Mechanicsburg, Pennsylvania. The original was dressed with a small jungle cock nail tied flat over a palmered hackle trimmed top and bottom, leaving the hackle sides to aid in floating and to imitate the legs.

The scarcity of jungle cock has necessitated the use of substitute feathers such as small body plumes from various common birds that are lacquered and trimmed to shape. The metallic-black neck feather from a cock pheasant is excellent for this purpose, and if you wish, it can be painted with a small white dot on top for better visibility.

To tie this tiny fly, I palmer two small black hackles of the appropriate size for 18 and 20 hooks and trim off the fibers on top and bottom, after which a lacquered feather that is long enough to reach the bend is tied in flat over the trimmed hackle.

It's a fairly easy procedure, requiring very little skill, except perhaps an ability to see and work with such small flies. The finished Leafhopper is shown in **Fig. 10.4**.

Chapter 11
Streamers and Bucktails

Streamers and bucktails should not really be called "flies" since they are imitations of the many different baitfish found in both freshwater and saltwater.

The main difference between streamers and bucktails is in the material used in the wing dressing. Streamers are generally dressed with hackle wings, while bucktails are dressed with hair from white deer tail that may be dyed or with any of the many synthetic hairs. Some patterns use a combination of the two materials, in which case they are most often called streamers.

In my travels around the country fishing and holding fly-tying clinics, I have had the opportunity to ask some anglers what they considered to be their favorite streamers. It was not really surprising that most favor the Wooly Bugger, Matuka, Muddler Minnow, and Matuka Sculpin, closely followed by the Black-Nosed Dace, the Black Ghost, and the Gray Ghost. However, I suggest that you try to get some information about favorite patterns for the particular area you will be fishing or buy the patterns when you get there and spend the first evening in camp at the vise.

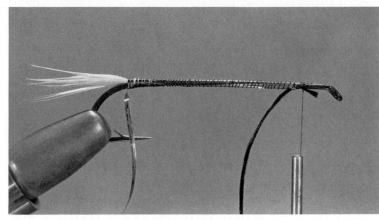

Step 1 Attaching the tail, ribbing, and floss.

Step 2 Attaching the throat.

Before you start, I suggest that you study the beginner's tying chapter and the chapter dealing with wet flies. Many of the tying techniques are explained in these chapters and therefore will not be repeated in this chapter.

The Black Ghost

I have chosen this famous streamer as a model for the tying instructions not only because it's an effective fly, but because it also gives me the opportunity to teach two important techniques, tying bucktail wings and tying hackle wings. The Black Ghost can be tied with either. Sometimes a combination of both is used, bucktail in the middle and feathers on the sides, and this is the one I like best. It seems to have a little more "fill" in the wing which gives it a better swimming motion.

Tying the Black Ghost Bucktail

HOOK: Mustad #9575, 6X long or Partridge CS17, 6X long, sizes 2 to 10
THREAD: Black, prewaxed 3/0 Monocord
TAIL: Yellow hackle fibers
WINGS: Four white neck or saddle hackles or white bucktail (or combination of both)

BODY: Black floss, ribbed with medium-wide, flat silver tinsel
THROAT: Yellow hackle fibers
CHEEKS: Jungle cock or substitute
HEAD: Black tying thread lacquered with clear head cement

Step 1: Attach the tying thread and wind it to the bend of the hook. Tie in the tail and a 6″ piece of flat silver tinsel. The tail should be about 1 1/2 hook gaps long. Wind the tying thread forward to 3/16″ from the eye, binding the material ends down on the shank in the process. Tie in a length of black floss that is long enough to be wound to the bend and back again to the tie-in spot. Your fly should now look like the one in the photo.

Step 2: Wind the floss on the shank evenly, over and away from you with each turn laying side by side. When you reach the bend, wind the floss back over the first layer to the front and tie it off. Grasp the tinsel and spiral it over the body to the front and tie it off. Trim away the surplus materials and tie in a bunch of yellow hackle fibers under the shank right at the spot where the other materials were tied off. The throat hackle should be about 1 1/2 hook gaps long. Be sure to leave room in the front for the wing and head by maintaining a 3/16″ space behind the eye.

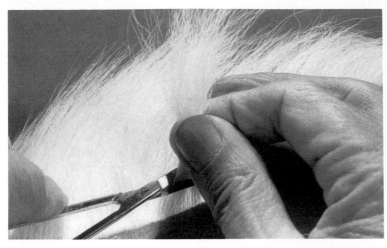
Step 3 Preparing the wing.

Step 4 Attaching the wing.

Step 3: Gather a bunch of bucktail with your fingers and hold it out at a right angle from the skin before cutting it. In this way the tips will be a little more even. Clean out the fuzz and short fibers at the butt ends and pull out any long unwanted hair. You can pull out some of the longer fibers and place them back in the bunch alongside the others with the tips even to get all the fibers lined up as much as possible. Do NOT use a hair stacker— that would make the wing look like a paint brush.

Step 4: Hold the hair on top of the hook with the tip ends reaching to the tip of the tail. Fasten it on the shank with five or six tight turns of thread. Then cut the butt ends on a long slant as shown.

Step 5: Select two jungle cock feathers or a substitute. Pull off the down and unwanted fibers from the stem and tie the feathers in, one on each side of the wing. They are attached by applying the thread over the fibers closest to the end of the feather, not directly on the stem (which would make it difficult to get them to lie correctly). Make them long enough to reach down the wing to above the tips of the beard (throat). Apply some penetrating cement on the bucktail butts before

Step 5 The finished Black Ghost.

winding a nice tapered head as shown. Tie off with a whip finish and apply several coats of Price's head cement for a fine, shiny finish. This finishes the bucktail wing and the fly.

Step 1 Preparing for the feather wing.

Tying the Black Ghost Streamer

Step 1: Tie in the body and bucktail exactly as explained in Steps 1 through 4 for the bucktail version above, except you should use a very small bunch of bucktail which serves only as an underwing. Check the photo carefully to determine the size of the hair bunch.

Step 2: Select four white saddle or neck hackles that are rather wide and webby in the butt ends. It's best to pick them from the left and right side of a whole saddle or neck to get the uniform texture and curvature you need. The feathers from the right side of the skin are for the right wing (near wing for a right-handed tier) and the ones from the left side are for the left (or far) wing.

Step 2 Selecting the wing feathers.

To prepare the feathers, place the two left feathers on top of each other. Measure the feathers so they are a 1/4″ longer than the distance between the tie-in spot (3/16″ from the eye) and the tip of the tail. While still holding the feathers on top of each other with the tips aligned, cut them to length. The fibers on the 1/4″ surplus are now pulled in reverse and set in heavy cement so the fibers are compressed against the stem, forming a flat surface.

Prepare the other two feathers in the same manner, and the wings, as shown in the lower part of the photo, are now ready to be tied in. By forming the flat surface of cemented fibers at the base of each wing, you can easily prevent them from turning and rolling when you tie them in.

Step 3 Attaching the wings.

Step 4 The finished Black ghost, feather-wing style.

Step 3: Tie in a wing on each side of the bucktail, followed by the jungle cock feathers. The wings can be tied in one at a time. The best way is to hold both sets of wings in place with your fingers and fasten them together with five or six tight turns of thread. Then tie in the jungle cock feathers one at a time.

Step 4: Trim the surplus feather stems; then wind and lacquer the head as explained before. This finishes the Feather-Wing Black Ghost.

The Wooly Bugger

The Wooly Bugger is a spin off of the famous Wooly Worm, a fly that has worked so well for so many years that an innovative fly tier decided that it was time for a change.

Undoubtedly he had some marabou leftovers on his tying bench, tied them on a hook at the bend and added a Wooly Worm body. What he probably didn't know at the time was that he had just created one of the most effective attractor streamers of recent years. It works well for all types of freshwater fishing and can be tied in many color combinations and sizes. It's important to add lead weight on the shank near the eye. This helps create the swimming motion applied with the rod tip as the Wooly Bugger is fished. In that way, its long marabou tail will "come to life" and attract the fish.

Tying the Wooly Bugger

HOOK:	Mustad #38941, 3X long, sizes 2 to 10
THREAD:	Color of the fly, prewaxed 3/0 Monocord
TAIL:	Blood marabou dyed brown, black, or olive
BODY:	Chenille— brown, black, or olive
HACKLE:	Saddle or neck hackle, natural brown, black, or dyed olive, palmered over the body
HEAD:	Tying thread, color of the fly

NOTE: Try combinations of the colors mentioned in the materials list. For example, black tail and brown body with black hackle. Instead of chenille, I sometimes use Seal-Ex in various colors with good results.

Step 1 Attaching the tail, chenille, lead, and hackle.

Step 2 The finished Wooly Bugger.

Step 1: Cover the shank with tying thread. Take 6″ of lead wire and double one end back to the length shown in the photo. Tie in the lead loop under the shank. Then wind the remaining lead back over the front 1/3 of the shank as shown. (See Step 1 of the instructions for tying the Matuka Sculpin later in this chapter for a close-up photo of the lead loop method.)

Apply some cement on the windings and lead. Then tie in a bunch of marabou at the bend. Select the desired color of chenille or dubbing. If you have decided to use chenille, it should be 1/3 hook gap in diameter. Prepare it by peeling off the fuzz on one end, exposing 1/4″ of the core. Tie it in under the shank at the same spot as the marabou; then wind the thread 1/8″ forward toward the front and tie in the hackle

on top by the tip. This leaves a little space to the rear of the hackle for one turn of chenille.

Step 2: Wind the chenille on the shank to 1/8″ from the eye and tie it off. Cut the surplus. Then grasp the hackle and double the fibers back as you spiral it over the body palmer style. (See doubling of hackle in the wet fly chapter, Chapter 6, in the section on tying the soft-hackle wet fly.) Take a couple of extra turns of hackle in front, forming a hackle collar. Tie off the hackle, cut the surplus, and wind a small head. Make a whip finish before cutting the thread and applying some cement on the head. This finishes the Wooly Bugger.

The Muddler Minnow

The Muddler Minnow is unquestionably the most famous of all streamer-type flies. It was developed by Don Gapen of Anoka, Minnesota. For many years it's been the model for many other similar flies, such as the Marabou Muddler, the Sculpin, and several of the better-known hopper patterns.

If you were purchasing your flies before you ventured into fly tying, it will probably interest you to note that the Muddler Minnow pattern you are about to tie is a little different than those available commercially. It will be tied in the true Gapen style, in which the head and deer hair collar are made with a single application of hair. In trimming the head, the collar is trimmed a little as well to give it a more Gapen-style appearance. In that way it will sink rather quickly instead of floating like a cork due to a heavily packed head.

This style of Muddler may not suit everyone, but I suggest you follow the instructions and try it. Who knows, you may like it.

Before you start, however, I recommend that you study the wet fly chapter as well as the beginner's tying practice, where you will find the tying technique for setting quill wings with my "slack loop" method, in addition to other important techniques.

Tying the Muddler Minnow

HOOK:	Mustad #38941, 3X long, sizes 1/0 to 12
THREAD:	Black, prewaxed 3/0 Monocord
TAIL:	Two sections of brown-mottled turkey wing
WINGS:	Small bunch of white-tipped squirrel tail, with brown-mottled turkey wing section on each side
BODY:	Flat gold tinsel
HEAD AND COLLAR:	Natural deer body hair, flared and trimmed to shape

NOTE: You can use 6/0 thread for the tail, body, and wing, and change to 3/0 Monocord for the head.

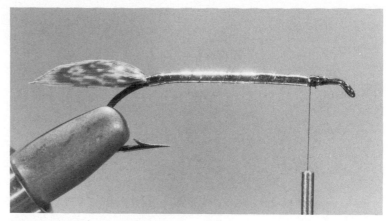

Step 1 Attaching the tail and body tinsel.

Step 1: Place a size 2 hook in the vise and cover the shank with tying thread. To prepare the tail feathers, cut two 1/8" wide strips of brown mottled turkey wing quill, one from a right and one from a left wing feather. (See Step 3 for illustration.) Hold them together on edge at the hook bend with the good sides out and tie them in on top of the shank with a few turns of thread. The tail should be about 1 1/2 hook gaps long and have the curvature shown in the photo. This is achieved by using the strip from the right wing feather for the near side, and the left strip for the far side.

Now fasten the feathers securely. Wind the tying thread forward over the butt ends to a position 3/16" from the eye, binding them down on the shank to serve as an underbody. Tie in a piece of medium-wide flat gold tinsel 8" long and wind it with side-by-side turns back to the tail without overlapping. Then wind back over the first layer to the front where it was tied in. Tie off the tinsel and cut the surplus. Your fly should now look like the one in the photo.

Step 2 Attaching the squirrel tail wing.

Step 4 Attaching the turkey wing feathers.

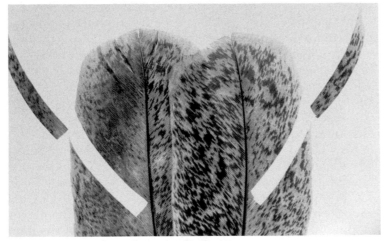

Step 3 Selecting the turkey wing feathers.

Step 2: Cut a small bunch of squirrel tail and pull out the short fibers and fuzz from the butt ends. Measure the hair so it extends from the tip of the tail to 1/8″ beyond the tie-in spot (3/16″ from the eye). Cut the butt ends straight across. Apply a little cement on the ends and tie in the hair bunch securely. Let the thread hang 3/16″ from the eye, where the wings are to be tied in.

Step 3: Select a left and a right brown-mottled turkey wing feather and trim out a segment from each. The segments should be about 2/3 as wide as the hook gap. Make sure they are long enough to reach from the tie-in spot to the middle of the tail.

Step 4: Tie in a quill section on each side of the squirrel tail underwing. To get the same curvature as the tail, use the strip from the right feather for the near side and the other for the far side. Use the tying method explained in the Chapter 6 in the section on setting the wing on the Gold-Ribbed Hare's Ear. Trim the surplus ends and let the tying thread hang 3/16″ from the eye. If you used 6/0 tying thread up till now, you should tie it off and tie in the heavier 3/0 Monocord for making the head.

Step 5 Preparing the deer hair collar.

Step 6 Attaching the deer hair collar.

Step 5: Cut a heavy bunch (about the diameter of a pencil) of natural deer body hair from the skin. Comb out the under-fur and short hair before aligning the tips as explained in Chapter 5 in the section on tying the Humpy. Cut the hair bunch straight across the butt ends so the bunch is 1/2″ longer than the distance between the hook point and the tie-in spot, 3/16″ from the eye. Hold it with your fingers as shown. The hair tips should be even with the hook point, and the eye should be about in the middle of the hair.

Step 6: While holding the hair as shown in Step 5, grasp it with the fingers of your other hand and hold it there, with your finger tips directly at the tie-in spot. The hair butts extending out in front of your fingers should be no more than 1/2″ long. Now take two loose turns of thread around the hair directly in front of your fingers. The fly should now look like the one in the photo.

Step 7 Flaring the deer hair collar.

Step 7: Pull the two thread loops tight so the hair butts flair out. Now spiral the thread through the hair to the hook eye, pulling each turn tight without winding any of the fibers down. Let the tying thread hang directly at the hook eye.

Step 8 Winding the head.

Step 10 Trimming the head.

Step 9 Preparing to trim the collar.

Step 8: Hold all the flaired hair back with your fingers while winding a small head. If there is not enough room in front for the head, just push back the hair on the shank a little.

Step 9: Tie off the thread with a whip finish and cut it. After tying in the hair, the rest of the fly might be somewhat askew. Straighten up the wing and release any trapped hair in the hair collar. Massage the butt ends of the deer hair back so they all slant toward the rear of the fly. When you are ready to trim the head, the fly should look like the one in the photo.

Step 10: Trimming the head may cause a problem at first, but after tying a few Muddlers you will soon get the hang of it. Trim the bottom flat and very close to the shank. Then shape the top and sides with the scissor blades wide open, trimming from behind while holding the fly with your fingers at the bend. Both the flared-out hair butts and the hair tips are trimmed to blend with the wing. This is a variation from the Muddler you normally see, but I can assure you that it not only looks better, it also sinks and fishes better. The finished fly should look like the one in the photo.

Step 11 The finished Muddler Minnow, top view.

Step 1 Attaching the lead, ribbing, and dubbing.

Step 11: Top view of the finished Muddler Minnow.

The Matuka

The first time I saw a Matuka was some thirty years ago in Bill Blades' tying room. Being rather secretive about his flies, he reluctantly explained that it was a New Zealand fly that was sent to him by a friend in England. "I am going to tie some," he said. "They might work for bass."

At the time we first discussed the fly, I must confess that it didn't impress me at all. Since then, after many years in obscurity, it has become one of the most popular streamers around.

Tying methods for the Matuka have eliminated the common problem of having the streamer feathers get trapped under the shank by the hook bend when being fished. Perhaps best of all, we now have a use for all the large hackles that were somewhat useless before. The Matuka can be tied in any size and color using almost any kind of hackle or body feathers. The ones I like the best are tied with grizzly hackles dyed olive, black, or brown with a body color to match. The Matuka should be fished close to the bottom for best results, and I apply the lead weight in the same way as for the Wooly Bugger explained earlier in this chapter.

Tying the Matuka

HOOK:	Mustad #38941, 3X long, or Partridge low-water salmon hook, Code N, sizes 2/0 to 8
THREAD:	Color of the fly, prewaxed 3/0 Monocord
BODY:	Seal-Ex dubbing, olive (#106), brown (#110), or black (#118)
RIBBING:	Medium oval gold tinsel
WINGS:	Four grizzly neck hackles dyed olive, brown, or black
HACKLE:	Two webby neck hackles, color of wings
HEAD:	Tying thread, color of the fly

Step 1: Place a size 1 low-water salmon hook in the vise and cover the shank with tying thread. Tie in the lead weight in the same manner as explained in the instructions for tying the Wooly Bugger. Tie in the ribbing tinsel under the shank at a point above the hook barb. Now prepare the Seal-Ex by drawing out a tapered layer of dubbing and rolling a point in the end. For this size 1 fly, the dubbing should be about 3" long. Tie in the dubbing by the point at the same spot as the tinsel and spiral it lightly around the tying thread in a clockwise direction.

Step 2 Winding the dubbing.

Step 3 Attaching the wing.

Step 2: Hold the dubbing and the tying thread together and wind the body, applying the dubbing in a direction over and away from you. Release the dubbing now and then or it will twist too much and give the fly a segmented body. Try to get a smooth taper; if it's too thin, use a heavier layer of dubbing next time. Tie off the dubbing in front, about 3/16″ from the eye for a size 1 fly.

Step 3: Select four large, rather webby neck hackles, two from the right side of the neck and two from the left. This will give a nice curvature when the hackles are tied in with the good side out. Place the feathers from their respective sides on top of each other; then place all four of them together with the dull sides toward the middle. While holding them

in that manner with the tips lined up, cut the hackle across the stems so the feathers are exactly twice as long as the distance between the hook eye and the end of the body. The hackle fibers in the butt end should be 1 1/2 hook gaps long. Now pull some fibers off the butt ends, exposing 1/4″ of the hackle stems.

Trim away the surplus dubbing in front of the body. Tie in the hackles in front of the dubbing and on top of the shank with several tight turns of thread, holding them on edge with the stems laying close side-by-side. Now hold the hackles together lengthwise on top of the body and separate the hackle fibers right at the tip of the body using a little moisture to keep them apart from the tail portion of the feathers.

Grasp the ribbing tinsel and take a couple of turns over the hackle stems, binding them down on the bare shank. Pull the turns tight and spiral the tinsel through the hackle fibers to the front, binding down the hackle stems on top of the body with each turn. It's important to separate and pull the hackle fibers toward the front before each turn of tinsel to avoid winding them down. Tie off the tinsel in front and use a dubbing needle to release any fibers that might have been trapped under the ribbing. The fly should now look like the one in the photo.

Step 4 The finished Matuka.

Step 4: Cut the surplus stems and tinsel. To make the hackle collar in front I ask you to study the tying method in the wet fly chapter, Steps 5-9 for tying the soft-hackle. The only difference is the type of hackle used. For the Matuka, select two large soft neck hackles with fibers that are two hook gaps long. Tie them both in by the tip at the same time and wind them together, doubling the hackle fibers before each turn. Take three or four turns for a full collar and tie them off. Cut the surplus and wind a small head in front before applying a whip finish and cutting the thread. Brush a good coat of clear cement on the head, and the Matuka is finished.

The Matuka Sculpin

Sculpins are the small, bottom-dwelling baitfish that dart and "crawl" around among the rocks in streams with the aid of their large pectoral fins. When you see them in the water, they appear in a mottled camouflaged coloration that varies in shade depending on the water quality and environment.

The artificial sculpin developed by Dave Whitlock is not an easy fly to tie. Before you attempt to tackle the highly complex tying techniques involved in dressing a sculpin, you must have mastered all the basics outlined in the beginner's tying practice chapter, and you should have done some simpler work with the spinning of deer hair.

I suggest that you study all the photos and read the instructions carefully several times before you start, so you get a clear picture of the tying procedures. If you have tied a sculpin before, perhaps the instructions and text will be helpful to you and in some way help improve your tying.

The materials list given here is for the Brown Matuka Sculpin. Other color variations are, of course, possible.

Tying the Brown Matuka Sculpin

HOOK:	Partridge low-water salmon hook, Code N, sizes 4/0 to 1
THREAD:	Yellow, prewaxed 6/0 for body, yellow or brown Kevlar
WEIGHT:	Lead wire, .030" diameter
RIBBING:	Medium-weight oval gold tinsel
BODY:	Light golden-brown Seal-Ex dubbing (#103)
WINGS AND TAIL:	Four medium brown furnace hackles tied Matuka style
PECTORAL FINS:	Two wide black feathers from a cock pheasant or prairie chicken
GILLS:	Bright red Seal-Ex dubbing (#122) or dyed natural fur dubbing
HEAD:	Light golden-brown, dark brown, and black elk or deer body hair

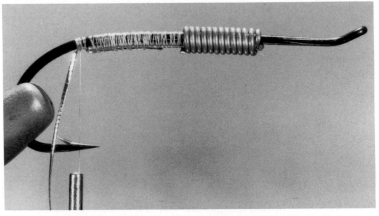

Step 1 Attaching the lead loop.

Step 3 Preparing the pectoral fin feathers.

Step 2 Tying in the body and hackle.

Step 1: Place a hook in the vise and measure the shank length from above the hook point to the eye. Attach the tying thread 1/3 of the shank length back from the hook eye and cover the rear 2/3 with tying thread. Take a 6″ piece of lead wire and double the end back as explained in Step 1 for tying the Wooly Bugger. The doubled over, shorter end should be as long as 2/3 of the body length. Tie in the lead wire under the shank; then wind the long end back to the middle of the rear body portion with close turns. It's important that the

first turn of lead is 1/3 of the shank length from the eye. Apply some cement on the lead and thread windings. Then tie in a 6″ length of ribbing tinsel on the shank at the end of the rear body portion.

Step 2: Tie in the body and hackle as explained in Steps 1-3 for tying the Matuka. The only difference is the front of the body, which should be tied off so there is 1/8″ of lead wire (about four turns of a .030″ wire diameter) exposed in front. This is done so the pectoral fins and gills can be attached there, leaving the front 1/3 of the shank bare. Now cut the surplus dubbing, ribbing, and hackle stems. Apply a generous amount of penetrating cement on the lead, hackle stems, and windings. Let the tying thread hang in front of the dubbed body.

Step 3: While the cement is drying, select two wide back feathers from a cock pheasant. Cut the feathers so they are 1/8″ longer than the distance between the tie-in in front of the body dubbing and a spot just short of the hook point. Reverse the lower 1/8″ of fibers and set them close to the

Step 4 Attaching the fin feathers.

Step 5 Dubbing the gills.

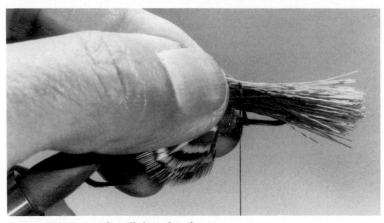

Step 6 Preparing the elk hair head.

stem with tying cement by stroking them into place with your fingers. By using this procedure, you can create a flat spot to fasten the feather with, instead of the bare stem which would make it roll all over the place. The pectoral fins are now ready to be tied in.

Step 4: Cover the lead wraps with additional windings of thread before tying in a fin on each side of the body. The first fibers should be as close to the tie-in spot as possible. The feathers should be slanting down a little with the upper edge almost parallel to the top of the body. Fasten them securely with tying thread and apply some cement on the windings.

Step 5: Trim off the surplus feather stems. To imitate the gills, roll some red dubbing on the tying thread and wind in on the 1/8″ portion in front of the body. Tie off the 6/0 thread and cut it; then attach a well-waxed Kevlar thread at a position that is 1/3 of the head space in front of the gill segment. Make a half hitch and let the thread hang in that position.

Step 6: Cut a bunch of light golden-brown elk hair 1 1/2 times the diameter of a pencil, and at least 1 1/2″ to 2″ long. Comb out the short hair and the underfur before lining up

the tips in a hair stacker. (This procedure is explained in the instructions for the Humpy in the dry fly chapter, Chapter 5.) Hold the hair bunched together on top of the hook with the tips reaching to the end of the pectoral fins. Grasp the bunch with the other hand and take two loose turns around the hair and hook shank as shown.

Step 7 Attaching the rear section of the head.

Step 8 Attaching the second application of elk hair.

Step 7: While holding the hair bunch tight between your fingers, lower the hair to the top of the shank as you gently start to pull the thread tight. As soon as the hair starts to flair, stop pulling. Start a third turn of thread, let go of the hair, and with the torque of the thread as you complete the turn, roll the hair bunch under the shank. Place your thumb on top of the shank and your bent index finger under the hair and pull the tying thread tight to flair it.

Separate the hair a little so the tips point toward the rear, and the butt ends forward. All the hair should now sit under the shank evenly distributed to each side. Let the thread hang at the tie-in position so the top of the head can be applied at the same spot. Apply a little cement on the windings and you are ready for the next step.

Step 8: Cut a bunch of dark brown elk hair a little smaller in diameter than the bunch placed under the shank. After cleaning out the short hair and underfur, even the tips in the hair stacker and hold the bunch on top of the shank with the tips extending to the end of the pectoral fins like the first bunch. Take two loose turns of thread around the hair and hook. Hold the hair bunch firmly on top of the shank while pulling the thread tight and flaring the butt ends. Take an extra turn of thread and pull it tight.

Separate the hair on top and below so the butt ends extend toward the front and the tops toward the rear before pressing them out to each side with your fingers. Apply some penetrating cement at the tie-in spot. Let the tying thread hang at the same position, ready for the next application of hair.

Step 9 Attaching the final application of elk hair.

Step 10 Preparing to attach the front section.

Step 11 Attaching the front section of the head.

Step 9: Cut a very small bunch of black hair, clean it out and tie it in on top of the brown, but with the tips just a little short of those of the first bunch. This method of tying in deer hair is called "stacking." Separate all the hair as before and take two loose turns of thread around all the hair. Then place your thumb on top and your index finger below to hold the hair in position while pulling the thread tight. Apply some more penetrating cement at the tie-in spot.

Step 10: Separate the upper and lower hair colors and push the entire structure back lightly against the lead wraps and gills. Hold the hair back while taking the thread to the front of it. Anchor the thread with two or three half turns and a half hitch. This finishes the first half of the head.

Step 11: The front part of the head is made in the same manner as the part you just completed, but there is an additional color included on top of the head. After applying the bottom hair, start the top of the head with a small bunch of light golden-brown (same color as the bottom). Then add a small bunch of black, over which you tie in a big bunch of dark brown.

Push all the hair lightly back against the first head portion; then take the thread to the front and apply a very small amount of black hair in front of it (on top only) to represent a black nose segment. Tie off the thread with a whip finish and cut it. If the head space is not completely filled out, you should increase the size of the hair bunches next time or make three stacks instead of two. You are now ready to trim the hair.

Matuka Sculpin   195

Step 12 Trimming the bottom of the head.

Step 14 Trimming the top of the head.

Step 13 Trimming the sides of the head.

Step 12: Take the sculpin out of the vise and hold it by the hook bend with your fingers. Trim the bottom first, starting in front with your scissors held flat as shown. It should be trimmed parallel with and as close to the hook shank as possible. Trim out the hair tips in the center of the hair collar to expose the red gills.

Step 13: Next, with your scissors wide open, trim each side of the head with straight cuts. Leave the head a little wider than it should be at this time. You can always trim off a little more later, but you cannot add to it. Notice the amount of hair left as a collar above the body and over the pectoral fins.

Step 14: Finish trimming the top and shaping the sides of the head, as shown in the photo.

Step 15 The finished head, top view.

Step 16 The finished Matuka Sculpin.

Step 15: Top view of the finished head.

Step 16: Side view of the finished sculpin. Apply some penetrating cement to the middle of the underside as well as to the nose and thread windings in front. Your Matuka Sculpin is now finished and ready to be fished.

Additional Sculpins

As I mentioned earlier, the coloration of sculpins may vary depending on the water quality and environment. Consequently, there is no definitive sculpin pattern. For instance, in addition to the brown pattern, I also tie a grizzly and an olive sculpin. They are all tied in the same manner on the same type of hook. Perhaps it's best to collect a sample of the sculpins from the water you are fishing and then design a pattern to match.

The main differences in the additional two sculpins I use are the following:

Grizzly Sculpin

BODY:	Buff Seal-Ex dubbing (#116)
WINGS AND TAIL:	Four natural grizzly neck hackles
PECTORAL FINS:	Two wide, well-marked grizzly hen body feathers, natural or dyed pale olive
HEAD:	Bottom—natural deer body hair; top—dark brown, black, and light golden-brown elk or deer hair

Olive Sculpin

BODY:	Pale olive-gray Seal-Ex dubbing (#105)
WINGS AND TAIL:	Four grizzly neck hackles dyed olive
PECTORAL FINS:	Two wide, well-marked grizzly hen body feathers, dyed olive
HEAD:	Bottom—pale olive elk or deer body hair; top—black, brown, pale olive, and dark olive

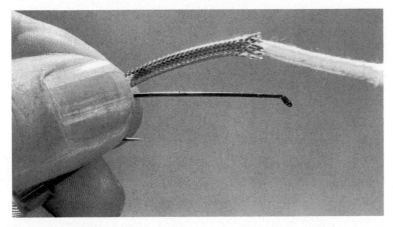

Step 1 Preparing the Mylar tubing.

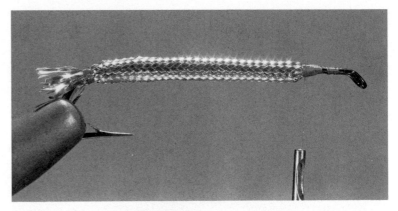

Step 2 Attaching the Mylar tubing.

The Zonker

The Zonker is a fairly new streamer fly. There are many streamers recommended for fishing in Alaska and other places, such as Marabou Muddlers and bucktail streamers, that could use the Zonker's flashy type of braided mylar body to telegraph their presence to the fish, but none of them lend themselves as well to a braided body as the Zonker.

The fur strips used in its unique design are available from your supplier in many different colors and are very easy to attach over the Mylar body.

Tying the Zonker

HOOK: Mustad #9575, 6X long, sizes 2 to 8
THREAD: Red, prewaxed 6/0, or 3/0 Monocord for large flies
BODY: Braided Mylar tubing, silver or gold, 1/8″ to 3/16″ diameter, over an underbody of wool or Seal-Ex dubbing, any color

WINGS: Rabbit fur strip, natural gray or white, or dyed chartreuse, tan, brown, olive, yellow, rust, purple, hot orange, or black

Step 1: For the size 2 hook we are using, cut a piece of silver Mylar tubing that is 3/16″ in diameter. It should be just a little longer than the shank. Remove the cotton center core and trim the ends clean on the tubing.

Step 2: Attach the tying thread and wind an underbody of any color wool or Seal-Ex dubbing. Some patterns I have seen are tied with an underbody made from metal to create a belly-shaped body. I don't use distended bodies because they reduce hooking effectiveness. Wind the underbody so it reaches from above the hook point to a point 1/4″ from the eye. Wind the tying thread back to the bend and slide the Mylar tubing on the shank from the front. Let it come all the way back to the bend by unraveling the braid a little in the end.

Now take several tight turns of thread to fasten the tubing to the shank and make a whip finish. If you have two bobbins with red thread, let one hang at the bend where it is now. If not, cut the thread and attach it in front. Wind over the front of the tubing to fasten it and let the tying thread hang 3/16″ from the eye.

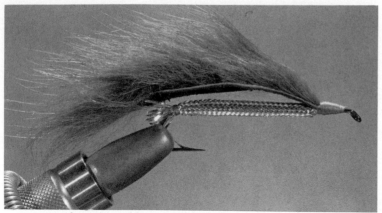

Step 3 Attaching the rabbit strip.

Step 4 The finished Zonker.

Step 3: Cut a strip of rabbit fur so it's 1 1/2 times the length of the body. Determine the "direction" of the hair. On the finished fly, it should be slanting toward the rear. Trim the hair off a 1/8" section of the front of the skin and taper the skin a little by trimming it with your scissors. Hold the skin with your hands and stretch it a little before tying in the trimmed portion in front on top of the shank with several tight turns of tying thread. Apply some cement and wind a nice tapered head before tying off and cutting the thread. This finishes the front of the fly.

Step 4: Attach the tying thread at the rear tie-in spot, apply some cement on top of the braided body and place the skin on top. Hold it tight toward the rear and moisten the hair a little so you can separate it at a place right over the tie-in spot. Now fasten the skin with half a dozen tight turns of thread. Make sure the skin is pulled very tight over the body. Tie off the thread and cut it before applying some cement on the windings. Trim the skin even with the hook bend and taper it a little along each side. Apply some tying cement along the edges of the skin on top of the body and add an extra coat on the head. This finishes your Zonker.

Making a Tandem Hook Arrangement

When it's necessary to use very large flies for lake trout, landlocked salmon, bass, or northern pike, it's often advantageous to increase your hooking potential without the use of very large hooks. With a tandem hook arrangement, almost any streamer or bucktail can be tied in very large sizes without the compromising effect of a large hook. Before you use them, however, you should check the local regulations where you are fishing. Some states and foreign countries allow only the use of single hooks.

A tandem arrangement consists of a main hook in front with a second hook fastened upside-down to a nylon-covered twisted-wire harness. The front hook is usually a size larger than the rear one, but that is a matter of preference. The arrangement I like best for freshwater streamers is a Partridge salmon hook Code M, size 2 in front, with a Mustad #3906, size 4, as a trailer. If I am going to use the flies in saltwater, I use Mustad #37007 stainless steel hooks in those same sizes.

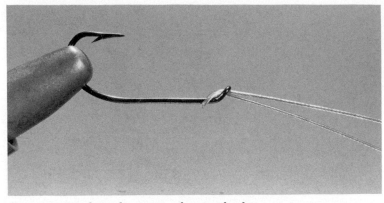

Fig. 11.1 Attaching the wire to the rear hook.

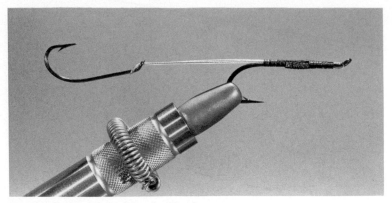

Fig. 11.2 The finished tandem hook.

Start by placing the rear hook in the vise upside-down. Cut a 6″ length of 15-pound test nylon-coated twisted wire and double it in the middle. Now straddle the hook shank from below with the wire and thread both ends through the eye. Pull the wire tight, and the hook in that way is looped to the wire as shown in **Fig. 11.1**. Remove it from the vise and clamp the front hook in the jaws right side up. Hold the two wire strands on top of the shank so there is a distance of 1″ between the bend of the front hook and the eye of the rear one. Now cut one of the wires to 3/8″ short of the eye of the front hook.

Attach the tying thread (3/0 nylon or Monocord) in the middle of the shank and insert the other wire end through the hook eye. Hold the wires on top of the shank with the short end 3/8″ from the eye and fasten them with several tight turns of thread. Cut the long wire so the end projects 1/2″ in front of the eye. Then bend it back under the hook shank. If you are going to fish for northern pike, I suggest that you extend the long wire end to 6″ in front of the eye of the hook and make a loop in the end for attaching your leader.

Wind a generous amount of thread on the entire shank and apply some cement. The finished tandem hook arrangement should look like the one in **Fig. 11.2**. When tying the

fly, let the wing material extend about 1″ beyond the bend of the rear hook so the total length of the finished fly is about 4″.

Selected Streamer Patterns

The additional streamer and bucktail patterns listed here were selected among hundreds of well-known flies. They were chosen for their ability to take fish in most streams and lakes throughout the country, including Alaska, and in some foreign countries where I have had the privilege of casting a fly. They are proven patterns for trout, bass, northern pike, lake trout, and also king and landlocked salmon.

Since hook selection for these flies is a matter of preference, I list only the most effective sizes for each pattern listed. However, I would like you to consider the following hooks which, in any event, are best suited for my personal needs. The detailed characteristics of the following hooks are described in Chapter 2.

The streamer hooks I recommend are: Mustad #9575, 6X long, limerick bend; Mustad #9672, 3X long, round bend; Mustad #79580, 4X long, round bend; Mustad #38941, 3X long, sproat bend; Partridge regular salmon, Code M.

ALASKA MARY ANN
HOOK:	Sizes 2 to 6
THREAD:	Black, prewaxed 6/0 or 3/0 Monocord
TAIL:	Red hackle fibers or floss
BODY:	Pale tan floss or creamish-white Seal-Ex dubbing (#115)
RIBBING:	Flat silver tinsel
WINGS:	White polar bear hair
CHEEKS:	Jungle cock
HEAD:	Black tying thread

BADGER STREAMER
HOOK:	Sizes 1 to 12
THREAD:	Black, prewaxed 6/0 or 3/0 Monocord
TAIL:	Black-barred wood duck flank feather strip
BODY:	Flat embossed silver tinsel
WINGS:	Underwing—small bunch of white bucktail reaching to tip of tail; a cream badger hackle on each side of same length
THROAT:	White bucktail, same length as wing
CHEEKS:	Wide strip of black-barred wood duck flank feather, 1/2 wing length
HEAD:	Black tying thread

NOTE: The fly can also be tied with yellow bucktail and furnace hackle wing, in which case the fly is called a Furnace Streamer.

BLACK GHOST
HOOK:	Sizes 2 to 10, 6X long
THREAD:	Black, prewaxed 3/0 Monocord
TAIL:	Yellow hackle fibers
WINGS:	Four white neck or saddle hackles or white bucktail (or combination of both)
BODY:	Black floss, ribbed with medium-wide, flat silver tinsel
THROAT:	Yellow hackle fibers
CHEEKS:	Jungle cock or substitute
HEAD:	Black tying thread

BLACK-NOSED DACE
HOOK:	Sizes 4 to 12
THREAD:	Black, prewaxed 6/0
TAIL:	Red yarn
BODY:	Flat silver tinsel (or embossed tinsel without the ribbing)

RIBBING:	Oval silver tinsel
WINGS:	White, black, and natural brown bucktail
HEAD:	Black tying thread

NOTE: Great care should be taken in keeping the wing in three distinct color layers and sparsely tied. Start with white; then add black in the middle and natural brown as the top layer.

BROOK TROUT
HOOK:	Sizes 2 to 12, 4X long
THREAD:	Black, prewaxed 6/0
TAIL:	Hackle fibers, green over red, 1 1/2 hook gaps long
BODY:	Yellowish-cream Seal-Ex dubbing (#117) or cream fur
RIBBING:	Flat or oval silver tinsel
THROAT:	Orange hackle fibers
WINGS:	Bottom to top—white, orange, and green bucktail in equal amounts, with whitetipped gray squirrel overwing
CHEEKS:	Jungle cock
HEAD:	Black tying thread

BROWN TROUT
HOOK:	Sizes 2 to 12, 4X long
THREAD:	Black, prewaxed 6/0
TAIL:	Light ginger hackle fibers, 1 1/2 hook gaps long
BODY:	White wool yarn or Seal-Ex dubbing (#115)
RIBBING:	Narrow flat or oval gold tinsel
THROAT:	None
WINGS:	Yellow on bottom with reddish-orange bucktail on top, in equal amounts, with red squirrel tail overwing
CHEEKS:	Jungle cock
HEAD:	Black tying thread

BUCKTAIL STREAMER
HOOK:	Sizes 1/0 to 10, 4 to 6X long
THREAD:	Black, prewaxed 6/0, 3/0 Monocord for larger sizes
TAIL:	None
BODY:	Embossed silver tinsel or braided Mylar tubing
WINGS:	Red over white bucktail

HEAD: Black tying thread

NOTE: *The wing can be made up of many different combinations such as green over white (for coho), plain white, yellow over white, etc.*

BUNNY FLY

HOOK:	Sizes 1/0 to 4, 6X long
THREAD:	Black, 3/0 Monocord
TAIL:	Narrow strip of rabbit fur, color of fly, 1/2″ long
BODY:	Narrow strip of rabbit skin wound forward over entire hook shank like a hackle, any color, natural or dyed
HEAD:	Black tying thread

NOTE: *The fur strips should be about 1/8″ wide. Zonker strips in various colors work well for this fly.*

GOLDEN DARTER

HOOK:	Sizes 1 to 10, 4X long
THREAD:	Black, prewaxed 6/0
TAIL:	Strip of brown mottled turkey wing, 1 1/2 hook gaps long
BODY:	Yellow floss
RIBBING:	Narrow flat or oval gold tinsel
THROAT:	Jungle cock body feather with white stripe tied flat
WINGS:	Four golden badger hackles, reaching to end of tail
CHEEKS:	Jungle cock, short

NOTE: *Jungle cock body feathers may not be available, but you can use teal flank feather as a substitute.*

GRAY GHOST

HOOK:	Sizes 2 to 6, 6X long
THREAD:	Black, prewaxed 6/0
TAG:	Flat silver tinsel
BODY:	Orange floss
RIBBING:	Flat silver tinsel
THROAT:	Four strands of peacock herl with small bunch of white bucktail under, both materials reaching slightly past the bend; under these, a golden pheasant crest feather, curving up and reaching to middle of body
WINGS:	Four olive-gray saddle hackles with a golden pheasant crest in the middle between them, reaching to just past hook bend

SHOULDERS:	Silver pheasant body feathers, 1/3 wing length
CHEEKS:	Jungle cock
HEAD:	Black tying thread with narrow red center band

HORNBERG STREAMER

HOOK:	Sizes 6 to 10, 3X long
THREAD:	Black, prewaxed 6/0
TAIL:	None
BODY:	Silver tinsel
WINGS:	Two yellow hackle tips or sparse bunch of calf tail with a mallard flank feather on each side, both materials reaching one hook gap beyond the bend; mallard feathers rolled to a point with cement
CHEEKS:	Jungle cock, 1/2 wing length
HACKLE:	Two grizzly hackles, wound dry fly style
HEAD:	Black tying thread

MAGOG SMELT

HOOK:	Sizes 1 to 10, 4X long
THREAD:	Black, prewaxed 6/0
TAIL:	Teal flank feather fibers, 1 1/2 hook gaps long
BODY:	Flat or embossed silver tinsel
THROAT:	Red hackle fibers
WINGS:	Bottom to top—white, yellow, and violet bucktail with four to six peacock herls as overwing
CHEEKS:	Teal flank feathers, 1/3 wing length
HEAD:	Black tying thread

MARABOU MUDDLER

HOOK:	Sizes 1/0 to 12, 4X long
THREAD:	Black, 3/0 Monocord or Kevlar
TAIL:	Red hackle fibers, 1 1/2 hook gaps long (optional)
BODY:	Silver Mylar tubing attached at the rear with red tying thread
WINGS:	Black, white, or yellow marabou reaching to tip of tail with two or three strands of peacock herl on each side
COLLAR:	Natural deer body hair
HEAD:	Natural deer body hair spun and trimmed to shape

NOTE: *Many combinations of different color marabou are often used, such as black and white, white and yellow, etc.*

MARABOU STREAMER

HOOK:	Sizes 1/0 to 12, 4X long
THREAD:	Black, prewaxed 6/0
TAIL:	Red wool short
BODY:	Embossed silver tinsel or Mular tubing
THROAT:	Red hackle fibers
WINGS:	Marabou with two or three strands of peacock herl, Crystal Hair, or Flashabou
HEAD:	Black tying thread

NOTE: The Marabou Streamer uses the same colors and color combinations as the Marabou Muddler.

MATUKA

HOOK:	Sizes 2/0 to 8, 3X long
THREAD:	Prewaxed 3/0 Monocord, color of the fly
BODY:	Seal-Ex dubbing, olive (#106), brown (#110), or black (#118)
RIBBING:	Medium oval gold tinsel
WINGS:	Four grizzly neck hackles dyed olive, brown, or black
HACKLE:	Two webby neck hackles, color of the wing
HEAD:	Tying thread, color of the fly

MATUKA SCULPIN, BROWN

HOOK:	Sizes 4/0 to 1
THREAD:	Yellow, prewaxed 6/0 for body, yellow or brown Kevlar for head
WEIGHT:	Lead wire, .030″ diameter
RIBBING:	Medium-wide oval gold tinsel
BODY:	Light golden-brown Seal-Ex dubbing (#103)
WINGS AND TAIL:	Four medium brown furnace hackles, tied Matuka style
PECTORAL FINS:	Two wide black feathers from a cock pheasant or prairie chicken
GILLS:	Bright red Seal-Ex dubbing (#122) or dyed natural fur dubbing
HEAD:	Light golden-brown, dark brown, and black elk or deer body hair

MICKEY FINN

HOOK:	Sizes 1 to 10, 4X long
THREAD:	Black, prewaxed 6/0
TAIL:	None
BODY:	Flat silver tinsel
RIBBING:	Oval silver tinsel
WINGS:	Yellow, red, and yellow bucktail, distinctly separated, with the top yellow layer twice the amount of the lower
HEAD:	Black tying thread

MUDDLER MINNOW

HOOK:	Sizes 1/0 to 12, 3X long
THREAD:	Black Monocord, prewaxed 3/0
TAIL:	Two sections of brown-mottled turkey wing
WINGS:	Small bunch of white-tipped squirrel tail, with brown-mottled turkey wing section on each side
BODY:	Flat gold tinsel
HEAD AND COLLAR:	Natural deer body hair, flared and trimmed to shape

NOTE: You can use 6/0 thread for the tail, body, and wing, and change to 3/0 Monocord for the head.

NINE THREE

HOOK:	Sizes 1 to 10, 4X long
THREAD:	Black, prewaxed 6/0
TAIL:	None
BODY:	Flat silve rtinsel
THROAT:	None
WINGS:	White bucktail with a green and black hackle on each side reaching 1 1/2 hook gaps beyond the bend
HEAD:	Black tying thread

RAINBOW TROUT

HOOK:	Sizes 2 to 12, 4X long
THREAD:	Black, prewaxed 6/0
TAIL:	Green hackle fibers
BODY:	Pinkish-white fur dubbing
RIBBING:	Flat or oval silver tinsel
THROAT:	Pink hackle fibers or bucktail
WINGS:	Bottom to top—white, pink, and green bucktail in equal amounts, with white-tipped gray squirrel tail overwing
CHEEKS:	Jungle cock
HEAD:	Black tying thread

ROYAL COACHMAN STREAMER

HOOK:	Sizes 1 to 10, 4X long
THREAD:	Black, prewaxed 6/0
TAIL	Golden pheasant tippet fibers, 1 1/2 hook gaps long
BODY:	Peacock herl with wide red floss center band
THROAT:	Brown hackle, wound as a collar and tied under as a throat
WINGS:	White bucktail or four white hackles, reaching to end of tail
HEAD:	Black tying thread

SPRUCE FLY STREAMER

HOOK:	Sizes 1 to 10, 3X long
THREAD:	Black, prewaxed 6/0
TAIL:	Three or four peacock sword tips
BODY:	Rear half, red floss; front half, peacock herl
WINGS:	Two to four badger hackles, reaching 1 1/2 hook gaps beyond the hook gap
HACKLE:	Soft badger hackle wound as a collar after wing is attached
HEAD:	Black tying thread

SUPERVISOR

HOOK:	Sizes 1 to 10, 4X long
THREAD:	Black, prewaxed 6/0
TAIL:	Short strand of red wool yard reaching to bend
BODY:	Flat silver tinsel
RIBBING:	Oval silver tinsel
THROAT:	White hackle fibers
WINGS:	White bucktail with two light blue hackles on each side, four to six strands of peacock herl over the top; reaching to 1 1/2 hook gaps beyond the bend
SHOULDER:	Pale green hackle tips, 1/3 wing length
CHEEKS:	Jungle cock
HEAD:	Black tying thread

WARDEN'S WORRY

HOOK:	Sizes 2 to 10 4X long
THREAD:	Black, prewaxed 6/0
TAIL	Thin section of red goose wing feather, 1 1/2 hook gaps long
BODY:	Yellowish-orange wool or Seal-Ex dubbing (#121)
RIBBING:	Oval gold tinsel
WINGS:	Natural brown bucktail reaching to end of tail
HACKLE:	Yellow hackle wound as a collar and tied down as a throat before wing is attached
HEAD:	Black tying thread

WESTERN BLACK GHOST

HOOK:	Sizes 2 to 10, 3 X long
THREAD:	Black, prewaxed 6/0
TAIL:	Yellow hackle fibers, 1 1/2 hook gaps long
BODY:	Black chenille
RIBBING:	Oval silver tinsel
WINGS:	White bucktail (calf tail for smaller flies)
HACKLE:	Black hackle wound as a collar after wing is attached
HEAD:	Black tying thread

WOOLY BUGGER

HOOK:	Sizes 2 to 10, 3X long
THREAD:	Prewaxed 3/0 Monocord, color of the fly
TAIL:	Blood marabou dyed brown, black, or olive
BODY:	Chenille—brown, black, or olive
HACKLE:	Saddle or neck hackle, natural brown, black, or dyed olive, palmered over the body
HEAD:	Tying thread, color of the fly

NOTE: Try combinations of the colors listed above. For example, black tail and brown body with black hackle, etc. Instead of chenille, I sometimes use Seal-Ex in various colors with good results.

ZONKER

HOOK:	Sizes 2 to 8, 6X long
THREAD:	Red, prewaxed 0 or 3/0 Monocord for large flies
BODY:	Braided Mylar tubing, silver or gold, 1/8″ to 3/16″ diameter, over an underbody of wool or Seal-Ex dubbing, any color
WINGS:	Rabbit fur strip, natural gray or white, or dyed chartreuse, tan, brown, olive, black, yellow, rust, purple, or hot orange
HEAD:	Red tying thread

Chapter 12
Atlantic Salmon Flies

When you look at a box of salmon flies, you know that you are looking at something quite different from just ordinary trout flies. Even though some of them might look as simple to tie, there is more involved in their dressing than meets the eye.

If you are tying wet flies or streamers for trout fishing, you are, to some extent, at liberty to use your creative mind in positioning the various parts, whether it's the number of ribbing turns, the tail length, or the hook you have chosen to tie them on. Salmon flies, however, are much more bound by tradition in their anatomy, proportions, and materials selected for their dressing. You must follow these traditions—if you want your flies to look like salmon flies, that is.

In this chapter I deal only with the simpler hair-winged flies, which, in my opinion, are just as important as the fully dressed feather-winged classics of the Kelson era. Some of the flies I have included were designed as hair-wings and have never been anything but hair-wings, while others are classics converted to hair. If you are interested in the fully dressed feather-wing classics, I suggest that you get my book

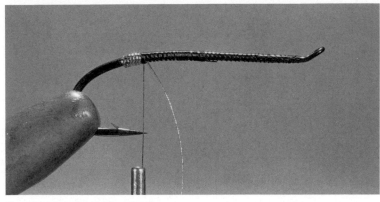

Step 1a Attaching the tinsel tag.

Salmon Flies, Their Character, Style, and Dressing, (Harrisburg, PA: Stackpole Books, 1978) in which I deal with all types of salmon flies.

Hair-Wing Salmon Flies

Perhaps the best example of simplicity combined with the beauty and effectiveness of hair-wings is the Lady Joan, a fly originated by Lee Wulff for his lovely wife, Joan Salvato Wulff.

Before you start to tie this salmon fly, however, I suggest that you study Chapter 4 on beginner's tying practice, as well as Chapter 6 dealing with wet flies. Many of the tying techniques used in salmon fly dressing are similar and will not be repeated in this chapter.

Tying the Lady Joan

HOOK:	Partridge single salmon, Code M, or double salmon, Code P, sizes 2 to 8
THREAD:	Black, prewaxed 6/0
TAG:	Medium-wide oval gold tinsel
TAIL:	None
BODY:	Hot orange seal's fur or Seal-Ex dubbing (#120)
RIBBING:	Medium-wide oval gold tinsel
HACKLE:	Yellow, wound as a collar and tied down as a throat
WINGS:	Black bear with white-tipped squirrel tail overwing
HEAD:	Black tying thread

Step 1: Place a size 4 hook in the vise with the barb and hook point exposed to act as a measuring guide for positioning the tag, which in turn determines the overall proportions for most salmon flies. Attach the tying thread and wind it to the middle of the shank; then tie in a 6″ length of medium-wide oval tinsel. Wind the thread toward the rear, binding down the tinsel under the shank in the process. Stop at a position directly above a point midway between the barb and the hook point. Then wind the thread forward to above the hook point. Grasp the tinsel and wind it on the shank with close turns to the thread position and tie it off under the shank. Let the remainder of the tinsel hang down for use as ribbing later.

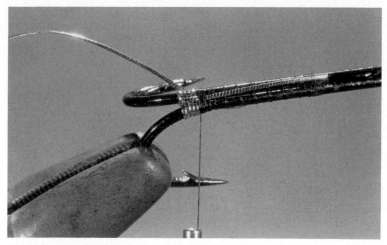

Step 1b Attaching the tag on a double hook.

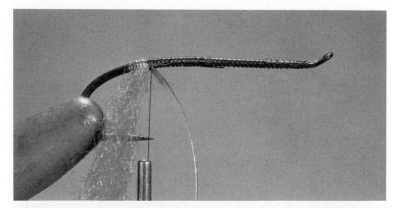

Step 2 Preparing the dubbing.

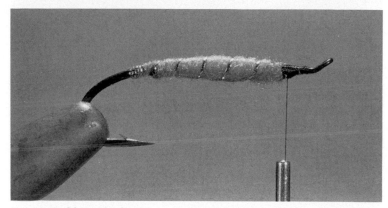

Step 3 Dubbing the body.

Step 1b: When tying the fly on a double hook, fasten it in the vise by the bend nearest to you and adjust the vise head to be level with the hook. Tie in the tinsel in the same manner as for a single hook and wind the thread to above the hook point. Now wind the tinsel on the hook working toward the rear, taking the last turn midway between the barb and the hook point. After the last turn, take the tinsel up between the two hook bends and pull it tight. To secure it, hold the end over the tag to the right and tie it off on top of the shank, directly in front of the first tinsel winding. After securing it tightly, cut the surplus tinsel in the middle of the shank and tie it in again on the far side directly in front of the tag for use as ribbing.

Step 2: Draw out a thin tapered layer of Seal-Ex dubbing and roll a point in the end; then tie it in by the tip in front of the tag as shown in the photo.

Step 3: Spiral the dubbing lightly around the thread in a clockwise direction and hold it while winding it on the shank with the thread to form a fairly thin, tapered body. Make sure there is plenty of room in front for the hackle, wing, and head. Tie off the dubbing and trim away the surplus.

Spiral the ribbing forward over the body to the front, taking five turns only. Tie off the tinsel under the shank and cut the surplus.

The reason for using only five turns of tinsel is not that the fish can count. Rather it comes from a tradition for all salmon flies. Body hackle, called for on some flies, is wound with the stem up close behind each turn of tinsel to protect it. If there were more than five turns, the hackle would be too dense, adversely affecting the fly's performance.

Lady Joan   209

Step 4 Attaching the hackle.

Step 5 Creating the head space.

Step 6 Preparing the wing.

Step 4: Select a soft hen neck hackle and use the portion near the base where the softest webby fibers are found. The fibers should be 1 1/2 hook gaps long. Prepare and tie in the hackle wet-fly style, as explained in Chapter 6 dealing with wet flies. Wind the thread forward almost to the eye of the hook. Apply three or four turns of hackle and tie it off on top of the shank. Do not cut the surplus. At this point, you have temporarily lost the head space in front, but it will be regained in the next step. Your fly should now look like the one in the photo.

Step 5: Divide the hackle fibers on top and pull them down to each side, holding them while laying the surplus hackle stem back over the top. Soften the stem a little with your fingernail; then wind a couple of turns of thread back over the stem, binding it down before cutting the surplus. Now hold all the fibers under each side of the hook shank while winding the thread back to the front of the body.

There should now be about a 1/8″ space in front for the wing and head. By laying the stem back instead of cutting it after tying off the hackle, you eliminate the little stump that always interferes when winding the small stubby head. That style of head is just as much a part of a well-dressed salmon fly as the rest of its anatomy.

Step 6: Cut a small bunch of black hair and even up the ends. Pull out the short hair and the underfur. If you hold the hair out at a 90-degree angle from the skin before cutting it, the ends should be fairly even. But whatever you do, you must not even the tips in a hair stacker—this would make the wing look like a paint brush. Now hold the hair with

Step 7 Trimming the wing butts.

Step 8 Attaching the squirrel tail overwing.

your fingers over the body as shown, with the tips reaching to the outside of the hook bend.

Step 7: While holding the hair as shown in Step 6, grasp it with the other hand so the fingers are right above the tie-in spot in front of the body. Trim away the butt ends straight across, close to your finger tips.

Step 8: Apply some cement on the butt ends and tie in the hair with four or five tight turns of thread. Make sure there is a little room in front between the butt ends and the eye. Let the thread hang directly in front of the body. Then prepare and tie in a small bunch of white-tipped squirrel tail of the same length over the black hair. The wing should now look like the one in the photo, with the tips even with the bend and the wing sitting parallel with the body.

Step 9: Wind a small, stubby head and whip finish before cutting the thread. Apply several coats of Price's Head Cement, and the Lady Joan is finished.

Step 9 The finished Lady Joan.

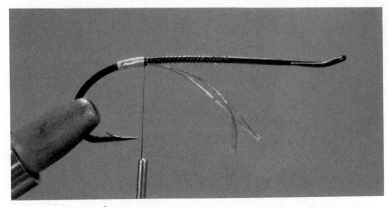

Step 1 Forming the tag.

Feather-Wing Classics, Converted

Most anglers who fish extensively for Atlantic salmon agree that this fine sport fish can be teased into taking contemporary sparsely dressed hair-wing patterns. Since fully dressed feather-winged flies of the classic vintage have always been as much a part of salmon fishing as the salmon themselves, a conversion scheme was created, and a few of the most popular classics were converted to hair. The bodies from the original dressings have been retained to some degree, although sometimes slightly reduced, and the multi-colored wings are made of hair with shades and colors that, when assembled, create a highly transluscent look and "lively" structure.

Fly tiers interested in a more expanded knowledge of fully dressed feather-wings should get my book *Salmon Flies*, mentioned earlier.

Tying the Green Highlander, Converted

HOOK: Partridge single salmon, Code M, or double salmon, Code P; or low-water single salmon, Code N, or low-water double salmon, Code Q, sizes 5/0 to 10
THREAD: Black, prewaxed 6/0

TAG: Fine oval silver tinsel and yellow floss
TAIL: Golden pheasant crest and strip of black-barred wood duck
BUTT: Black ostrich herl
BODY: Rear quarter, yellow floss; rest, bright green seal's fur or Green Highlander Seal-Ex dubbing (#124)
RIBBING: Oval silver tinsel
HACKLE: Grass-green hackle over seal's fur
THROAT: Bright yellow hackle
WINGS: Golden pheasant tippet in strands with a small bunch of mixed yellow, orange, and green polar bear hair tied in together; natural brown bucktail over as a main wing
SIDES: Narrow strips of black-barred wood duck flank feather
CHEEKS: Jungle cock (optional)
HEAD: Black tying thread
NOTE: The polar bear hair can be substituted for with Crystal Hair, Fishair, or bucktail in the same colors.

Step 1: For better illustration and clearer details, I have selected a size 3/0 low-water hook for this tying practice. Attach the tying thread and tie in a 4″ length of the finest oval silver tinsel under the middle of the shank. Continue winding the thread toward the rear, binding the tinsel down under the shank in the process. Stop directly above a point midway between the barb and the hook point. Wind the thread forward a little and take three or four turns of tinsel around the shank toward the front. Tie it off under the shank and wind the thread over the end to a point above the hook point. Do not cut the surplus; it will help form the underbody later.

Tie in a 6″ length of floss and form the floss part of the tag by winding it back to the tinsel, then forward over the first layer of floss to the tie-in position. Tie it off under the shank. Do not cut the surplus tinsel or floss unless the ends are excessively long, in which case they may be trimmed no shorter than 1/4″ from the eye. Your fly should now look like the one in the photo, and you are ready to add the tail.

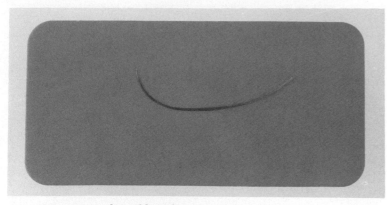

Step 2 Preparing the golden pheasant crest.

Step 2: Select a single topping (crest) from the head of a golden pheasant. It should be long enough to reach from the front of the tag to the outside of the hook bend plus a little extra for tying it in. Pull off the fuzz and excess fibers at the base; then let it soak in lukewarm water for a few minutes. Take it out and stroke off the excess water and place it on a piece of plastic or glass. Shape it with your dubbing needle to the desired curvature and let it dry completely. I sometimes make up several tails at a time and store them for future use.

Step 3: Form a smooth surface with tying thread and tie in the golden pheasant crest tail in front of the tag with several

Step 3 Attaching the tail.

turns of thread, keeping the fibers bunched well together with the tip of the tail even with the hook bend. Do not cut the surplus. Now select a section, 1/8″ wide, from a black-barred wood duck flank feather and double it lengthwise. Tie it in, on edge, over the crest tail with the tip reaching to the middle of the crest. Cut the surplus of that feather only and wind a thread segment 1/16″ wide, directly in front of the tag to serve as a foundation for the herl butt and to secure the tail material tightly. The fly should now look like the one in the photo.

Step 4 Attaching the ostrich herl butt.

Step 5 Attaching the ribbing and floss.

Step 4: Select a long ostrich herl, either natural or dyed black. The fibers on each side of the stem should be about 1/8″ long for the size fly we are tying and fairly even in length throughout the herl. If you closely examine the texture of the herl, you will notice that the fibers are almost flush with the stem on one side, making the stem very pronounced on the other. This is one of nature's gifts to the fly tier, as it makes the ostrich herl very easy to work with.

Tie in the herl directly in front of the tag, with the pronounced side of the stem toward the front, securing it with a couple of turns of thread. Hold the herl straight up and start winding it on the hook over and away from you. Take about six close turns or as much as needed to cover the 1/16″ thread segment in front of the butt, stroking the fibers back like a wet fly hackle as you take each turn. Tie off the herl

and cut the surplus. The result will be a neat butt that will do justice to any "well-dressed" salmon fly.

Step 5: When a particular dressing calls for a number of different materials in the body construction, each will occupy a certain portion of the hook shank. In most cases, the body length is calculated from approximately 3/16″ from the eye, where the body starts, to the butt. The body for a Green Highlander is 1/4 yellow floss and 3/4 seal's fur or Seal-Ex dubbing.

Start by tying in a 4″ length of medium-wide oval silver tinsel on the far side of the hook, directly in front of the black herl butt, leaving the surplus end long. Let it hang down in that position so it's ready to be used as ribbing when the rest of the body is completed. Now wind the tying thread forward to 1/4 of the body length from the butt and tie in 4″ of yellow floss.

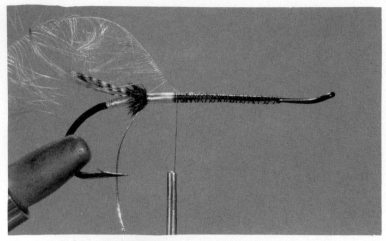

Step 6 Attaching the hackle.

Step 7 Forming the body.

Step 6: Wind the floss segment in the same manner as the tag and tie it off at the tie-in position. Now cut all the long material ends to just 3/8" from the eye and spiral the thread forward over the remainders, binding them down parallel to the hook shank without twisting them. Then wind the thread back to 1/16" in front of the floss segment. In this way the material ends will serve as an underbody. Select a soft hackle 3 1/2" long with fibers at the tip end a shade shorter than the hook gap. Prepare the hackle wet-fly style as explained in Chapter 6 on wet flies.

Place the hackle on top of the body projecting over the hook eye. Place it with the underside up and the tip at the tie-in spot in front of the floss segment. Tie it in with a few turns of thread, making sure that there is a good amount of stem between the lowest hackle fibers and the shank. Now pull the hackle toward the rear, thus doubling the hackle stem at the tie-in spot. Hold it there while winding some thread over it so the hackle stem is directly in front of the floss. This will insure against the hackle accidentally being pulled out under tension when the fibers are doubled back. The hackle should now sit pointing toward the rear with the good side (shiny side) up.

Step 7: Place the hackle out of the way and dub some seal's fur on the tying thread or prepare a thin layer of Seal-Ex dubbing as explained in Step 2 for tying the Lady Joan. The dubbing should be about 3" long. Wind the dubbing on the shank over and away from you toward the front and tie it off 3/16" from the eye. Then cut away or peel off any surplus. Grasp the ribbing tinsel and spiral it up the body with five turns and tie it off in front under the shank.

Cut the surplus tinsel and grasp the hackle with your hackle pliers, holding it straight up with the good side facing front. Double the hackle fibers back as explained in Chapter 6 for tying soft-hackle wet flies. Use a little saliva on your fingers as you double the fibers back after each turn. Wind the hackle over the dubbing in palmer fashion, with each turn following close behind each turn of ribbing tinsel. Take a couple of close turns in the middle of the head space in front and tie it down as a throat, as explained in Step 4 for tying the Lady Joan. The fly should now look like the one in the photo.

Step 8 Attaching the wing.

Step 9 Preparing the sides and cheeks.

Step 8: For the wing, tie in a small bunch of golden pheasant tippet fibers so the tips reach to above the herl butt. Directly over those, tie in a mixed bunch of yellow, orange, and green polar bear hair just slightly longer than the tippet fibers. Now cut a bunch of natural brown bucktail and remove the short hair and fuzz from the end. Measure it so it reaches from the tie-in spot in front to just inside the tail. Cut the butt ends even across, apply a little cement, and tie it in over the polar bear hair to serve as the main wing. Secure the wing firmly with several tight turns of thread that cover the butt ends. Be sure there is still about 3/16" of room left in front for the hackle and head.

Step 9: For the sides and cheeks, select a left and a right black-barred wood duck flank feather and cut a section 1/8" wide from each. The strip shown to the left in the photo is for the right side (near side) of the wing, and the one to the right is for the other side. The segments should be long enough to reach above the herl butt from the tie-in spot. Also, the feather strips must not be damaged. For the cheeks, prepare two jungle cock feathers like the one shown in the photo by pulling off the soft down and fibers from the butt ends. They should be long enough to reach the middle of the wing. If you don't have jungle cock feathers, the fly will be very acceptable without them.

Step 10 Attaching the sides and cheeks.

Step 11 The finished Green Highlander, Converted.

Fig. 12.1 Low-water and semi-low-water salmon flies.

Step 10: Tie in a wood duck strip on each side of the wing. They should sit in the middle of the wing and reach above the herl butt. Now tie in the jungle cock feathers on top of the wood duck with the tips reaching to the middle of the wing.

Step 11: To finish the fly, select a webby, yellow neck or saddle hackle with fibers as long as 1 1/2 times the hook gap or at least a little longer than the green hackle wound in front of the body. Prepare it as explained in the instructions for tying the soft-hackle wet fly in Chapter 6 and Step 3 for tying the Lady Joan. However, it's not tied under as a throat but, rather, wound as a collar. Wind the thread back on the hackle fibers while holding them toward the rear after the hackle is wound, thus creating a small head. Tie off the thread with a whip finish and cut it. Apply several coats of Price's Head Cement, and your fly is finished.

Low-water Salmon Flies

These are merely small flies tied on large hooks of wire thinner than the standard diameter. The fly is usually started by tying the tag and tail in the middle of the shank (like the Crossfield to the left in **Fig. 12.1**). The fly to the right is the same fly tied semi-low-water style. As you can see, the fly is a little larger because the tag was started above the point of the hook. These types of flies are often used when fishing low, clear water, so you will not spook the fish.

Selected Salmon Fly Patterns

The following patterns were selected among the better-known flies for their effectiveness in fishing for Atlantic salmon almost anywhere they're found. The hooks I use for most of my flies are made by Partridge of England and are described in the hook chapter, Chapter 2. Before leaving on a fishing trip, it's always best to obtain some information about hook sizes appropriate for the area you are planning to fish. All the flies included in the following list can be dressed on single or double, regular or low-water irons.

BLACK BEAR

HOOK:	Sizes 2 to 12, single or double
THREAD:	Black, prewaxed 6/0
TAIL:	Two narrow strips of black crow wing quill
BODY:	Black wool or Seal-Ex dubbing (#118)
THROAT:	Small bunch of black bear hair, dressed sparse and reaching to hook point
WINGS:	Black bear hair reaching to end of tail
HEAD:	Black tying thread

BLACK BOMBER

HOOK:	Sizes 2 to 12, single or double
THREAD:	Black, prewaxed 6/0
TAG:	Fine oval silver tinsel and yellow floss
TAIL:	Golden pheasant crest
BODY:	Black wool or Seal-Ex dubbing (#118)
RIBBING:	Oval silver tinsel
THROAT:	Black
WINGS:	Black squirrel or black bear hair
CHEEKS:	Jungle cock
TOPPING:	Golden pheasant crest
HEAD:	Black tying thread

NOTE: A topping should be attached in front and should follow the upper edge of the wing, meeting the tip of the tail in the rear.

BLACK LABRADOR

HOOK:	Sizes 2 to 10, single
THREAD:	Black, prewaxed 6/0
TAIL:	Heavy bunch of black bear hair or dyed calf tail, one body length
BODY:	Black wool or Seal-Ex dubbing (#118), dressed heavy and cigar shaped
HACKLE:	Black, wound as a collar with fibers extending to the hook point
HEAD:	Black tying thread

BLACK RAT

HOOK:	Sizes 2 to 12, single or double
THREAD:	Red, prewaxed 6/0
TAG:	Fine oval silver tinsel
TAIL:	Small golden pheasant crest
BODY:	Black seal's fur or Seal-Ex dubbing (#118)
RIBBING:	Flat or oval silver tinsel
WINGS:	Gray fox guard hair with small amount of underfur left in
CHEEKS:	Jungle cock (optional)
HACKLE:	Grizzly, wound as a collar and tied back to blend with wing
HEAD:	Red tying thread

BLUE CHARM

HOOK:	Sizes 4 to 12, single or double
THREAD:	Black, prewaxed 6/0
TAG:	Fine oval silver tinsel and yellow floss
TAIL:	Golden pheasant crest
BUTT:	Black ostrich herl (optional)
BODY:	Black floss
RIBBING:	Oval silver tinsel
THROAT:	Deep blue hackle fibers
WINGS:	Woodchuck guard hair or eastern pine squirrel tail
HEAD:	Black tying thread

BLUE RAT

HOOK:	Sizes 2 to 12, single or double
THREAD:	Red, prewaxed 6/0
TAG:	Fine oval gold tinsel
TAIL:	Four short peacock sword fibers, no longer than to bend
BODY:	Rear half—kingfisher blue floss; front half—peacock herl
VEILING:	Length of blue floss over rear body half, reaching to just short of tail length
RIBBING:	Oval gold tinsel

WINGS: Gray fox guard hair with small amount of under-fur left in
CHEEKS: Jungle cock reaching to middle of wing; blue kingfisher outside
HACKLE: Small bunch of soft grizzly hackle fibers tied over the wing, with a similar bunch tied in as a throat
HEAD: Red tying thread

BUTTERFLY
HOOK: Sizes 4 to 12, single or double
THREAD: Black, prewaxed 6/0
TAIL: A good-sized bunch of red hackle fibers, one body length
BODY: Bronze peacock herl
WINGS: White goat hair or calf tail, slightly longer than the body, divided into two bunches in splayed fashion, set low
HACKLE: Several turns of soft brown hackle, wound dry fly style
HEAD: Black tying thread

COPPER KILLER
HOOK: Sizes 4 to 12, single or double
THREAD: Black, prewaxed 6/0
TAG: Fine copper wire and small segment of pale green floss
TAIL: Small bunch of golden pheasant tippet fibers, extending to bend
BUTT: Red wool or Seal-Ex dubbing (#122)
BODY: Flat copper tinsel
RIBBING: Copper wire
HACKLE: Hot-orange, wound as a collar and tied back but not under
WINGS: Fox squirrel tail hair, reaching to hook bend
HEAD: Red tying thread

COSSEBOOM
HOOK: Sizes 2 to 12, single or double
THREAD: Black, prewaxed 6/0
TAIL: Olive-green floss, 1 1/2 hook gaps long
BODY: Olive-green floss
RIBBING: Embossed silver tinsel
WINGS: Gray squirrel tail, reaching to the hook bend
CHEEKS: Jungle cock (optional)

HACKLE: Lemon-yellow, wound as a collar and tied back to blend with the wing
HEAD: Red tying thread

COLBURN SPECIAL
HOOK: Sizes 1 to 8, single or double
THREAD: Black, prewaxed 6/0
TAG: Fine oval silver tinsel
TAIL: Black hair over green hair in two equal sections
BODY: Fluorescent green floss with black ostrich herl butt in center
WINGS: Black hair over green hair in two equal sections
HACKLE: Yellow, wound as a collar
HEAD: Black tying thread
NOTE: There is a series of flies under the name "Colburn". They are tied exactly alike except for the color.

COLBURN, BLUE
TAIL: Squirrel dyed blue
BODY: Medium blue floss
WINGS: Gray squirrel dyed blue
HACKLE: Blue
NOTE: See full pattern above.

COLBURN, CLARET
TAG: Oval silver tinsel
TAIL: Squirred dyed claret
BODY: Claret floss
WINGS: Gray squirrel dyed claret
HACKLE: Black
NOTE: See full pattern above.

CROSSFIELD
HOOK: Sizes 4 to 12, single or double
THREAD: Black, prewaxed 6/0
TAIL: Golden pheasant crest
BODY: Embossed silver tinsel
THROAT: Medium blue hackle fibers
WINGS: Gray squirrel tail
HEAD: Black tying thread

FOX
HOOK: Sizes 4 to 12, single or double
THREAD: Black, prewaxed 6/0

TAG:	Fine oval silver tinsel and fluorescent yellow-orange floss
TAIL:	Golden pheasant crest
BUTT:	Black ostrich herl
BODY:	Black floss
RIBBING:	Oval silver tinsel
THROAT:	Black hackle fibers
WINGS:	Gray fox guard hairs
CHEEKS:	Jungle cock, short (optional)
HEAD:	Black tying thread

GREEN BUTT

HOOK:	Sizes 2 to 12, single or double
THREAD:	Black, prewaxed 6/0
TAG:	Fine oval silver tinsel and bright green fluorescent floss, wound over white silk and lacquered
TAIL:	Golden pheasant crest
BODY:	Black wool or Seal-Ex dubbing (#118)
RIBBING:	Oval silver tinsel
THROAT:	Black hackle fibers
WINGS:	Soft black bear or black squirrel hair
HEAD:	Black tying thread

NOTE: This fly can be dressed with a red or orange butt, in which case it's called either a Red Butt or Orange Butt. The rest of the fly remains the same.

GRAY RAT

HOOK:	Sizes 2 to 12, single or double
THREAD:	Red, prewaxed 6/0
TAG:	Fine oval silver tinsel
TAIL:	Small golden pheasant crest
BODY:	Underfur from a gray fox
RIBBING:	Flat gold tinsel
WINGS:	Gray fox guard hair with small amount of underfur left in
CHEEKS:	Jungle cock (optional)
HACKLE:	Grizzly, wound as a collar and tied back to blend with the wing
HEAD:	Red tying thread

GRIZZLY KING

HOOK:	Sizes 2 to 12, single or double
THREAD:	Black, prewaxed 6/0

TAIL:	Narrow strip of red goose or small bunch of red hackle fibers
BODY:	Green floss
RIBBING:	Flat silver tinsel
WINGS:	Gray squirrel tail hair
CHEEKS:	Jungle cock (optional)
HACKLE:	Grizzly, wound as a collar and tied back to blend with the wing
HEAD:	Black tying thread

HAIRY MARY

HOOK:	Sizes 4 to 12, single or double
THREAD:	Black, prewaxed 6/0
TAG:	Fine oval gold tinsel
TAIL:	Golden pheasant crest
BODY:	Black floss
RIBBING:	Oval gold tinsel
THROAT:	Bright blue hackle fibers
WINGS:	Reddish-brown fitch tail or squirrel
HEAD:	Black tying thread

LADY JOAN

HOOK:	Sizes 2 to 8, single or double
THREAD:	Black, prewaxed 6/0
TAG:	Medium-wide oval gold tinsel
TAIL:	None
BODY:	Hot orange seal's fur or Seal-Ex dubbing (#120)
RIBBING:	Medium-wide oval gold tinsel
HACKLE:	Yellow, wound as a collar and tied down as a throat
WINGS:	Black bear with white-tipped squirrel tail over-wing
HEAD:	Black tying thread

LAXA BLUE

HOOK:	Sizes 4 to 12, single or double
THREAD:	Black, prewaxed 6/0
TAG:	Fine oval silver tinsel and fluorescent yellow-orange floss
TAIL:	Golden pheasant crest
BODY:	Silver Doctor blue floss
RIBBING:	Oval silver tinsel
THROAT:	Silver Doctor blue hackle
WINGS:	Gray squirrel dyed blue
HEAD:	Black tying thread

ORANGE BLOSSOM

HOOK:	Sizes 2 to 12, single or double
THREAD:	Black, prewaxed 6/0
TAG:	Fine oval silver tinsel and golden-yellow floss
TAIL:	Golden pheasant crest and Indian crow
BUTT:	Black ostrich herl
BODY:	Embossed silver tinsel
WINGS:	Palest natural brown bucktail
HACKLE:	Bright orange, wound as a collar and tied back to blend with the wing, tips extending to hook point
HEAD:	Black tying thread

PROFESSOR

HOOK:	Sizes 2 to 12, single or double
THREAD:	Black, prewaxed 6/0
TAG:	Fine oval gold tinsel
TAIL:	Small bunch of red hackle fibers
BODY:	Yellow floss
RIBBING:	Oval gold tinsel
WINGS:	Gray squirrel tail
HACKLE:	Soft natural brown hackle, wound as a collar and tied back to blend with the wing
HEAD:	Black tying thread

ROGER'S FANCY

HOOK:	Sizes 2 to 12, single or double
THREAD:	Black, prewaxed 6/0
TAG:	Fine oval silver tinsel and fluorescent yellow floss, wound over white silk and lacquered
TAIL:	Three or four peacock sword fibers, reaching to the bend
BODY:	Bright green wool or Seal-Ex dubbing (#124)
RIBBING:	Oval silver tinsel
THROAT:	Bright yellow hackle fibers, fronted by bright green hackle fibers
WINGS:	Gray fox guard hair with small amount of underfur left in
CHEEKS:	Jungle cock, fairly short (optional)
HEAD:	Black tying thread

RUSTY RAT

HOOK:	Sizes 2 to 12, single or double
THREAD:	Red, prewaxed 6/0
TAG:	Fine oval gold tinsel
TAIL:	Three or four short peacock sword fibers, reaching to hook bend
BODY:	Rear half—yellow floss; front half—peacock herl
VEILING:	Length of yellow floss over rear half, extending to middle of tail
WINGS:	Gray fox guard hair with small amount of underfur left in
CHEEKS:	Jungle cock (optional)
HACKLE:	Grizzly, wound as a collar after wing is tied in
HEAD:	Red tying thread

NOTE: A very interesting effect can be achieved by using fluorescent yellowish-orange floss instead of yellow. It gives the fly a "Jock Scott" look.

SILVER RAT

HOOK:	Sizes 2 to 12, single or double
THREAD:	Red, prewaxed 6/0
TAG:	Fine oval gold tinsel
TAIL:	Short golden pheasant crest
BODY:	Flat silver tinsel
RIBBING:	Oval gold tinsel
WINGS:	Gray fox guard hair with a small amount of underfur left in
CHEEKS:	Jungle cock (optional)
HACKLE:	Grizzly, wound as a collar and tied back to blend with the wing
HEAD:	Red tying thread

Hair-Wing Conversions

In addition to the preceding list of dressings for standard hair-wing salmon flies, I have designed a scheme by which many of the most important classic fully dressed feather-wing flies can be converted into very attractive hair-wing patterns. The ones included in the following list are by no means the only ones that can be converted, and you may find others that you can work on yourself.

AKROYD

HOOK:	Sizes 3/0 to 6, single low-water
THREAD:	Black, prewaxed 6/0
TAG:	Flat silver tinsel
TAIL:	Golden pheasant crest and tippet in strands
BODY:	Rear half—light orange seal's fur or Seal-Ex dubbing (#121); front half—black floss
RIBBING:	Oval silver tinsel over rear body half; flat silver tinsel and twist over front half
HACKLE:	Lemon hackle over orange seal's fur, black heron hackle over black floss
THROAT:	Teal flank feather, wound as a collar and tied under
WINGS:	White or natural brown bucktail set flat and slightly divided
CHEEKS:	Jungle cock, 1/3 wing length and slanting down (optional)
HEAD:	Black tying thread

BLACK DOSE (CANADIAN)

HOOK:	Sizes 3/0 to 10, regular single or double
THREAD:	Black, prewaxed 6/0
TAG:	Fine oval silver tinsel and yellow floss
TAIL:	Golden pheasant
BODY:	Black floss
RIBBING:	Oval silver tinsel
HACKLE:	Very soft black hackle, wound as a collar and tied back to blend with wing
WINGS:	A few strands of golden pheasant tippet, over which is a mixed bunch of yellow, scarlet, and blue polar bear, bucktail, Fishair, or Crystal Hair, with a main wing of natural red fox squirrel tail over
CHEEKS:	Jungle cock (optional)
HEAD:	Black tying thread

DURHAM RANGER

HOOK:	Sizes 3/0 to 10, regular single or double
THREAD:	Black, prewaxed 6/0
TAG:	Fine oval silver tinsel and yellow floss
TAIL:	Golden pheasant crest and Indian crow
BUTT:	Black ostrich herl
BODY:	Equal sections of yellow floss, orange, fiery

brown, and black seal's fur or Seal-Ex dubbing, palmered with a badger hackle dyed yellow

RIBBING:	Flat silver tinsel and twist
WINGS:	Gray squirrel or fox guard hair dyed yellowish-orange
SIDES:	Jungle cock, reaching to middle of wing (optional)
CHEEKS:	Blue kingfisher, 1/4 the length of jungle cock
HACKLE:	Very soft blue hackle, wound as a collar and tied back to blend with the wing
HEAD:	Black tying thread

NOTE: Seal-Ex numbers for body—orange, (#121); fiery brown, (#123); black, (#118).

GREEN HIGHLANDER

HOOK:	Sizes 5/0 to 10, regular or low-water, single or double
THREAD:	Black, prewaxed 6/0
TAG:	Fine oval silver tinsel and yellow floss
TAIL:	Golden pheasant crest and strip of black-barred wood duck
BUTT:	Black ostrich herl
BODY:	Rear quarter, yellow floss; rest, bright green seal's fur or Green Highlander Seal-Ex dubbing (#124)
RIBBING:	Oval silver tinsel
HACKLE:	Grass-green hackle over seal's fur only
THROAT:	Bright yellow hackle
WINGS:	Golden pheasant tippet in strands with a small bunch of mixed yellow, orange, and green polar bear hair tied in together; natural brown bucktail over as a main wing
SIDES:	Narrow strips of black-barred wood duck flank feather
CHEEKS:	Jungle cock (optional)
HEAD:	Black tying thread

NOTE: The polar bear hair can be substituted for with Crystal Hair, Fishair, or bucktail in the same colors.

JOCK SCOTT

HOOK:	Sizes 3/0 to 10, regular single or double
THREAD:	Black, prewaxed 6/0
TAG:	Fine oval silver tinsel and yellow floss
TAIL:	Golden pheasant crest and Indian crow

BUTT: Black ostrich herl
BODY: Rear half—golden-yellow floss veiled above
                and below with toucan feathers and butted with
                black ostrich herl; front half—black floss pal-
                mered with soft black hackle
RIBBING: Fine oval silver tinsel over rear half, wider flat
                and round tinsel over front half
THROAT: Speckled guinea fowl
WINGS: A small mixed bunch of scarlet, yellow, and
                blue polar bear hair, bucktail, Fishair, or Crys-
                tal Hair, with a main wing of fairly dark, natural
                brown bucktail over
SIDES: Narrow strip of black-barred wood duck 2/3
                down middle of wing
CHEEKS: Jungle cock with short kingfisher feather on
                outside (optional)
HEAD: Black tying thread
NOTE: On smaller flies, the flat tinsel ribbing is left out, and a
wider oval silver tinsel is used.

NIGHT HAWK
HOOK: Sizes 3/0 to 10, regular single or double
THREAD: Black, prewaxed 6/0
TAG: Fine oval silver tinsel and yellow floss
TAIL: Golden pheasant crest and blue kingfisher or
                dyed hen neck feather
BUTT: Red wool or Seal-Ex dubbing (#122)
BODY: Flat silver tinsel
RIBBING: Oval silver tinsel
THROAT: Black hackle
WINGS: Black bear or natural black squirrel tail
CHEEKS: Jungle cock with short blue kingfisher feather
                on outside (optional)
HEAD: Red tying thread

SILVER DOCTOR
HOOK: Sizes 3/0 to 10, regular single or double
THREAD: Black, prewaxed 6/0
TAG: Fine oval silver tinsel and golden-yellow floss
TAIL: Golden pheasant crest and blue kingfisher
BUTT: Scarlet wool or Seal-Ex dubbing (#122)
BODY: Flat silver tinsel
RIBBING: Oval silver tinsel
THROAT: Pale blue hackle with teal in front

WINGS: A few strands of golden pheasant tippet, over
                which is a mixed bunch of yellow, scarlet, and
                blue polar bear, bucktail, Fishair, or Crystal
                Hair, with a main wing of natural red fox squir-
                rel tail over
SIDES: Strips of black-barred wood duck 1/8″ wide
                down the middle of wing, reaching to above
                the butt
HEAD: Scarlet wool, Seal-Ex dubbing (#122), or red
                tying thread

SILVER GRAY
HOOK: Sizes 3/0 to 10, regular single or double
THREAD: Black, prewaxed 6/0
TAG: Fine oval silver tinsel and golden-yellow floss
TAIL: Golden pheasant crest and strands of black-
                barred wood duck
BUTT: Black ostrich herl
BODY: Flat silver tinsel, palmered with badger hackle
RIBBING: Oval silver tinsel
THROAT: Widgeon or teal
WINGS: A few strands of golden pheasant tippet, over
                which is a small mixed bunch of white, yellow,
                and green polar bear hair, bucktail, Fishair, or
                Crystal Hair with a main wing of gray squirrel
                tail over
CHEEKS: Jungle cock (optional)
HEAD: Black tying thread

THUNDER AND LIGHTNING
HOOK: Sizes 3/0 to 10, regular or low-water, single or
                double
THREAD: Black, prewaxed 6/0
TAG: Oval gold tinsel and yellow floss
TAIL: Golden pheasant crest and Indian crow
BUTT: Black ostrich herl
BODY: Black floss, palmered with a deep-orange
                hackle
RIBBING: Oval gold tinsel
THROAT: Guinea fowl
WINGS: Natural red fox squirrel hair or dark brown
                bucktail
CHEEKS: Jungle cock
HEAD: Black tying thread

Chapter 13
Steelhead Flies

Because I live in the East, I have not had the good fortune to do much steelhead fishing, and even though "freshwater steelhead" are now entering rivers in both Michigan and New York, I had to rely on several experts and my own notes from occasional trips to the Pacific Northwest to select a list of patterns that will work for both summer and winter fishing.

These brightly colored flies are much like those used for Atlantic salmon, and in the last few years steelhead anglers have begun dressing their flies on salmon hooks. This makes sense since salmon hooks are not only very strong but also have a sproat bend which aids the fly in swimming upright with much more consistency.

I suggest that you study Chapter 12 dealing with hair-wing Atlantic salmon flies and use the tying instructions for those when dressing your flies for steelhead.

The Egg Fly

There is one important steelhead fly, however, that needs special attention, and that's the egg fly. It can be tied with

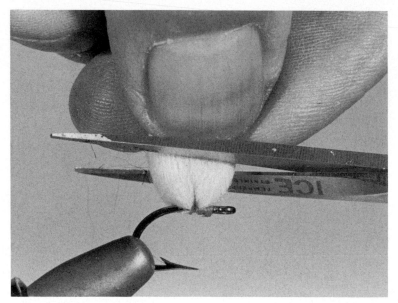

Step 1 Attaching the Glo-Bug yarn.

Step 2 Trimming the yarn.

a single or double egg and with or without hackle. This unusual contraption is not only used for steelhead but also for Pacific salmon and lake-run rainbows and browns.

Tying the Glo-Bug Egg Fly

HOOK:	Mustad #9174 3X short, sizes 4 to 8
THREAD:	Red Kevlar thread
BODY:	Hot orange or pink Glo-Bug yarn, fluorescent

Step 1: Place a size 6 hook in the vise and attach the tying thread securely in the middle of the shank. Now cut four 2"

pieces of Glo-Bug yarn. Bundle the pieces together and tie them in on top of the shank with two or three tight turns of thread. Pull hard on the Kevlar thread to tighten the yarn securely.

Step 2: Gather the yarn between your fingers and pull it upward. Hold it there while taking several turns of thread around the hook shank in back and front of the tie-in spot. Tie off the thread in front and cut it, then apply a drop of cement without getting any on the yarn. Hold the yarn tightly upward with your fingers and cut across it about a hook gap above the shank with a pair of heavy, sharp scissors.

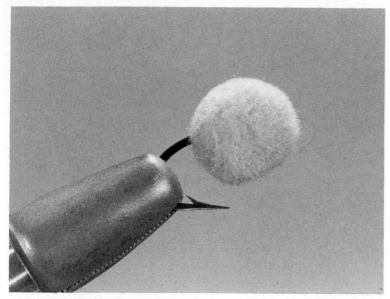

Step 3 The finished Glo-Bug Egg Fly.

Step 3: When the yarn is cut, it should flare, as shown in the photo. Help its distribution a little with your fingers, and the egg fly is finished.

Selected Steelhead Flies

In addition to the list of patterns specifically designed for steelhead, there are several of the hair-wing Atlantic salmon flies that can be used. If you are interested in expanding your knowledge of steelhead patterns, I can highly recommend Trey Combs' book *Steelhead Fishing and Flies* (Portland, Oregon: Salmon, Trout, Steelheader, 1976).

BABINE SPECIAL
HOOK:	Partridge salmon hook, Code M, sizes 2 to 8
THREAD:	Red, prewaxed 6/0
WEIGHT:	Lead wire, .015″ to .025″
BODY:	Two red or hot orange chenille balls, as large as hook gap
HACKLE:	Red hackle center, white hackle front
HEAD:	Red tying thread

BRAD'S BRAT
HOOK:	Partridge salmon hook, Code M, sizes 2 to 8
THREAD:	Black, prewaxed 6/0
TAG:	Gold tinsel
TAIL:	Orange and white hackle fibers, mixed
BODY:	Rear half—hot orange Seal-Ex dubbing (#120); front half—red Seal-Ex dubbing (#122)
RIBBING:	Flat gold tinsel
HACKLE:	Brown
WINGS:	Bottom third—orange bucktail; top two-thirds—white bucktail
HEAD:	Black tying thread

FALL FAVORITE
HOOK:	Partridge salmon hook, Code M, sizes 2 to 8
THREAD:	Black, prewaxed 6/0
BODY:	Embossed silver tinsel
HACKLE:	Scarlet
WINGS:	Hot orange bucktail or polar bear hair
HEAD:	Black tying thread

NOTE: Sometimes tied with a tail of scarlet hackle fibers.

GOLDEN DEMON
HOOK:	Partridge salmon hook, Code M, sizes 2 to 8
THREAD:	Black, prewaxed 6/0
TAIL:	Golden pheasant crest feather
BODY:	Oval gold tinsel
HACKLE:	Hot orange
WINGS:	Natural brown bucktail; jungle cock each side (optional)
HEAD:	Black tying thread

GOLDEN GIRL
HOOK:	Partridge salmon hook, Code M, sizes 5/0 to 4
THREAD:	Black, prewaxed 6/0
TAIL:	Orange hackle fibers
BODY:	Flat gold tinsel
HACKLE:	Orange neck or saddle hackle
WINGS:	Orange polar bear with golden pheasant tippet each side, reaching to bend
HEAD:	Black tying thread

KALAMA SPECIAL
HOOK: Partridge salmon hook, Code M, sizes 2 to 8
THREAD: Black, prewaxed 6/0
TAIL: Scarlet hackle fibers
BODY: Yellow wool or Seal-Ex dubbing (#119)
HACKLE: Golden badger, palmered
WINGS: White bucktail or polar bear hair
HEAD: Black tying thread

ORANGE HERON
HOOK: Partridge low-water salmon, Code N, sizes 5/0 to 2
THREAD: Red, prewaxed 6/0
BODY: Rear two-thirds—orange floss; front third—orange seal fur or Seal-Ex dubbing (#120)
RIBBING: Oval silver tinsel
HACKLE: Gray heron (substitute: pheasant rump feather), palmered
THROAT: Teal flank feather
WINGS: Four hot-orange hackle tips, reaching to bend
HEAD: Red tying thread

PAINT BRUSH
HOOK: Partridge salmon hook, Code M, sizes 2 to 6
THREAD: Orange, prewaxed 6/0
BODY: Flat gold tinsel palmered with heavy orange neck or saddle hackle
HACKLE: Pale blue, fronted with deep purple
HEAD: Orange tying thread

PURPLE PERIL
HOOK: Partridge salmon hook, Code M, sizes 2 to 8
THREAD: Black, prewaxed 6/0
TAG: Oval silver tinsel
TAIL: Purple hackle fibers
BODY: Purple chenille
RIBBING: Oval silver tinsel
HACKLE: Purple
WINGS: Red fox squirrel tail, reaching to bend
HEAD: Black tying thread

SILVER COMET
HOOK: Partridge salmon hook, Code M, sizes 2 to 8
THREAD: Red, prewaxed 6/0

WEIGHT: Lead wire, .015″ or .025″
TAIL: Orange calf tail
BODY: Flat or oval silver tinsel
HACKLE: Orange and yellow, mixed
EYES: Bead eyes, 1/8″ diameter
HEAD: Red tying thread
NOTE: This fly can also be tied in black, gold, orange, yellow, and mixed.

SKUNK
HOOK: Partridge salmon hook, Code M, sizes 2 to 8
THREAD: Black, prewaxed 6/0
TAIL: Scarlet hackle fibers
BODY: Black chenille
RIBBING: Oval silver tinsel
HACKLE: Black
WINGS: White calf tail or polar bear
HEAD: Black tying thread

SKYKOMISH SUNRISE
HOOK: Partridge salmon hook, Code M, sizes 2 to 8
THREAD: Black, prewaxed 6/0
TAIL: Scarlet and yellow hackle fibers, mixed
BODY: Red chenille
RIBBING: Oval silver tinsel
HACKLE: Scarlet and yellow, mixed
WINGS: White calf tail or polar bear
HEAD: Black tying thread

UMPQUA SPECIAL
HOOK: Partridge salmon hook, Code M, sizes 2 to 8
THREAD: Red, prewaxed 6/0
TAIL: White hackle fibers
BODY: Rear half— yellow wool; front half— red chenille
RIBBING: Oval silver tinsel
HACKLE: Brown
WINGS: White calf tail or polar bear
HEAD: Red tying thread

WINTER'S HOPE
HOOK: Partridge salmon hook, Code M, sizes 5/0 to 2
THREAD: Orange, prewaxed 6/0
BODY: Flat silver tinsel

HACKLE:	Deep purple over pale blue
WINGS:	Two yellow hackle tips inside two orange hackle tips
HEAD:	Orange tying thread

Steelhead Dry Flies

GREASE LINER

HOOK:	Partridge dry fly salmon, Code 01, sizes 4 to 8
THREAD:	Black, prewaxed 6/0
TAIL:	Dark deer body hair, 1/2 body length
BODY:	Black seal fur or Seal-Ex dubbing (#118)
HACKLE:	Grizzly wound wet fly style, sparse
WINGS:	Dark deer body hair, reaching to end of body
HEAD:	Wing butts trimmed like small Muddler head, top only

OCTOBER CADDIS

HOOK:	Partridge dry fly salmon, Code 01, sizes 4 to 10
THREAD:	Black, prewaxed 6/0
TAIL:	Golden pheasant crest, 1 1/2 hook gaps long
BODY:	Orange fur or Seal-Ex dubbing (#121)
HACKLE:	Soft brown hackle, applied after wing is tied in
WINGS:	Brown squirrel tail tied forward and divided over hook eye
HEAD:	Black tying thread

STEELHEAD BEE

HOOK:	Partridge dry fly salmon, Code 01, sizes 6 to 12
THREAD:	Black, prewaxed 6/0
TAIL:	Red fox squirrel tail
BODY:	Alternated bands of brown, yellow, brown; yarn or chenille
HACKLE:	Sparse brown hen, applied after wing is tied in
WINGS:	Red fox squirrel tail tied forward and divided over hook eye
HEAD:	Black tying thread

STEELHEAD CADDIS

HOOK:	Partridge dry fly salmon, Code 01, sizes 4 to 12
THREAD:	Black, prewaxed 6/0
BODY:	Rabbit fur to middle of shank, low-water style
WINGS:	Brown mottled turkey wing quill segment, twice the body length
COLLAR:	Natural deer body hair
HEAD:	Wing butts trimmed like Muddler head, short

Chapter 14
Saltwater Flies

Saltwater fly rodding is a very exciting and challenging addition to light-tackle sport fishing. Leading tackle manufacturers have spared no effort in providing anglers with heavier fly rods and lines specifically designed to handle the often large flies needed to entice hefty saltwater gamefish. However, there are still some trout anglers who listen in disbelief when you tell them about hooking and landing tarpon weighing 70 to 100 pounds on a fly rod with a leader tippet of 15-pound test. And on top of that, the flies in some cases are only about 3″ long. I guess you just have to see it to believe it.

Flies for saltwater fishing are constructed in the same basic manner as many of the freshwater streamers and bucktails, but they are often simpler in their dressing, lacking the fancy trimmings found on some trout flies. It's important to concentrate on selecting material that is not water-absorbent to ease the pick-up after each cast. This is particularly important when using very large flies. While flies for saltwater fishing can best be described as long tail-and-head affairs, there is one thing of extreme importance, and that's their size. They should be carefully selected to match the baitfish the fish are feeding on.

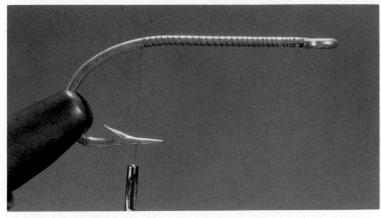

Step 1 Attaching the thread.

The Keys Tarpon Fly

This fly was designed for tarpon fishing in the Florida Keys and other places where you are casting to visible fish on the move. In addition to the colors given in the materials list below, the Keys Tarpon Fly can be dressed in many other color combinations, such as red and white, grizzly and yellow, and orange and white. The hackle collar, however, always matches the color combination of the tail.

Tying the Keys Tarpon Fly

HOOK: Mustad #34007, stainless, sizes 5/0 to 1
THREAD: Red, 3/0 Monocord
TAIL: Fairly wide saddle hackles, 3″ long, two orange and two bright yellow
HACKLE: Four or five turns of orange and yellow webby saddle hackles with fibers 1 1/2 hook gaps long, wound together dry fly style
BODY: Front 1/2 of hook shank covered with red tying thread and lacquered

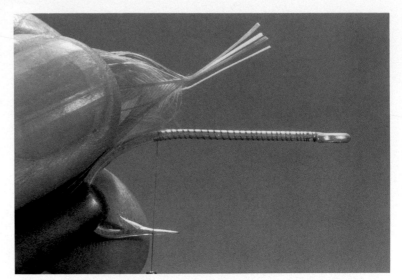

Step 2 Preparing the tail.

Step 1: Attach the tying thread close to the eye and wind it with close turns back to the bend. Stop at a point above midway between the barb and the hook point where the tail will be tied in.

Step 2: Select two orange and two bright yellow, fairly wide saddle hackles of the same length, about 3 1/2″ long. Place the two yellow hackles on top of each other with the glossy sides together and the tips even. Then place an orange hackle on each side with the glossy sides inward and the tips lined up with the yellow ones. Put the glossy sides inward to splay the feathers outward when they are tied on. Hold the hackles tightly between your fingers while pulling the fuzz and soft lower fibers from a 1/2″ length of the four hackle stems as shown. If there are still some soft fibers left on the hackles, it's all right. That gives a little more life to the fly.

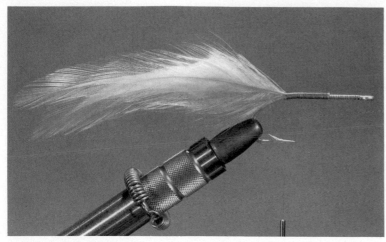

Step 3 Attaching the tail.

Step 4 Attaching the hackle.

Step 5 The finished Keys Tarpon Fly.

Step 3: Tie in the four hackles securely at the bend. They should sit side-by-side in a horizontal position. Cover the hackle stems completely with tying thread and let the thread hang by the bobbin directly in front of the first fibers on the tail where the hackle is to be tied in.

Step 4: To make the hackle collar, select one orange and one bright yellow saddle hackles. They should be fairly webby and of the same length and texture as the ones used for the tail. Prepare them by pulling off the fuzz and soft fibers at the butt ends in the same manner as you prepared the tail hackle. Tie them in together on top of the hook with the glossy sides up. Wind the tying thread over the stems to the middle of the shank and let the thread hang in that position.

Step 5: Wind the hackle on the shank dry fly style as shown in the photo. Tie off the hackle in the middle of the shank and cut the surplus. Wind a smooth layer of red tying thread on the forward portion of the shank and whip finish. Apply several good coats of Price's Head Cement or Hard-As-Nails fingernail polish, and your fly is finished.

Step 1 Attaching the tail.

Step 2 Selecting the wing hackles.

The Dirty Water Tarpon Fly

This pattern was designed specifically for fishing in places like Casa Mar in Costa Rica, where I have taken tarpon on both white and black patterns. These are the only two colors you will need. The major difference between this and the Keys pattern is the heavier dressing and the large bead eyes. The beads are there not only to aid the fly in getting down deep but also to "push" water so the fish can feel the vibrations of the swimming fly in the cloudy and dirty water that is often found at the mouth of rivers like the Colorado in Costa Rica. The hooks for these flies, as for all other saltwater flies, must be very carefully sharpened before dressing the fly. Setting a hook in a tarpon's mouth is like setting a hook in a cinder block.

Tying the Dirty Water Tarpon Fly

HOOK: Mustad #34007, stainless, sizes 6/0 to 4/0
THREAD: White, 3/0 Monocord
TAIL: White bucktail or Fishair, with six to eight strands of pearl Flashabou over
BODY: White tying thread
WINGS: Six very wide and webby white saddle or neck hackles, 3″ long, tied splayed

COLLAR: Red calf tail, one hook gap long
EYES: 3/16″ bead eyes
HEAD: Red tying thread

NOTE: This materials list is for the white pattern. See the Selected Patterns listing at the end of this chapter for the black pattern.

Step 1: Attach the tying thread and tie in a bunch of bucktail or Fishair on the shank at a position above the hook point. The hair should be about 2″ long. Next, tie in Flashabou of the same length over the bucktail and wind a body of tying thread reaching to 3/8″ from the eye, covering all the material ends in the process. Tie off the thread, cut it off, and attach some red 3/0 Monocord at the tie-off position. Your fly should now look like the one in the photo.

Step 2: The most important feature on this fly is the wing, and the feathers must be very carefully selected. Pick three feathers from the left side and three from the right side of either a saddle or neck skin to assure you of getting the correct curvature in the stems. The feathers should be 3 1/2″ long and about 1″ wide at the butt end. The butt end should be very webby and appear nearly solid, as shown.

Step 3 Attaching the wings.

Step 4 Attaching the collar.

Step 3: Place the three feathers from their respective sides on top of each other and even up the tip ends. Pull off the fuzzy fibers from 1/2″ of the stems, leaving them bare. Then tie in a feather bunch on each side of the shank with the dull sides out so they sit in a flared-out position. After the feathers are tied in, fan them a little so you can see the three stems on each side. Wind thread up on the lower fibers a little and fasten the feathers securely on the shank. Trim the hackle stems if needed so they are 1/8″ short of the eye and bind them down securely with tying thread. Let the thread hang by the bobbin 3/8″ from the eye.

Step 4: Cut a heavy bunch of red calf tail and even up the tips as much as possible with your fingers. Spread it evenly around the shank in front of the wing as a collar and fasten it with several turns of thread. The hair should be a hook gap long and cover the entire circumference evenly. Trim the butt ends of the hair if needed so they are just short of the eye before covering them completely with tying thread. Let the thread hang just a little ahead of the hair collar where the bead eyes will be tied in next.

Step 5 The finished Dirty Water Tarpon Fly.

Step 1 Attaching the tail.

Step 5: Cut two bead eyes from a chain with a pair of wire cutters, leaving them linked together. Hold them on top of the hook 1/16″ in front of the hair collar and fasten them securely with crisscross windings and some head cement or Crazy Glue. Now form a neat tapered head with tying thread and tie off. Apply several good coats of Price's Head Cement or Hard-As-Nails fingernail polish, and the fly is finished.

The Lefty's Deceiver

This is a fly I would not want to be without. It imitates many of the large and small baitfish found in the ocean and can be dressed in many different color combinations and sizes, all of which have taken fish from New Zealand to the North Atlantic. I have seen the fly's originator, Lefty Kreh, carry patterns ranging to 12″ in length, but he admits that the most popular are 4″ to 6″ long. The one I like most is 4″ long and is dressed with a white tail and a red hair collar in front. It suits me just fine and not only for fishing the salt. I have taken some fine bass and northern pike in freshwater with it as well.

Tying Lefty's Deceiver

HOOK:	Mustad #34007, stainless, sizes 6/0 to 4
THREAD:	White or red, 3/0 Monocord or Kevlar Super Thread
TAIL:	Six to eight long white saddle hackles with six to eight strands of silver, pearl, or gold Flashabou on each side, 1/2 as long as tail
BODY:	Silver tinsel
COLLAR:	White or red polar bear, bucktail, or Fishair, reaching a hook length past the bend
TOPPING:	Six to eight strands of peacock herl or Flashabou, reaching to tip of tail (optional)
HEAD:	Red or white tying thread

NOTE: Color combinations are wide open, but white, yellow, black, red, green, blue, and combinations of those colors can be used. A grizzly hackle is sometimes tied on each side of the tail.

Step 1: Attach the tying thread on a size 5/0 hook and wind it to the bend, covering the entire shank in the process. Select six 4″ to 5″ long white saddle hackles and place them on top of each other in two groups of three with their glossy sides out. Now place the two bunches together with the dull undersides toward the middle.

Step 2 Winding the body tinsel.

Step 3 Attaching the collar.

While holding all the hackles bunched together with the tips even, pull the fuzzy fibers from 1/2" of the stems and tie in the whole bunch at the bend right above the hook point. After securing it firmly, tie in six to eight strands of silver Flashabou on each side so they reach to about the middle of the tail. Your fly should now look like the one in the photo.

Step 2: Tie in a 6" length of silver tinsel 3/8" from the eye. Wind it on the shank to the bend, then back over the first layer to the tie-in spot, and tie it off. Trim the surplus and let the tying thread hang by the bobbin at the tie-off position.

Step 3: Cut a good-sized bunch of red hair and even up the tips as much as possible with your fingers or in a hair stacker. Tie it on in front so it encircles the shank as a collar. If that is troublesome at first, try to tie in the hair in small bunches, one at a time. The tips of the hair should reach about a hook length past the bend. Trim the surplus ends and wind some tying thread over the butt ends to secure the hair firmly.

Step 4 The finished Lefty's Deceiver.

Step 4: Tie in six to eight strands of peacock herl so they form a dark line along the upper part of the entire fly. They are tied on in front and reach to the tip of the tail. Trim the surplus. Then wind a nice tapered head, and the Deceiver is finished, with the exception of several good coats of Price's Head Cement or Hard-As-Nails fingernail polish.

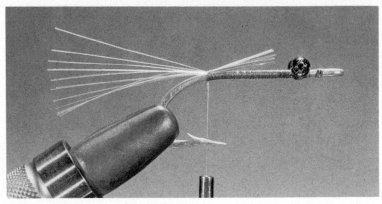

Step 1 Attaching the eyes and tail.

Bonefish Flies

Fishing for bonefish is one of the most exciting experiences one can have in saltwater flyfishing. Since you fish on relatively shallow flats, a hooked fish is often half way out of the water when running, going sixty miles an hour and reminding you of a duck taking off from a pond. It's not unusual for even small four- or five-pound fish to spool you off on the first run, so you must have plenty of backing on the reel. I recall one fish on Christmas Island in the Pacific that spooled me off four times before it tired out.

Bonefish flies are typical examples of simplicity and size. The mouth of a 10-pound bonefish is only about 2″ when open, and any flies larger than 1″ to 2″ in length will simply be refused. The Crazy Charlie is a dynamite fly designed for fishing the white sandy flats at Christmas Island where there is no grass, just white sand and coral stumps. It will not work well in Caribbean waters, where the bead eyes, which help the fly to sink and swim upside down, will hang up on the grass-covered bottom. In the list of additional patterns later in this chapter, I have included other flies better suited for grass-covered flats.

Tying the Crazy Charlie

HOOK:	Mustad #34007, stainless, sizes 4 to 6
THREAD:	Tan, 3/0 Monocord
TAIL:	Eight to ten strands of silver Flashabou or pearlescent Fly Flash, reaching to the bend
BODY:	1/16″ wide pearlescent tinsel with Larva Lace or 1/32″ clear Swannundaze wound over
WINGS:	Very sparse bunch of white calf tail, reaching to the tips of the tail
EYES:	Two 1/8″ silver bead eyes
HEAD:	Tan tying thread

NOTE: I soak the white calf tail in a pot of coffee for 24 hours to attain an off-white shade. This fly can also be tied with wings that are yellow, pink, or tan, and a gold body and gold bead eyes. Gold with a tan wing is my second choice.

Step 1: Attach the tying thread in front. Wind it on the shank to the bend and back to 1/8″ from the eye. Cut two bead eyes from a chain so they are joined together and fasten them on top of the shank with crisscross windings, as shown. Then apply some cement or Crazy Glue so they are tightly secured. Now wind the tying thread back to a position above midway between the barb and the hook point and tie in eight to ten strands of pearlescent Fly Flash.

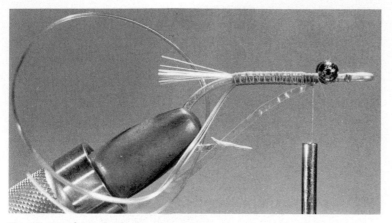

Step 2 Attaching the body materials.

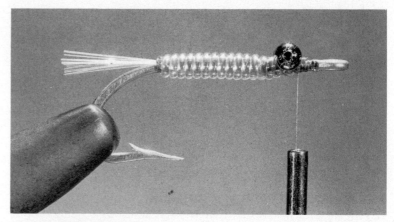

Step 3 Winding the body.

Step 2: Wind the thread forward to the bead eyes, binding down the ends of the Fly Flash in the process. Cut the tail material so it extends to just past the bend. Tie in a 4″ length of clear Swannundaze in front and wind the thread back to the bend, binding it down on the shank in the process. Wind the thread back to the front and tie in a 6″ length of pearlescent tinsel 1/16″ wide.

Step 3: Wind the tinsel on the shank back to the bend, then forward over the first layer to the eye, and tie it off. Cut the surplus tinsel and wind the clear Swannundaze forward over the body with turns laying side by side. Tie off the Swannundaze by bringing it forward between the eyes and tying it off just in front of them. Cut the surplus and fasten the end securely with tying thread.

Step 4: Place the fly upside-down in the vise and tie in a small bunch of calf tail, fastening it just in front of the bead eyes. Form a small head with tying thread, and tie it off with a whip finish. Cut the thread, apply some cement on the head, and your fly is finished.

Step 4 The finished Crazy Charlie.

Selected Saltwater Patterns

This list of additional patterns by no means includes all the flies that are used in saltwater fly rodding. Rather, it is merely a list of the ones I have found to be most effective for fishing almost anywhere in the world. As fly tiers, however, we should never hesitate to experiment with different materials and tying methods in hope of coming up with patterns that are more effective than those already proven.

General Use Patterns

BENDBACK, YELLOW AND RED

HOOK:	Mustad #34007, stainless, sizes 5/0 to 1
THREAD:	Black, 3/0 Monocord
TAIL:	None
BODY:	Yellow chenille
WINGS:	Yellow over red bucktail as long as three times the body length, with four to eight strands of silver Flashabou of same length on each side, on the outside of which is a grizzly hackle dyed red, 1/2 as long as wing
HEAD:	Black tying thread

NOTE: When tying Bendback patterns, it's important that you bend the hook shank up a tiny bit 1/8″ from the eye. This makes it ride upside-down, making it relatively weedless. It's much superior to a keel hook, since it hooks the fish better. Don't bend it too much or the body portion gets way below the wing and you will miss the strike.

BENDBACK, WHITE AND CHARTREUSE

BODY:	White chenille
WINGS:	Chartreuse over white, silver Flashabou, natural grizzly
HEAD:	Black

NOTE: See full pattern above.

BENDBACK, BROWN AND WHITE

BODY:	Yellow chenille
WINGS:	Brown over white, silver Flashabou, natural grizzly
HEAD:	Black

NOTE: See full pattern above.

CHESAPEAKE SILVER SIDES

HOOK:	Mustad #34007, stainless, size 1/0
THREAD:	Black, 3/0 Monocord
TAIL:	None
BODY:	Flat silver tinsel
THROAT:	White bucktail, twice the hook length
WINGS:	White bucktail same length as throat, over which is a small bunch of light green bucktail, followed by dark green bucktail a little longer than the others, topped with six to eight strands of black bucktail the same length
SIDES:	Four to six strands of silver Flashabou down each side
HEAD:	Black tying thread

CUDA FLY

HOOK:	Mustad #34007, stainless, sizes 5/0 to 1/0
THREAD:	Red, prewaxed 3/0 Monocord
BODY:	Blue over green over white Fishair, each bunch about 1/16″ diameter and 6″ to 10″ long
HEAD:	Red tying thread, tapered from the bend to the eye

NOTE: It's important to apply some glue to the very tip end of the Fishair to hold the fibers together. If you don't, the fly will "blossom" when being fished and spoil the retrieve. Lefty Kreh calls this fly a "throw-away fly"—one barracuda and you can put on another.

DIRTY WATER TARPON FLY, BLACK

HOOK:	Mustad #34007, stainless, sizes 6/0 to 4/9
THREAD:	Black, 3/0 Monocord
TAIL:	Black bucktail or Fishair with six to eight strands of pearl Flashabou over, on top of which are six to eight peacock herls
BODY:	Black tying thread
WINGS:	Six very wide, webby black saddle or neck hackles 3″ long, tied splayed
COLLAR:	Red calf tail, one hook gap long
EYES:	3/16″ bead eyes
HEAD:	Red tying thread

GLASS MINNOW

HOOK:	Mustad #34007, stainless, sizes 4/0 to 1/0
THREAD:	Black, 3/0 Monocord

BODY:	Silver tinsel overwound with clear Swannundaze or Larva Lace
WINGS:	Green over white bucktail with four to six strands of silver Flashabou each side, wing twice as long as hook
EYES:	White lacquer with black center applied with small round sticks
HEAD:	Black tying thread with clear lacquer

NOTE: As with most saltwater flies, you can make different combinations of dyed bucktail to change the wing color of the Glass Minnow. Solid white with a bunch of peacock herl over is also very effective.

LEFTY'S DECEIVER

HOOK:	Mustad #34007, stainless, sizes 6/0 to 4
THREAD:	White or red, 3/0 Monocord or Kevlar Super Thread
TAIL:	Six to eight long saddle hackles with six to eight strands of silver, pearl, or gold Flashabou on each side, 1/2 as long as tail
BODY:	Silver tinsel
COLLAR:	White or red polar bear, bucktail, or Fishair, reaching a hook length past the bend
TOPPING:	Six to eight strands of peacock herl or Flashabou, reaching to tip of tail (optional)
HEAD:	Red or white tying thread

NOTE: Color combinations are wide open, but white, yellow, black, red, green, blue, and combinations of those colors can be used. A grizzly hackle is sometimes tied on each side of the tail.

SEA-DUCER, YELLOW AND RED

HOOK:	Mustad #34007, stainless, sizes 5/0 to 1/0
THREAD:	Red, 3/0 Monocord
TAIL:	Six to eight saddle hackles, 4" to 6" long with webby fluff at butt end left in, with six strands of silver Flashabou each side as long as tail
BODY:	Two yellow saddle hackles wound heavy, dry fly style
HEAD:	Small, wound with red tying thread

NOTE: You can make any color combinations for this large hackle fly. White and red with a natural grizzly hackle on each side of the tail is one of my favorites.

STRAWBERRY BLONDE

HOOK:	Mustad #34007, stainless, sizes 5/0 to 1/0
THREAD:	Black, 3/0 Monocord
TAIL:	Red bucktail, twice the hook length
BODY:	Silver tinsel
WINGS:	Orange bucktail, reaching to just short of the tail's tip
HEAD:	Black tying thread

OTHER BLONDE PATTERNS

These are common color variations of the Strawberry Blonde listed above.

PLATINUM:	White tail; silver body; white wing
HONEY:	Yellow tail; gold body; yellow wing
PINK:	Pink tail; gold body; pink wing
BLACK:	Black tail; silver body; black wing
ARGENTINE:	White tail; silver body; blue wing
KATYDID:	White tail; silver body; dark green wing
IRISH:	Light-green tail; silver body; yellow over red wing
MICKEY FINN:	Yellow tail; silver body; yellow over red wing

Bonefish Flies

The wings on all the flies included below are tied under the shank in the manner described in the tying instructions.

BEAD-EYED CHENILLE FLY

HOOK:	Mustad #34007, stainless, sizes 4 to 6
THREAD:	Tan, 3/0 Monocord
BODY:	Rear two-thirds—gold tinsel with Larva Lace or 1/32" clear Swannundaze wound over; front third—fine tan chenille, crisscrossed between the bead eyes
WINGS:	Tan calf tail
EYES:	Two 1/8" gold bead eyes
HEAD:	Tan tying thread

NOTE: This fly can also be tied with yellow chenille and either tan or yellow calf tail wings.

BLACK CHENILLE FLY
HOOK: Mustad #34007, stainless, sizes 4 to 6
THREAD: Black, 3/0 Monocord
BODY: Black chenille wound on shank and crisscrossed between the bead eyes
WINGS: Red calf tail
EYES: Two 1/8″ silver bead eyes
HEAD: Black tying thread

BONEFISH SPECIAL
HOOK: Mustad #34007, stainless, sizes 4 to 6
THREAD: Black, 3/0 Monocord
TAIL: Orange hackle fluff or marabou, one hook gap long
BODY: Gold tinsel with Larva Lace or 1/32″ clear Swannundaze wound over
WINGS: White calf tail or bucktail with narrow grizzly hackle on each side, reaching to tip of tail
HEAD: Black tying thread

CRAZY CHARLIE
HOOK: Mustad #34007, stainless, sizes 4 to 6
THREAD: Tan, 3/0 Monocord
TAIL: Eight to ten strands of silver Flashabou or pearlescent Fly Flash, reaching to the bend
BODY: 1/16″ wide pearlescent tinsel with Larva Lace or 1/32″ clear Swannundaze wound over

WINGS: Very sparse bunch of white calf tail, reaching to even with the tips of the tail
EYES: Two 1/8″ silver bead eyes
HEAD: Tan tying thread
NOTE: I soak the white calf tail in a pot of coffee for 24 hours to attain an off-white shade. This fly can also be tied with wings that are yellow, pink, or tan, and a gold body and gold bead eyes. Gold with a tan wing is my second choice.

HORROR
HOOK: Mustad #34007, stainless, sizes 4 to 6
THREAD: Black, 3/0 Monocord
BODY: Yellow chenille, 1/2 shank length only
WINGS: Brown calf tail or bucktail tied in to sit raised, 1/3 hook length from eye, in middle of chenille body, with rest of body chenille wrapped over wing butts in front
HEAD: Black tying thread, small

SNAPPING SHRIMP
HOOK: Mustad #34007, stainless, sizes 4 to 6
THREAD: Tan, 3/0 Monocord
BODY: Small segment of hot orange Seal-Ex dubbing (#120); rest—buff Seal-Ex dubbing (#116)
WINGS: Brown calf tail or bucktail reaching one hook gap beyond hook bend, with optional slim grizzly hackle dyed tan on each side, same length as wing
HEAD: Tan tying thread

Chapter 15
Cork and Hair Bugs

It is said that Theodore Gordon, father of dry fly fishing in America, used some sort of cork bug early in the 20th century. Whether it was intended to perform as a popping bug is not known. In any case, as far as I know, it was E.H. Peckinpaugh of Chattanooga, Tennessee, who is credited with introducing the cork-bodied bass bug, the forerunner of our modern popping bugs. Since then, popping bugs have evolved and are being made of deer hair in many different styles.

Casting a cork or hair bug to the edge of lily pads, under overhanging trees, or near stumps and grassy lakeshores will give you plenty of action from bluegills, bass, and northern pike.

The construction of cork and hair bugs is fairly simple if you follow the instructions carefully and have a basic knowledge of fly tying. However, you should not expect to succeed the first couple of times you try to spin and trim deer hair.

There is no set color scheme for these artificials, and the patterns I have included consist of color combinations that both the fish and I have found attractive. Because there are

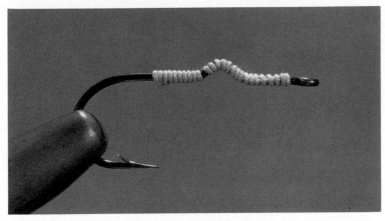

Step 1 Covering the shank with cotton thread.

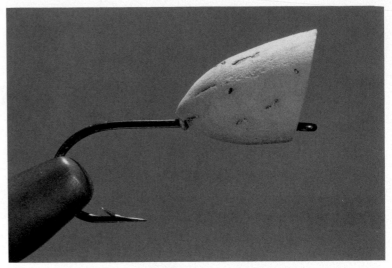

Step 2 Mounting the cork head.

few standard patterns and because so much is left up to the individual in creating cork and hair bugs, no additional patterns are listed at the end of this chapter.

The Cork-Bodied Popper

HOOK: Mustad #33903 or similar, with kink, sizes 1/0 to 10
THREAD: Brown cotton thread for the head, pre-waxed 6/0 for the feathers
HEAD: Pre-shaped cork, painted with clear lacquer
TAIL: Four soft, wide grizzly neck hackles
HACKLE: Two grizzly neck hackles, tied wet-fly style
EYES: Painted, white with black center
NOTE: For good balance with maximum hooking potential, the relation between the hook and head size must be carefully balanced. My suggestion is that the head diameter be equal to one hook gap and the shank be long enough so the end of the head will be right above the hook point. This should leave bare shank equal to one hook gap behind the head to accomodate the feathers.

Step 1: Place a size 2 hook in the vise and cover the shank from the eye to above the hook point with cotton thread. Tie off the thread and cut it.

Step 2: Select a head of the proper size that is pre-shaped and slotted. Apply some Duro Super Glue in the slot and on the shank. Then mount the head as shown in the photo. I usually make up several bugs at one time and let them dry thoroughly before continuing. If there is an opening in the slot after the glue is dry, it should be filled with plastic wood which you can purchase in a hobby shop or hardware store. Sand it flush after it dries. Be careful not to get any Super Glue on your fingers. Read the instructions on the glue pen before you use it.

Step 3 Painting the eyes.

Step 4 Selecting the tail hackles.

Step 3: Sand the head with fine sandpaper before applying two or three coats of clear lacquer or head cement, letting it dry between applications. Sometimes additional coats are needed to get a nice finish. To make the eyes, choose two dowel sticks, one with a diameter equal to the size eye needed and the other with a smaller diameter for the center of the eye. Daub the white paint on with the large dowel first. Let the white dry a little before using the smaller dowel to apply the black center. The sticks must have smooth ends. For best results, dip the end so you get only a drop of paint on it; then daub it lightly onto the head on both sides.

Step 4: Select four soft, fairly wide neck hackles for the tails, two from the right side of the neck and two from the left. Select hackles that will provide tight curvature. These hackles are found around the upper half of the neck. Line up the tips of the four hackles and cut them to 1 1/2 times the length of the hook shank. Pair up the hackles so the good sides are toward the middle and the hackles curve out as shown.

Step 5 Attaching the tail and hackle.

Step 6 The finished Cork-Bodied Popper.

Step 5: Attach the tying thread and tie in the hackles together securely on top of the shank. Then prepare two hackles with fibers that are 2 hook gaps long. Tie them in by the tips with the good sides out. Wind the thread to behind the head. Apply some cement on the tie-in windings. (See instructions for preparing and winding hackle in the section on tying a soft-hackle fly in Chapter 6.)

Step 6: Wind the hackles simultaneously, doubling the fibers back before each turn like a wet-fly hackle. Tie off the hackles close to the head and trim away the surplus stems. Wind over the butt ends and apply a whip finish before cutting the thread. Give the windings a few drops of head cement, and your cork-bodied popper is finished.

The Deer-Hair Bug

HOOK: Mustad #3366, sizes 2/0 to 10
THREAD: Olive Kevlar thread
TAIL: Four soft, fairly wide yellow neck hackles
HACKLE: Two yellow neck hackles, soft
HEAD: Olive deer or elk body hair with yellow center band, trimmed to shape

NOTE: When tying this fly, you can choose either to make the head and do the trimming before tying in the feathers or to tie in the feathers and then make the head.

Step 1 Attaching the tail and hackle.

Step 2 Selecting the deer hair.

Step 3 Preparing the deer hair.

Step 1: Tie in the tails and hackle above the hook point on a size 1 hook in the same manner as explained in the instructions for tying the cork bug. Let the tying thread hang at the tie-in spot in front of the hackle above the hook point where the first bunch of deer or elk hair is to be tied in.

Step 2: Select some medium-textured deer or elk hair dyed olive. The hair must be at least 2″ long for the size fly we are tying. Gather a bunch of hair with your fingers and cut it off close to the skin. Don't make the bunches too big to start. They should be about a 1/4″ in diameter when lightly compressed between your fingers. Comb out the fuzz and underfur before proceeding to the next step.

Step 3: Trim the butt ends so the hair bunch is not less than 1 1/2″ long and hold it as shown in the photo, with 1/2″ to 3/4″ projecting out in front of your finger tips. The larger the head, the longer the hair in front of your fingers must be.

Step 4 Attaching the first deer hair bunch.

Step 5 Attaching the second deer hair bunch.

Step 4: Holding the hair in the manner described in Step 3, press it down around the shank with your finger tips right in front of the hackle. Take two loose turns of thread around the hair and hook shank and pull them tight, thus making

Step 6 Preparing for additional bunches.

the hair butts flare out while the hair tips are held tight between your fingers. Continue by taking a couple more turns of thread through the hair and pulling them tight.

Step 5: Stroke the hair butts back and move the thread through to the front of them. Take two or three turns of thread around the shank to secure this first bunch of hair. Now cut another bunch and clean it out like the first one but cut off the tip portion, leaving a hair bunch that is 1 1/4" long. Hold it at an angle in front of the previous bunch and take two loose turns around the hair and hook shank. If need be, trap the thread loops with your fingers to hold them in place.

Step 6: Pull the thread loops tight to make the hair spin and flare. As you tighten the loops, let go of the hair and continue in the same motion by taking a couple of additional turns of thread through the hair to help it spin around the hook shank. Take the thread forward through the hair and secure it on the shank as before. Now hold your fingers behind the first bunch of hair and push the second bunch tight back against it. Apply a couple of drops of cement on the windings, and you are ready for the next bunch of hair.

Step 7 Finishing the head.

Step 8 Trimming the bottom.

Step 7: Continue to add hair bunches as explained in Step 6. When you reach the middle of the body, just switch from olive to yellow hair and make one application for the yellow band. Then continue with olive, leaving just enough space in front for the head.

When the last application is made, don't wind the thread forward through the hair. Instead, separate the hair on top and tie in a slightly smaller and shorter bunch of yellow hair. Pull it down tight in the space while holding it with your fingers to prevent it from spinning around. In that way it will cause the hair above the hook to extend forward over the eye for a "pop" effect when the bug is being fished. Now take the thread through the hair and wind a small head in front. Tie off with a whip finish or use a half-hitch tool before cutting the thread.

Step 8: Take the bug out of the vise and trim the bottom first. It should be flat with rounded corners and should be trimmed as close to the hook shank as possible.

Step 9: Trim the sides to the shape shown in the photo.

Step 9 Trimming the sides.

Step 10 Trimming the top.

Step 11 The finished Deer-Hair Bug, front view.

Step 10: Last, trim the hair on top. It's best to trim it on a slant first. Then round the corners to blend with the rest of the head to finish it off.

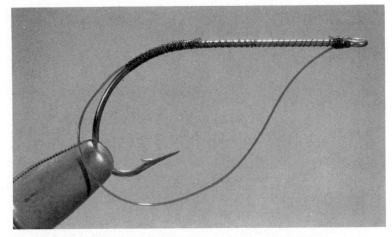

Fig. 15.1 The finished snag guard.

Step 11: Front view of the finished bug.

Making a Snag Guard

There are times when it's necessary to fit your cork and hair bugs with a snag guard to prevent them from hanging up in grass and debris that may be present in the water you are fishing. It's a fairly simple device for which I usually use a piece of monofilament.

The Mustad stinger hook illustrated in the photo is equipped with a length of 25-pound-test Cortland Flat Cobra line (**Fig. 15.1**). That will do well for larger flies, but you should choose monofilament for smaller flies so that it will give when the fish are taking the bug.

Tie the monofilament in at the bend above the hook point and wind over it down the bend a little to keep it in place on top of the shank. Apply some cement on the windings and let the monofilament hang loose in the back. When the fly is finished, the snag guard is taken under the hook and up through the eye and tied off. It should clear the hook point by a distance equal to 1/3 of the hook gap.

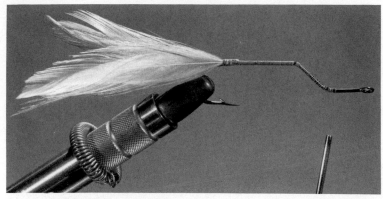
Step 1 Attaching the tail hackles.

The Weedless Hammerhead

This artificial is one of the most important flies I have used for bass and northern pike. It does not imitate an insect, as such, but it is representative of frogs, small birds, mice, and any other such creatures you might find around lakes and ponds. The keel hook is an important factor in the overall scheme of its effectiveness.

HOOK:	Mustad #79666, keel hook, sizes 1 to 6
THREAD:	Red Kevlar thread
TAIL:	Two red and two white soft neck hackles, one hook length
BODY:	Long bunch of white bucktail
RIBBING:	Red Kevlar thread
WINGS:	Natural brown bucktail
HEAD:	Yellow deer body hair with black insert on top, trimmed

NOTE: This fly can be tied in any color combination. Red and white is best for pike. Olive, yellow, and green combinations are best for bass.

Step 2 Attaching the bucktail body.

Step 1: Pair up the tail hackles so there is one white and one red in each pair and tie them in using the instructions given for the cork bug. Wind the thread forward to the horizontal head space, covering the entire shank in the process.

Step 2: Cut a bunch of white bucktail with enough fibers to cover the circumference of the shank. Pull out the fuzz and short hairs. Trim the bunch so it reaches from the hook eye to midway along the tail. Tie it in on the angled shank portion close to the head space. The hair should be distributed evenly around the shank. Apply some penetrating cement on the windings, and your fly should look like the one in the photo.

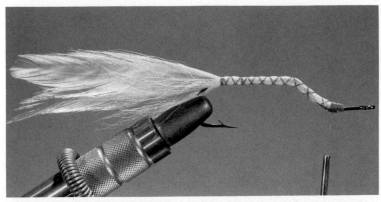

Step 3 Completing the body.

Step 4 Attaching the wing.

Step 5 Preparing the deer hair head.

Step 3: Starting at the tie-in spot, hold the bucktail along the shank and spiral the tying thread over it to the back bend, thus binding it down all around the shank to form the body. Take four or five close turns at the tail and spiral the thread back to the front. Let the tying thread hang right above the tie-in spot while brushing some clear cement on the whole body.

Step 4: Turn the hook and tie in a bunch of natural brown bucktail, long enough to reach above the barb. You should only use 1/3 of the head space for tying in the bucktail; the rest is for the head. Apply some penetrating cement on the windings and let the thread hang right in front of them.

Step 5: Cover the front shank with tying thread and let it hang directly in front of the wing butts. Cut a very heavy bunch of deer hair and comb out the fuzz and underfur. Hold the hair under the shank as shown and take two loose turns around it and the shank.

Step 6 Flaring the hair.

Step 8 Attaching the second deer hair bunch.

Step 7 Applying cement.

Step 9 Attaching the black deer hair.

Step 6: Pull the thread loop tight while holding the hair so it flares under the shank. Take a couple of extra turns of thread through the hair and press with your thumb on top and index finger below while pulling the thread tight.

Step 7: Apply some penetrating cement on top of the head and let it soak down into the hair a little.

Step 8: Tie in another bunch of hair, this time on top of the

shank, and fasten it securely with some extra turns of thread. Part the hair and apply some penetrating cement.

Step 9: Tie in a small bunch of black deer body hair in the middle of the top bunch of hair. Take a couple of extra turns of thread through it. Hold all the hair back while taking the thread to the front and tying it off with a half-hitch tool.

Step 10 Trimming the top.

Step 11 Trimming the sides.

Step 12 Trimming the bottom.

Step 13 Finishing the trimming.

Step 10: Take the fly out of the vise and hold it by the bend while trimming the head flat on top as shown.

Step 11: Trim each side quite wide. Round the corners a little in front.

Step 12: The bottom is now trimmed like the front of a Boston whaler fishing boat. Trim it so the body and the underside of the head form a continuous curve toward the eye.

Step 13: Fine-trim the lower part of the sides to blend with the bottom and apply some cement to the tie-off windings.

Step 14 The finished Weedless Hammerhead, front view.

Step 1 The finished Hammerhead Baitfish, bottom view.

Step 14: Front view of the finished bug. I sometimes apply a light coat of cement on the head in front to make it more solid.

The Hammerhead Baitfish Imitation

All the hammerheads are tied as "non-patterns" with incidental color schemes except one, the injured baitfish. It represents one of the many small fish found in both freshwater and saltwater. It should be fished by imitating the erratic movement of a struggling fish. The basic materials list and method of dressing is like the "non-pattern", above, but with the following changes:

TAIL: Two badger neck hackles
BODY: Braided silver Mylar tubing
GILLS: Red calf tail, trimmed
HEAD: White deer body hair with black insert on
               top, trimmed

Step 1: Tie in the tail in the usual manner. Make the body of braided Mylar using the instructions given in Chapter 11 for tying the Zonker, Steps 1 and 2, but leave out the material wound on the shank. The unraveled Mylar should reach 1/3 of the way along the tail. Tie in some red calf tail on the shank close to the head space. Finish the head in the usual manner, trimming the red calf tail when finishing the bottom. This will expose the red gill effect as seen in the photo of the underside of the head of the finished fly.

Appendix

ABDOMEN: The posterior body portion of an insect.

ADULT: A mature insect; artificial dry fly.

APEX: The tip of an insect's wing.

ATTACH: To fasten by tying, usually a beginning procedure, like "attach the tying thread," etc.

BARB: The part of a hook near the hook point that prevents it from pulling out once it has entered, a fly tier's reference point for placement of material.

BEARD: A part of the fly, usually hackle fibers tied under the shank in front of the body, representing legs.

BEND: Part of a hook at the rear of the shank.

BOBBIN: A tool designed to hold the spool with thread; any sort of spool containing material.

BOBBIN THREADER: A fine, looped wire designed to thread the material through the tube of a bobbin.

BUTT: A general term for the base or bottom or heavy end of a feather, fiber, or material with different diameters in their respective ends; also, a segment of wool or herl wound on the shank to end or divide the body.

CAPE: A name often used instead of rooster neck, as in "hackle cape."

EYE: The part of a hook to which the leader is attached. A part often used as a reference point for measurement.

EVEN UP: To align hair or feather tips or butts.

EXCESS: Leftover material to be cut off or in some way hidden.

FIBERS: Individual filaments of feather, hair, or fur.

FINE: Measurement relating to smallest width of tinsel; relative measurement with reference to amount.

FLUE: Barb of filament of herl from peacock or ostrich.

GUARD HAIR: The long, fine hair on an animal's pelt.

HALF HITCH: A loop with a half twist used to prevent thread from unraveling. A half hitch can be done manually or with a half-hitch tool.

HACKLE TIP: The tapered, short-fibered end of the hackle.

MIXED: Fibers of different sorts or color blended together.

PALMER: Method of winding hackle, tinsel, floss, or other material up the body in open spirals.

RIBBING: Any material spiraled up the body.

SECURE: To fasten with thread or cement.

SEGMENT: A strip of feather, division of body, or any one part of a material or section consisting of more than one.

STACK: To superimpose one material on top of another.

TAPER: A graduation that evenly decreases in dimension (in either direction).

THORAX: The front half or one-third of an insect.

TIE IN: To fasten a material with tying thread.

TIE OFF: To whip finish or half hitch thread after applying a material or to finish the head of a fly.

THROAT: A hackle wound as a collar divided on top and tied under the shank to represent legs or front of streamer or other such flies. (Also see "beard".)

WHIP FINISH: A method of securing the tying thread at the head of the finished fly.

WEB: The discolored, meshed portion of a hackle close to the stem.

Index